Studies in
The Book of Acts
VOLUME THREE

VICTORIOUS CHRISTIANITY

MARTYN LLOYD-JONES

CROSSWAY BOOKS

A DIVISION OF
GOOD NEWS PUBLISHERS
WHEATON, ILLINOIS

Library of Congress Cataloging-in-Publication Data
Lloyd-Jones, David Martyn.
    Victorious Christianity / Martyn Lloyd-Jones.—1st U.S. ed.
        p. cm. — (Studies in the book of Acts ; v. 3)
    Includes bibliographical references.
    ISBN 1-58134-514-3 (alk. paper)
    1. Bible. N.T. Acts V-VI—Criticism, interpretation, etc. I. Title. II. Series.
BS2625.52.L57   2003
252'.058—dc21   2003011443

RRD			13	12	11	10	09	08	07	06	05	04	03
15	14	13	12	11	10	9	8	7	6	5	4	3	2	1

Contents

1

THE IRRATIONALITY OF UNBELIEF

Then the high priest rose up, and all they that were with him, (which is the sect of the Sadducees,) and were filled with indignation, and laid their hands on the apostles, and put them in the common prison. But the angel of the Lord by night opened the prison doors, and brought them forth, and said, Go, stand and speak in the temple to the people all the words of this life. And when they heard that, they entered into the temple early in the morning, and taught. But the high priest came, and they that were with him, and called the council together, and all the senate of the children of Israel, and sent to the prison to have them brought. But when the officers came, and found them not in the prison, they returned, and told, saying, The prison truly found we shut with all safety, and the keepers standing without before the doors: but when we had opened, we found no man within. Now when the high priest and the captain of the temple and the chief priests heard these things, they doubted of them whereunto this would grow. Then came one and told them, saying, Behold, the men whom ye put in prison are standing in the temple, and teaching the people. Then went the captain with the officers, and brought them without violence: for they feared the people, lest they should have been stoned. And when they had brought them, they set them before the council: and the high priest asked them, saying, Did not we straitly command you that ye should not teach in this name? And, behold, ye have filled Jerusalem with your doctrine, and intend to bring this man's blood upon us.

> *Then Peter and the other apostles answered and said, We ought
> to obey God rather than men. The God of our fathers raised up
> Jesus, whom ye slew and hanged on a tree. Him hath God exalted
> with his right hand to be a Prince and a Saviour, for to give
> repentance to Israel, and forgiveness of sins. And we are his
> witnesses of these things; and so is also the Holy Ghost, whom
> God hath given to them that obey him.*
>
> —Acts 5:17-32

This fifth chapter of Acts is an astonishing chapter. It starts with the amazing incident of the death, the judicial death, of Ananias and Sapphira. That is followed by a wonderful manifestation of the power of God through the apostles, a passage we have considered together.[1] Luke tells us:

> *And by the hands of the apostles were many signs and wonders
> wrought among the people. . . . Insomuch that they brought forth the
> sick into the streets, and laid them on beds and couches, that at the
> least the shadow of Peter passing by might overshadow some of
> them. There came also a multitude out of the cities round about unto
> Jerusalem, bringing sick folks, and them which were vexed with
> unclean spirits: and they were healed every one.*
>
> —Acts 5:12, 15-16

Then comes the incident that we shall now consider. We read, "The high priest rose up, and all they that were with him . . . and were filled with indignation" (v. 17). Here is a further episode in the life of the early church, and we are looking at it for the same reason that we have been looking at the other incidents. We are concerned to discover what the Christian church is, what her message is, and what she is meant to do in this world. And it is here in Acts, and here alone, that we have the authentic account of the origin of the church.

I must emphasize that we are dealing with historical facts; without them, there would never have been a church at all. There is no other explanation for its existence, as the authorities in Jerusalem had to find out. They were confronted by a great problem. They perceived that the apostles were "unlearned and ignorant men" (Acts 4:13); they marveled at this and could not understand it. And that, of course, is the continuing marvel. The church came into being and continued in existence and was able to do the astounding things that are recorded, not only in the book of Acts but also in her subsequent history down the centuries until today, because certain events took place—the events described in the Gospels and the early chapters of Acts.

Now I say again that if we are really anxious to know what Christianity is about and what the church is, it is in the Book of Acts that we can discover it. Here we have the great fundamental principles put before us in a clear and definite manner, and these are the principles that must still govern the life of the church. A church that cannot link herself up with these truths is not a Christian church. She may be an institution. She may still call herself a Christian church. But if she does not conform to the principles that are laid down here, she has no right to that name.

The great problem that is confronting so many at the present time is that there is confusion both within and, still more, outside the church about what the church is. People are in trouble, and they look to the church. But when they ask, "What is her message?" they find no clear answers. That is why it is important that we should go back and consider this early history. This, and this alone, is authentic Christianity. It is an astonishing story all the way through.

The incident we are now studying must amaze us. There is something almost incredible about it. Look at how the story opens: "Then the high priest rose up, and all they that were with him, (which is the sect of the Sadducees,) and were filled with indignation, and laid their hands on the apostles, and put them in the common prison."

"Then"—that is, immediately after the events that have just been recorded. What are they? Well—and this is what makes the reaction of the religious leaders so astonishing—Luke has just told us of the sudden deaths of Ananias and Sapphira, that startling and dramatic event. And then he records an unusual display of miraculous, supernatural power. Here were people coming in from the surrounding towns and countryside bringing their sick friends and relatives, and, we are told, they were all healed. This was a visible fact, and it was this that filled the high priest and the Sadducees with indignation.

Now it is really extraordinary that the religious leaders reacted the way they did. We can all understand people being afraid as a result of those events. You suddenly see a man drop dead, and in three hours his wife drops dead in the same way. That is enough to frighten anybody. So we read, "And great fear came upon all the church, and upon as many as heard these things" (v. 11).

We can also understand why the people "magnified" the apostles (v. 13). It may have been that the citizens of Jerusalem were credulous, that they were even a little bit superstitious; but I suggest that anybody hearing of the sudden judicial deaths of a man and his wife, and seeing such extraordinary miracles enacted before their very eyes, would surely have reacted with amazement. They would have felt that this was wonderful and would have been favorably disposed toward men who had been given such power. But what is surprising is that any group of people could have reacted with such anger—an anger so great that it led the Sanhedrin to arrest and imprison the apostles. And this is the phenomenon that I would like to consider with you now.

The New Testament records are very honest; they not only give us one side but give us all sides. In the case of Luke's account of Ananias and Sapphira, we have already seen an example of this honesty—Luke tells us the whole truth about those two people. This is quite unlike the methods of big business and advertising agencies. They have a policy of never admitting there is anything wrong with their products. But in the Scriptures we are told about the failures as well as the successes, the opposition as well as the support. And that is the case in the incident we are now studying. Here we are looking at an amazing picture of unbelief.

Now I call your attention to the unbelief of the religious leaders because it is just as important for us to understand the nature of unbelief as it is for us to understand belief. We have already considered the elements of belief: first, the fear of the unseen and of the power of God that, second, leads to a readiness to listen, a readiness to accept and to obey the message of the Gospel, and, third, the power of the Holy Spirit, bringing about, not some temporary, superficial reaction, but a profound change in men and women, as a result of which they become part of the body of Christ.

So we have indulged in what may be called the anatomy of belief, and now we come to the anatomy of unbelief. It is equally important for us to understand unbelief because it sometimes happens that people are brought to belief by their realization of the character of unbelief. They see how terrible it is, how horrible, how foolish and mad; and seeing that, they turn from it and believe.

So these records not only give us the positive, but also the negative pictures. It is all designed to open our eyes and understanding and bring us to a belief in this great Gospel of salvation. And, of course, we should be very grateful to God for the negative pictures. I have often put it like this: We always find it easier to grasp a point or a principle when we see it in somebody else rather than in ourselves. We are so well disposed toward ourselves, on such good terms with ourselves and always so protective of ourselves, that we never really see the truth about ourselves. But when we see one of our faults in somebody else, we at once recognize it. A good example is the story of David and Nathan (2 Sam. 12). Just as Nathan said to David, so the Gospel says to us, "Thou art the man" (v. 7), and the truth is brought home to us. That is the value of the historical incidents and the illustrations that we find given us with such profusion in the pages of the Bible.

Furthermore, we must remember the great principle that as belief does not change through the centuries, so unbelief does not change either. Somebody may say to me, "I see what you're going to do. You're going to show us the unbelief of the chief priests and the Sadducees. But that was nineteen hundred years ago and more. We're in the twentieth century now. What has all that got to do with us?"

And the answer is that unbelief is always the same; it does not change at all. There was unbelief in the first century, and there is still unbelief today. Of all the modern fallacies, there is none quite so pathetic and so feeble as the fallacy of thinking that there is something new about unbelief. Ask the average man today why he is not a Christian, and he will almost invariably tell you that it is because he is "a twentieth-century man" [Editor's note: Martyn Lloyd-Jones went home to heaven in 1981.] In his ignorance he has an idea that in the past, people swallowed Christian teaching because they did not know any better. They were all Christians. But *he*, ah, no, he is from the twentieth century!

But here is the answer: The Gospel was rejected in the first century too. The Son of God is being rejected today in exactly the same way as He was rejected two thousand years ago, and after He died, His disciples suffered the same hatred and rejection. There is never any change. Christ remains the same, belief and faith are the same, unbelief is the same. So as we analyze the behavior of these members of the Sanhedrin in their unbelief, we find nothing but the simple truth about all who still reject the Gospel, all who turn their backs upon it, all who dislike it.

What, then, are we told here? First of all, we are told something about the nature of unbelief, and this is always the starting point. Why is it that anybody should be a nonbeliever? If you do not accept the Gospel, why is it? Have you ever thought about that? And this profound question is answered here for us. Here were men who had rejected the apostles, as they had previously rejected our Lord with the words, "Away with Him! Crucify Him! We want nothing to do with Him. Give us Barabbas."

What, then, is the nature or cause of unbelief? And our first answer, negatively, is that unbelief is not intellectual. This is a point I want to emphasize because I know that at the present time it is the proud boast of those who scoff at religion—we see them on our television screens and read their articles—that they are rejecting Christianity for intellectual reasons. They claim they are people who have great ability, great understanding, and great powers of reasoning. And today, of course, they especially maintain that they are governed by a scientific outlook. The scientific outlook, they claim, is calm, dispassionate, and unemotional. Scientists have no preconceived notions—prejudice is the mark of religious people—and with truly detached minds they look on the facts objectively, assessing with a kind of Olympian calm the views that are placed before them.

The idea today is that men and women are not Christians because, as a result of their objective investigation, they have come to the conclusion that Christianity is not true. They say they are sorry about this. Not long ago I heard a man saying, "I wish I could believe. I wish I had faith." And I am sure he meant it—I am not saying he was dishonest. But the trouble was that he was mistaken.

That man said, "I wish I could . . ." But he thought belief was impossible for any intelligent person. So what about this? Well, I could go on for hours on this subject, but there is no need. I can deal with it very simply. First, if you could prove to me that no one with a great intellect ever believed the Gospel, then you would be in a powerful position, but you just cannot do that. Men and women of outstanding intelligence have believed this Gospel, and that at once raises a doubt about this modern position.

Second, there have been people in this world—some recorded here in the Scriptures and many others since then—who were at first bitter opponents of the Gospel. They dismissed it and ridiculed it. They proved to themselves that it was all wrong. But later they became Christians—the same people. Why did they make this change? There is no evidence that they developed brain tumors. There is no evidence that their brains began to degenerate owing to arteriosclerosis or some other cause. Some of them changed over when they were comparatively young, and not only that, they gave abundant proof afterward that their minds were still functioning with the previous brilliance. If the same people, with the same brains, having first rejected the Gospel, later believed it, giving good reasons for the change, then surely that is evidence enough in and of itself.

Or, third, you will sometimes find two brothers, who have grown up together, with very much the same gifts, going to the same school and doing equally well, both of them at the top of their class, and both going on to university where they achieved almost identical and outstanding results, and one is a Christian and the other is not. What accounts for the difference in belief? You cannot possibly say it is a matter of intellect, because everybody agrees that you really cannot choose between them. That, again, is enough to dispose once and forever of the argument that the modern clever person cannot be a Christian.

But then some people say, "I'll accept that, but isn't it a question of knowledge?" I find people, even bishops, writing books saying that because of the increase in scientific knowledge you cannot expect a man of the twentieth century to believe what people formerly did. We know many things today that were not known in the past, and it is these things that now make it impossible for us to believe.

All I would say in reply is that if modern knowledge is the cause of unbelief, what was the cause of the unbelief of the religious leaders in Jerusalem? Since they rejected the Gospel too, they must obviously have had some other reason for their unbelief. Unbelief is not, therefore, a question of knowledge. If it could be shown that everybody in the past believed the Gospel and that unbelief has only come in since we split the atom, then, of course, you would have a watertight case, but not otherwise. There was as much unbelief in the past as there is in the present.

But in addition to that, take all this new knowledge. It is very wonderful—I am not here to say a word against it. Anyone who says anything against modern knowledge and discoveries and inventions is just a fool. But I would point out that the increase in knowledge has nothing to do with the subject we are discussing. You split the atom. Does that tell you any more about yourself? Does the fact that the Russians have landed an instrument on the moon—which is a marvelous achievement, let us give them due credit for it—does that explain why you committed that same sin again last night that you said a week ago you would never do again? Does it help you with that? Does all this increase in knowledge tell you anything more about human beings—what they are, who they are, or what they are doing in this world? Does it tell you how to live a clean and a straight and a moral life, how to die or what lies beyond death? Jodrell Bank[2] cannot see through death. Sputniks cannot tell you anything about the soul or about God or about the great fundamental issues of life. Modern knowledge is irrelevant.

Those are the negatives. What, then, is the cause of unbelief? Here it is: "Then the high priest rose up, and all they that were with him . . . and were filled with indignation"—it has been suggested that a better translation is "anger" or "jealousy"—"and laid their hands on the apostles, and put them in the common prison." Now we are beginning to get at it, are we not? Is this a picture of a calm, cool, scientific, unprejudiced observer? Of course not. There is no such person, and there never has been.

Some of us have had a little scientific training. I myself spent two years engaged in scientific research. And I saw as much prejudice in scientific circles as I have ever seen anywhere else. The idea that scientists are impartial, that they could never be jealous of one another and never know anything about malice or spite—put that kind of theory to scientists and just watch their expressions. No, no! This is the deception of the devil; this is where he fools us. I make so bold as to say that the cause of unbelief is not man's ability to reason but is always the result of irrationality. Unbelief is entirely a matter of feeling and prejudice, as we see here in Acts 5, and as we see equally clearly from the way in which was our Lord was treated.

We are told in the twenty-fourth verse, "Now when the high priest and the captain of the temple and the chief priests heard these things, they doubted of them whereunto this would grow." These leaders knew about the healing of the man at the Beautiful Gate of the temple. They had heard these "unlearned and ignorant" apostles expounding the Scriptures with eloquence and understanding. They had heard of the deaths of Ananias and Sapphira. They had seen extraordinary manifestations of supernatural power. They did not understand it; they could not explain it. Yet they did not adopt the truly scientific attitude, which would have been, surely, to say, "We cannot dispute the facts. Facts are facts, after all. These things are happening, and it's obvious that they are not caused by these men alone. There must be something else. What is it? Let's watch; let's see what this will lead to." Instead of adopting that attitude of humble inquiry and tolerance and fair play, instead of giving the apostles an opportunity, they dismissed these events. They were filled with angry jealousy and annoyance and indignation, and they tried to put a stop to all this preaching and teaching.

And let me prove to you that it is still the same today. Look at modern men and women. Look how tolerant they are. They are so tolerant that they are prepared not only to excuse but to legitimize moral perversion. "You see," they say, "in the past we've judged this behavior with passion. We've regarded people as criminals and have called certain actions sinful perversions. But that's all wrong. We've grown out of that now, and we really must look at these actions in an intelligent and scientific manner." So they are prepared to tolerate something that breaks the very laws of nature. I am sorry for perverts, but I am talking now about the principle, and I think the worst thing you can do for such people is praise them and make them feel that they are normal. They are not.

But though it is the boast of modern men and women that they will tolerate even perversion, even foulness, they will not tolerate the Gospel. Listen to these tolerant gentlemen speaking about the Gospel; listen to them on the radio, and notice the sneering asides, the contempt, the bitterness. There is no fair play here, no readiness to allow possibilities, only total rejection and that with harshness and scorn. Why? That is the question that confronts us, and the explanation is here before our eyes: They "were filled with indignation . . . they doubted of them whereunto this would grow" (vv. 17, 24).

What was the matter with these religious leaders? Unfortunately, we all know something about unbelief; we have all been guilty of it. These men reacted as they did because of their jealousy and pride. They were the leaders; they were the chief priests; they were the Sadducees, the leading party in the Sanhedrin.[3] They were the important people, and in the past the populace had looked up to them. So they were guarding their position. They were proud of their learning; they were proud of their knowledge; they were proud of the fact that the people had always listened to them. But now they saw these uneducated men occupying the center of the stage with the crowd running after them and listening to them, and they were furious! They did not worry about miracles or the sudden deaths of Ananias and Sapphira. All that mattered to them was their position, their great position.

I can understand these Sadducees very well. Notice that the record puts emphasis on their party: "The high priest rose up, and all they that were with him, (which is the sect of the Sadducees)." Of course, the Sadducees had a real problem because they did not believe in the supernatural or in life after death, and therefore they had always taught that there was no such thing as resurrection. They did not believe in angels either. There is something almost humorous about this, is there not? Do you see their predicament? Here were these apostles, able to do marvelous things and claiming that it was because of Jesus of Nazareth—the Jesus whom the Sadducees, along with the other religious leaders, had condemned and succeeded in putting to death, and who had been buried. But the apostles said he had risen and was exercising power from heaven. Resurrection!

But still more humiliating for the Sadducees at this point was the fact that after they had the apostles thrown into the common prison, with the doors locked and the keepers on guard, on the first night the angel of the Lord opened the prison doors and brought the prisoners out. Angels!

Now when you have always said that resurrection is impossible and that there is no such thing as an angel, and everybody has believed you, then when things begin to happen that prove that both are true, you are obviously in trouble. Your whole position is shaken, and people tend to laugh at you. When you come with your great pomp and ceremony in the morning and say, "Bring out the prisoners please," and the soldiers go to the prison and come back saying that they have found the prison intact, with all the doors locked and the guards standing before them, but that there are no prisoners inside the prison, then you are indeed in trouble.

Now this is an old first-century narrative, but what a perfect picture it is of modern men and women who reject the Gospel. They have always said that there is no God. They have always said that there are no miracles and that Jesus Christ was only a man. But then something happens that they cannot explain, and some fool of an ignoramus who calls himself a Christian seems to be able to live a better life than they can and is able to help people in misery and distress in a way that they cannot. Furthermore, things happen through this ignoramus that they cannot explain. And they are in trouble. Their whole attitude, their whole position, is threatened. People are turning from them. That is the crux; that is the real cause of unbelief. What will people think of you if you become a Christian? What about your intellectual respectability?

That is why most people are not Christians; that is what is really happening within them. The whole mental framework of the modern, literate, educated, sophisticated, scientific man or woman comes crashing down to the ground—it becomes valueless if the Christian faith is accepted. And, of course, that is a terrible thing and a blow to their pride. That is why men and women do not believe the Gospel.

But then have you noticed the element of hatred and rage in the response of these religious leaders—"filled with indignation"? And you see the same rage today. Why can people not talk quietly and calmly about the Christian faith? Why can they not write about it in a rational manner? Why must they always scoff and jeer? Why this anger? Why this passion? Now I am not inventing facts. You know this as well as I do; you are as aware of it as I am. Why is it considered clever to pour scorn upon the Gospel? Why did those people deal with the Son of God as they did? Why is He still treated in the same way, together with all He stands for and all He came to do? Why are His followers still hated?

We are told that the disciples were thrown into "the common prison." There were divisions in first-century prisons. And there was no lower prison than the common prison. This was the prison into which the felons were thrown, the men who were guilty of the vilest and foulest crimes. But nobody said, "These followers of Jesus have committed no glaring crimes. They are not drunkards or murderers. Let's lock them up in the better part of the prison, at any rate until we have investigated further." No! The common prison. And that is the modern attitude; that is always the attitude of unbelief. It consigns everything to do with Christianity into the common prison. Thus Christ was crucified between two thieves. Is this the calm, rational, dispassionate, scientific approach to truth? Not at all. Here feeling and passion are shouting at you.

And then notice the use of authority and force, the attempt to silence the apostles, indeed the very attempt to destroy the Christian church. Again, that has always been the characteristic of unbelief. I could take you through the centuries, and we could study the history of the treatment of the saints, and we would always find the same story. Look at the way the religious leaders treated our Lord. Look at the way they treated the first Christians. Look at the treatment of Christians in the first and second centuries—the massacres, the cruelty, the branding with hot irons. Look at what happened in the Middle Ages and the treatment meted out to the Reformers in London and elsewhere, to the Puritans and the Covenanters in Scotland, and to the early Methodists. In the seventeenth century and afterward men had both their ears cut off and were branded with hot irons because of their faith.

Why do people behave with such cruelty? This is unbelief, but why this continuing passion? Is it not obvious to you? This is not intellectual detachment. This is not a calm, scientific view of truth. This is jealous anger, hatred, raging malice, and spite.

"Ah," you say, "but there's none of that today."

Is there not? Is there no persecution [in England] today? I happen to be in a position to know something about this, and, alas, it is the simple truth that there is grievous persecution today. Sometimes people have been in danger of losing their positions in high educational circles because of their belief. In all walks and departments of life people are held back because they are Christians. You can see the persecution in the articles that are written. People are ridiculed and jeered at for their faith and because they are trying to live a Christian and a moral life. You can be a pervert and you will be praised. It is said that there is something marvelous about this, this wonderful love. But if you are a Christian, then the opponents of Christianity will whisper and wink at one another, and when they get an opportunity, they will keep you down. Unfortunately, I am simply putting facts before you. And yet we are asked to believe in the cool detachment of the scientific observer and investigator. Away with such nonsense! Indignation is still the cause of unbelief.

I say again that opposition to the Christian faith is nothing but sheer irrationality. It proves that it is irrational by opposing such a good thing. What were the religious leaders in Acts rejecting? We are told here that the angel appeared to the apostles and said to them, "Go, stand and speak in the temple to the people all the words of this life." The apostles had been imprisoned because they had been speaking "the words of this life." So what was it that filled their enemies with fury? This is the most amazing thing of all, and if you do not agree that it is irrational, then I suggest there is something wrong with your thinking. Were these leaders rejecting some unintelligent, emotional sob story? There is no evidence of that. Were they rejecting something primitive and debased or something that was in any way whatsoever opposed to man and his best interests? Did the apostles' teaching put fetters on the human intellect? Was it morally or spiritually harmful?

And the answer is this: "the words of this life." What is that? Oh, here it is: "God so loved the world, that he gave his only begotten Son, that whosoever believeth in him should not perish, but have everlasting life" (John 3:16). Men and women reject the message that the great God who made this world and made us all, the God who is over all and is our eternal Judge, the one against whom we have sinned and whom we have reviled and spat upon, is nevertheless a God who so loved us that He planned a way to set us free— the way of salvation. The apostle Paul puts it in these words: "The grace of God that bringeth salvation hath appeared" (Titus 2:11). This is good news; it is the Gospel.

If the message of the Gospel were that God is a great tyrant waiting to pounce upon us and to crush us, always keeping us down and stultifying our minds and our spirits and our souls, and forcing us to live a kind of hell all our lives, I would understand people rejecting it. But it is the exact opposite. It is not God putting up an impossible legal code and saying, "Keep that and I will forgive you, and if you do not I will damn you." No; it is God saying, "Though you have failed and sinned against Me, My love is such that I am preparing this way of salvation for you"—the grace of God. What I find so amazing is, that is what unbelievers are rejecting.

Look at those members of the Sanhedrin and their actions as recorded in Matthew 26. Look at this one on whom they are spitting. Look at the one on whom the Roman soldiers put the crown of thorns and a reed in His hand (Matt. 27). Look at them as they mock Him and jeer at Him and spit upon Him—literally—and laugh at Him in His agony on that cross. Why are they doing this to Him? What has He done? Who is He?

He is none other than the Son of God who has come into this world. He is the most amazing person the world has ever seen. We are told that he "went about doing good" (Acts 10:38). Here is a man who mixed with tax-collectors and sinners, when the best and most respectable religious people would not be seen anywhere near such people. He sat down among them. He ate with them and spent His time with them. He allowed a poor fallen woman to wash His feet with her tears and to wipe them dry with her hair. Here is one who had a word of kindness for everybody. Here is one who had encouragement to give to the hopeless. Look at Him: He restored people who were diseased; He gave sanity to the insane; He healed the blind, the lame, the deaf; He raised the dead. Here is the person they are spitting on.

Listen to His teaching. Why, common soldiers, on hearing Him one day, had to say, "Never man spake like this man" (John 7:46). Others had to admit that they had never heard such gracious words as those that fell from His lips. If only everybody lived by His teaching today, our world would be a very different place. If only everybody practiced the Sermon on the Mount, there would be no industrial problems, there would be no social problems, there would be no moral problems, there would be no international problems. That is the one they are crucifying; that is the one they are treating with scorn and derision.

But what am I speaking about? What is He doing on that cross? He could have avoided it, He could have evaded it—He said so Himself; but He went there deliberately, because, as He put it, He had come into this world "to seek and to save that which was lost" (Luke 19:10). He came because He is the greatest benefactor in the universe. He came because of His great heart of compassion and love. He came to set men and women free, to deliver them from the punishment they so richly deserve, to deliver them from the shackles and the bondage of the world, the flesh, and the devil. He came to make them children of God, to give them new life, and to prepare them for a glorious eternity. That is why He came; the death was a part of it, the burial was a part of it, the resurrection was a part of it, and the sending of the Holy Spirit was a part of it.

Now I ask you in all seriousness and soberness: Is such opposition rational? Is it rational to gnash your teeth against such a person? Is it rational to throw into the common prison men who tell you about Him and who show you why He came, who He is, and what He offers you?

"Go," said the angel, and "[let them know] all the words of this life." Life! If our Lord had offered some sort of slavery, then it would have been rational to oppose Him. I know that many people think of Christianity as slavery. They have listened to the devil, who says, "Don't become a Christian—it will turn you into half a person. Christianity means repression.

Christianity is a teaching that tells you, 'Don't do this, don't do that, don't do the other, and have nothing to do with sex, heterosexual or homosexual.' Both are right," says the devil, "just carry on. Don't listen to Christianity because if you do, you will be living a cramped, confined life. You will lose everything that is wonderful and happy and will become a little person and live a little life in a little world." The devil says all that, and if you are not a Christian, you may be mad enough to listen!

"Go," says the angel, "stand and speak in the temple to the people all the words of this life." Here is *life*! Life is what you need, and the world cannot give it to you. Does drinking alcohol give you life? That is slavery; that is cutting out your highest faculties; that is crippling your mind, interfering with your judgment and your understanding of what is right. Getting drunk is not life. It is existence on an animal level.

Here is life, in the message preached by the apostles. Here is something that delivers the whole person. Here is a truth that is bigger than humanity and the world; it is the truth of God, and it stretches through death to eternity. Here is a great worldview that explains everything and all that nothing else can explain. It not only gives you intellectual life—it gives you a new moral nature, and it gives you a new joy and a new appreciation.

I am sorry for people who are not Christians. They do not know what it is to be really happy; they do not know what it is to have real life and joy and vigor and enthusiasm. That other life is a life that drags you down; it cripples you and leaves you a wreck and an empty husk. Here is life: "I am come that they might have life, and that they might have it more abundantly" (John 10:10). It begins here; then it grows, it expands, and it continues throughout eternity. That is what people are rejecting with such scorn and anger, with such bitterness and annoyance, as though they have been insulted.

The Gospel tells you that you can be born again, that you can have a new start, that you can have a new principle of life and a power put into you with the Spirit of God dwelling in you, a power that will set you free. And yet that is what so many people hate. Their great minds do not seem to help them very much, do they? They do not help them to keep sober or to be loyal to their marriage contracts. Their minds do not keep them from their perversions. No, no; their great minds do not help them in any respect except in some mechanical, superficial ways. But here is life that is life indeed, life that is eternal. To reject this, and to reject it with passion, is nothing but a demonstration of utter irrationality.

The final proof of irrationality is this: The members of the Sanhedrin ordered the apostles to be seized and thrown into the common prison. They had the authority, the power, and they were going to put a stop to this preaching and healing. But—and there it is, this Christianity, this "but" that comes in, this blessed "but," God, the power of God—"The angel of the Lord by night opened the prison doors, and brought them forth, and said, Go, stand and speak . . ." Defy them; do the thing they are telling you not to do.

The unbeliever is such a fool. He not only rejects the most glorious person the world has ever seen, he not only rejects the most glorious teaching the world has ever heard, he not only rejects life and the offer of eternal salvation, but he is mad enough to defy the living God! He thinks he has power—the power of knowledge, the power of authority, the power of science, the power of the twentieth century—and he locks the prison doors; he is going to put an end to this thing. But he cannot! Those who have been put in prison always come out.

These leaders ought to have known better; that is why we must emphasize that word "then" in verse 17: "*Then* the high priest rose up." When? After the deaths of Ananias and Sapphira. The fools! Why did they not see the power of God there, after all the miracles? They were standing against that, not against men. They were not opposing ignorant and uneducated men, but the power of God. And they became the laughingstock of the populace whom they had thought they could impress. That is the final irrationality and madness of unbelief.

If you reject this Gospel, you are not rejecting me, the preacher, you are rejecting God. The power of God. Here it is, in one incident. Lock the door of the common prison, put the guards there—but the angel of the Lord sets them free!

And that is a summary of the whole of the subsequent history of the church. In the first century clever people thought they could put an end to Christianity. Throughout the centuries they were of the same opinion, and by sword and stake, by hanging and other physical means, and in intellectual ways, as we see today, they have done their utmost to destroy the faith. But it is all futile. God has settled this once and forever.

The devil brought out his last reserves when he brought about the death and burial of the Son of God, and he thought he had triumphed. But the resurrection is the eternal answer. Though men and devils and hell still do all they can to finish Christianity and lock it up once and forever, the doors will always be opened, and the messengers, whom they think they have killed off, will be standing and addressing the world and its peoples, and the Gospel will be leading many to salvation and to life.

The final irrationality of sin is that it is not pitting itself against a man or a human teaching but against the living God. And whatever this twentieth century may do:

> *Jesus shall reign where'er the sun*
> *Doth his successive journeys run;*
> *His kingdom stretch from shore to shore,*
> *Till moons shall wax and wane no more.*
>   Isaac Watts

Oh, I plead with you, see your irrationality. Repent, acknowledge your folly and your error, and believe the Gospel. "Believe on the Lord Jesus Christ, and thou shalt be saved" (Acts 16:31) and will be given life, and life more abundant.

2

"ALL THE WORDS OF THIS LIFE"

The angel of the Lord by night opened the prison doors, and brought them forth, and said, Go, stand and speak in the temple to the people all the words of this life. . . . Then Peter and the other apostles answered and said, We ought to obey God rather than men.

—Acts 5:19-20, 29

We have begun a consideration of this remarkable incident in the life of the early church and of the apostles in particular. All these incidents in the life of the early church are full of wonder and amazement, and the reason for that, as we have been seeing, is that here we are reminded that we are in the realm of the supernatural, the divine, the miraculous, and these incidents are recorded and put before us in order that we may be perfectly clear about that.

In our last study we saw that this incident gives a portrayal of unbelief, but now we shall look at it from a different standpoint and consider what it tells us about the message of the church, how she ever got this message, and therefore what the church herself really is. If we really want to know how it ever came to pass that someone who was regarded as nothing but a Jewish carpenter, an uneducated man, should become the central figure of all human history, and His cause and His people the dominating force in the world over many centuries, if we want to understand all that, then there is only one thing to do. We must come back here to the story that we have in this book, to the story of how the church ever came into being. And in that connection, nothing is more important than her message, because it is the message that has always done the work.

The church spread as the result of preaching. So nothing can be more important than to understand the character and content of her message. And this is particularly important at the present time because here, surely, is the great and the central problem. People are asking why the Christian church should go on. They want to know whether she is just an anachronism in this modern world, whether we can justify her continued existence. They ask, "Why should we listen to the Gospel?"

Now the vast majority will not listen because they say that the gospel message has nothing to do with them, that it is irrelevant and out-of-date. So we must face this great question. We must be able to answer people when they ask us, "What right have you to address the world? What right have you, with the world as it is today, to stand up and just go on repeating that old message?" That is the challenge that we must meet, and we are very ready to do so.

Or, to put it another way, Why is it that people are so confused about the Gospel? There is still a lot of discussion about it. Though people do not attend places of worship, they like to listen to the discussions and interviews, and they read the articles. The church's teaching is still a topic of interest in the press and on television and radio.

I suggest that the difficulty people have with the Gospel is dealt with in the incident that we are now considering. This passage emphasizes that their problem is not so much because of particular aspects or statements but stems from the essential truth of the Gospel and people's wrong approach to it. In other words, people have problems listening to the Gospel because they totally misunderstand its nature. And unfortunately, to make matters worse, this lack of understanding is not only true of the world outside the church, but of many who are inside, as we see from their books and articles. Then when we listen to them speaking, we are doubly certain.

Now in general the difficulty is that all teaching on religious issues seems to have become vague and uncertain. The great idea is that whatever may have been true in the past has now changed. Because we are now living in an atomic, scientific age, our first task should be to seek for a new message, a message that is adequate for "the modern man" and will be of help to people at a time such as this.

Now that approach ultimately raises the whole question of authority. What is our authority in these matters? What authority does the Christian church possess? And I contend that the church can only justify her continuance in terms of one particular authority. If she does not make sure of that, if she is not certain of it, then, as the phrase puts it, "She's finished."

Authority! This is the fundamental issue in all these early chapters of Acts. These apostles, these simple, uneducated men, were able to act with authority. At the Beautiful Gate of the temple Peter and John were confronted by a lame man. He was over forty years old, and he had never walked in his life, but they looked at him and said, "In the name of Jesus Christ of Nazareth rise up and walk" (Acts 3:6); and he did!

But in a few hours these two apostles were standing on trial before the great Sanhedrin in Jerusalem, facing a most imposing array of dignitaries and legal authorities. They had no advocate, they did not have the money for one, and they knew, furthermore, that nobody could defend them. But Peter did not hesitate to look straight into the eyes of these great authorities and say:

> *Ye rulers of the people, and elders of Israel, If we this day be examined of the good deed done to the impotent man, by what means he is made whole; be it known unto you all, and to all the people of Israel, that by the name of Jesus Christ of Nazareth, whom ye crucified, whom God raised from the dead, even by him doth this man stand here before you whole. This is the stone which was set at nought of you builders, which is become the head of the corner. Neither is there salvation in any other: for there is none other name under heaven given among men, whereby we must be saved.*
>
> *Acts 4:8-12*

Authority, even in the presence of this great authority, the Sanhedrin!

And now here, in Acts 5, we have a kind of repetition of that trial because the apostles have once more been arrested and thrown into prison. But this time they are delivered miraculously from their imprisonment and are commanded by the angel, "Go, stand and speak in the temple to the people all the words of this life." And Peter says to the authorities, "We ought to obey God rather than men" (v. 29).

And I repeat that the problem facing the church today concerns the whole question of authority. So let us consider what we are told here. The first principle is that the church succeeded, she did what she did, she turned the world upside-down, she became a great power among men—why?—because she knew that she was delivering the message of God. That is what stands out in the passage we are now studying. The angel gave the apostles God's command. And when the Sanhedrin said, "Did we not straitly command you that ye should not teach in this name? and, behold, ye have filled Jerusalem with your doctrine, and intend to bring this man's blood upon us," Peter's defense was that they were obeying God.

And obedience to God is the point at which we must always start. That is the character of this message. It is, as we read in 1 Thessalonians 2:2, "the gospel of God." The Gospel is not a theory that has been worked out by human beings. The whole notion of "seeking after truth," of "trying to discover a message" completely contradicts the plain teaching of the church in the first century and in every period of reformation and revival. The Gospel is not a human discovery or the result of thought and meditation, of discussion and dialogue, of delving into the opinions of philosophers. It is not the result of a process of "sharpening mind with mind." No; it is something quite different.

The trouble at the present time is that the whole emphasis is placed upon what is called "the quest for truth." I could quote you great names who have been teaching this. They have put their views into print; so why should I not quote them? I read an article by the present Archbishop of Canterbury[4] in which he writes, "The quest for faith is even better than faith itself." The whole emphasis is upon this search.

It is said that the thrilling thing about living in the twentieth century is that we are now in a new realm. We now have new knowledge, and the past is finished. Just as we are sending men into outer space and are discovering hitherto unknown facts about the moon, we are discovering fresh truth about "ultimate reality." And there is nothing more fatal, says the Archbishop in his article, than "orthodoxy." Orthodoxy is static. If you think you have arrived at truth, there is nothing left to hope for. It is the quest itself that is wonderful. It extends ever on before you; so you are traveling and seeking all your life. And we are told that it is the business of the church to stimulate men and women to enter upon this great quest for faith.

I remember reading a book in which the author uses the following illustration. Suppose a man came to you and said that he had a gift in each hand. In his right hand he had the quest for truth, and in his left hand he had truth itself. And suppose the man said, "You can choose one of these gifts—which one will you choose?" The author of this book then wrote, "I would undoubtedly choose the gift in the right hand." He preferred the quest for truth to truth itself.

Now that is of the essence of the modern position: Men and women are dissatisfied, but they feel they are on a great adventure, seekers and searchers after the truth, this truth that will give them happiness and joy and peace.

They will never arrive, but they will have made some progress, and their successors will follow on from where they left off. So on and on they go, and they are always traveling. Now that is the exact opposite of what we read here. "Go, stand and speak in the temple to the people all the words of this life." This message is not our discovery or our intuition. It does not come as the result of our seeking. It is given by God.

We are told so often in the Scriptures that the message is God's gift that it is almost impossible to understand how anyone claiming the name Christian can say anything else. Take, for instance, the magnificent opening statement of the letter to the Hebrews:

> *God, who at sundry times and in divers manners spake in time past unto the fathers by the prophets, hath in these last days spoken unto us by his Son, whom he hath appointed heir of all things, by whom also he made the worlds.*
>
> Heb. 1:1-2

You see what the writer is saying—God is speaking! And do you not realize that at once we have crossed the great watershed? We are no longer in the realm of human beings. To embark on a quest is all right when we are dealing with scientific matters, quite all right if we are trying to explore outer space and find out about the surface of the moon. Let men and women experiment; let them seek out information by the process of trial and error. It is absolutely all right. They set out, and they discover. Wonderful!

But where Christianity is concerned, we are in the realm of revelation. The apostle Paul told the Thessalonians how thankful he was that they had recognized that the Gospel had come from God: "For this cause also thank we God without ceasing, because, when ye received the word of God which ye heard of us, ye received it not as the word of men, but as it is in truth, the word of God, which effectually worketh also in you that believe" (1 Thess. 2:13).

At the beginning of 1 Thessalonians 2, Paul writes in a wonderful way of God's revelation: "But as we were allowed of God to be put in trust with the gospel . . ." (v. 4). That is diametrically opposed to saying, "I, Paul, as the result of my researches and my deep meditation upon life and its attendant problems, have come to a major conclusion and am developing a theory. My new idea is explored in my latest book where you will see that I am introducing a new school of thought—the school of Paul—following on from the schools of Plato, Socrates, and Aristotle."

Paul writes in the same way in his letter to the Corinthians. The foolish people in Corinth had been comparing and contrasting Paul and Apollos, arguing about who was the better preacher and who had the better message. Paul says, "You have misunderstood the whole thing. Apollos and I are nothing. We have not discovered anything. We are not preaching what *we* think. 'We preach not ourselves, but Christ Jesus the Lord' (2 Cor. 4:5). We are but 'stewards of the mysteries of God' (1 Cor. 4:1). We are but custodians and guardians. We have simply been given the great privilege of handling this message." And Paul tells his readers how careful he is lest he in any way misrepresent the Gospel. "We have this treasure in earthen vessels" (2 Cor. 4:7).

God committed the gospel message to men—that is the teaching all the way through the New Testament. Take the apostles. Peter and John were just ordinary fishermen, and they and the others, as the authorities rightly said, were nothing but "unlearned and ignorant men" (Acts 4:13). Is it not monstrous to suggest that these men were preaching a message they had worked out for themselves, that they were like the Greek philosophers, propounding their ideas and putting forward a new view of life? The whole idea is so ridiculous that it is amazing that anybody could possibly believe it.

What had happened to Peter and John? Why was it that they could stand up and address the Sanhedrin as they did? There is only one answer: They had been given their message. They had followed their blessed Lord and Master for three years; they had heard all His teaching and had seen what had happened to Him. And after His resurrection, He had taken them through the Scriptures. He had given them the message and had put them in charge of it. They were simply repeating exactly what He had told them to say.

And as we have seen, our Lord had also given His message to the apostle Paul. In Acts 26 we can read Paul's account of his own calling into the ministry. We are told that on the road to Damascus, Paul met the Lord, who said to him:

> *Rise, and stand upon thy feet: for I have appeared unto thee for this purpose, to make thee a minister and a witness both of these things which thou hast seen, and of those things in the which I will appear unto thee; delivering thee from the people, and from the Gentiles, unto whom now I send thee, to open their eyes, and to turn them from darkness to light, and from the power of Satan unto God, that*

they may receive forgiveness of sins, and inheritance among them which are sanctified by faith that is in me.

Acts 26:16-18

That was Paul's calling.

In Ephesians 3 Paul describes his calling in this way: "the dispensation of the grace of God which is given me to you-ward: how that by revelation he made known unto me the mystery" (Eph. 3:2-3). And he writes to the Corinthians: "And last of all he [the Lord] was seen of me also. . . . For I am the least of the apostles, that am not meet to be called an apostle, because I persecuted the church of God" (1 Cor. 15:8-9).

Now are we clear about this? I do not stand in the pulpit Sunday by Sunday to give my own ruminations on life during the past week. That is not preaching the Gospel. I do not simply try to tell how I see things. I am an expositor; it is all here before me, in the Bible. I am simply putting this biblical message forward in my own language, trying to make it plain and clear. The Gospel is God's message. As it was the message of the early church and the message of the church throughout the running centuries, so it is my message.

And that brings me to my second point. Because the Gospel is the message of God to men and women, it must be an unchanging Gospel. That is logical, is it not? As the hymn says:

> *O Word of God incarnate,*
> *O Wisdom from on high!*
> *O Truth unchanged, unchanging. . . .*
>
> W. W. How

"Unchanged"! "Unchanging"! Why? Because it is from God. Do you see how relevant this is to the modern position?

I can give you additional reasons for saying that the Gospel is an unchanging message. This was the message that saved people in the first century. It is the message that has been saving people in every other century. And since people do not change, they must have the same message in this century. The church came into being by preaching the message of the Gospel. She was given both the authority and the message. This is the only message, the only way whereby we can be saved. Peter had already said that to these people in Jerusalem: "Neither is there salvation in any other: for there is none other name under heaven given among men, whereby we must be saved" (Acts 4:12). This is not a matter of dispute—it is a question of fact.

Do you know of anything, other than the Gospel, that can save people? With all our advances and increase in knowledge, why is our world as it is? We do not seem to be very successful at saving society or at saving the world, do we? And we cannot save ourselves. People in the first century were victims of drink and sex and drugs, and they still are! They are no more able to overcome these addictions now than then. There is only one power that can do this impossible thing: It is the Gospel, the same message.

Now it is characteristic of men and women that they are always subject to changing whims and fashions in human thought. I can demonstrate this by pointing to the popularity at different times of different types of teaching. In the ancient world there were rival schools of philosophy, and ever since there have been great swings in academic opinion. Look at the last hundred to a hundred and fifty years. Until comparatively recently, the scientific outlook was purely materialistic. It is no longer that; today materialism is ridiculed. We now have a new and completely different physics—astrophysics or whatever name you may like to call it.

Anybody who has ever been a student has seen the way in which ideas change. The medical textbooks that some of us used thirty or forty years ago are now hopelessly out-of-date. Indeed, I recently heard of a group of doctors who solemnly asserted that anyone who qualified as a doctor before 1945 could not possibly understand modern medicine. At one time the one cure for every illness was to bleed a patient; so there were barber surgeons who bled everybody and undoubtedly killed thousands. Today there is a different view!

Now some people are foolish enough to think that because there are changes and fashions in thinking, all ideas must change, including the Christian message. But if you start by realizing that we are concerned here, not with human thought, but with God's thought, then you see how ridiculous it is to think that the message should in any way be affected by changing fashions. God cannot change. God is. And God is what God always was. There is no beginning; there is no end. He is the eternal I AM. And when He speaks, His words must therefore be the eternal and unchanging truth.

It is very important to understand that the Gospel is dependent, not on changing human nature, but on the unchanging God, and this is where so many go astray today. Their slogans are: "A new message for this atomic age!" "A new message for this scientific age, this post-war world!" "Modern man and his needs!" But that is rubbish. As we have seen, men and women always remain the same. Their needs are the same, and their difficulties are no greater. People had problems with the Gospel at the very beginning, and they still have problems. And the Gospel remains unaffected by the changing scenes of time because it is the message of God.

"Go," said the angel, "stand and speak in the temple to the people all the words of this life."

"You leaders tell us not to preach," said Peter, "but 'We ought to obey God'—who has given us the message—'rather than men.'"

That brings us to the next proposition, which is that the Gospel is a particular message: "all the *words* of this life." "Words"! This is not something vague and nebulous, not simply philosophical musings or poetic outpourings, not fancies and imaginations, not playing with ideas or embarking on a quest for truth. The Gospel is a definable message; there is no difficulty about knowing what it is.

Of course, I am well aware that when I say we can know what the gospel message is, I am regarded as being beyond the pale in every possible sense! The very suggestion is anathema—the Christian faith is a quest for truth, it is said, and it is the seeking that is thrilling! But there would never have been a church if the early Christians had taken that view. Seeking is all right for people who have been through Cambridge or Oxford and have studied philosophy and so on. They can explore ideas and write books to one another. It is marvelous and exciting, and the intellectuals follow it all.

But what, I ask you, about Tom, Dick, and Harry in the street? What do they know about this quest for truth and reality and clever philosophical arguments and disputations? It has nothing to give them. We must all face the fact that the masses of the people are outside the church in this country. Why? There is nothing wrong with the message. I read in the Gospel, "The common people heard him gladly" (Mark 12:37), and there is something wrong with a church that does not appeal to "the common people."

The Gospel is a clearly defined message—there is no doubt about that at all. This is emphasized everywhere in the New Testament. Let me give you one or two examples. The apostle Paul, writing to the Corinthians, reminds them of what he had preached to them:

Moreover, brethren, I declare unto you the gospel which I preached unto you, which also ye have received, and wherein ye stand; by which also ye are saved, if ye keep in memory what I preached unto you, unless ye have believed in vain. For I delivered unto you first of all that which I also received, how that Christ died for our sins

*according to the scriptures; and that he was buried, and that he rose
again the third day according to the scriptures; and that he was seen
of Cephas, then of the twelve.*

                                                              1 Cor. 15:1-5

And Paul says, as we have seen:

*I am the least of the apostles, that am not meet to be called an apos-
tle, because I persecuted the church of God. But by the grace of God
I am what I am. . . . Therefore whether it were I or they, so we
preach, and so ye believed.*

                                                            1 Cor. 15:9-11

In other words, the Gospel is not only a clearly defined message—it was
the one message that was preached by all the apostles. Paul did not belong to
the company that had accompanied our Lord during His life here on earth.
At that time he had been a persecutor, a blasphemer, a self-righteous Pharisee.
But he had been apprehended on the road to Damascus and was given a commission, and this was the message that he had been given. Paul says, "It is the
same message. They know what it is; I know what it is. There is no confusion, no uncertainty with respect to what it is."

How tragic it is that men and women should stumble here, at the very
approach to the Gospel. Their souls are lost; they are miserable; they cannot live; they cannot die; they are "without a hope to cheer the tomb," all
because of this initial misunderstanding. This is not an uncertain message.
It was preached dogmatically by the apostles, and it has been preached dogmatically ever since whenever the church has been truly functioning as a
church.

But now I want to take this a step further. Not only *can* this Gospel be
clearly defined, it *must* be clearly defined, and we must differentiate between
the Gospel and all false teachings, including any teaching that wrongly represents itself as a gospel. Paul says to the Galatians, "I marvel that ye are so
soon removed from him that called you into the grace of Christ unto another
gospel: which is not another; but there be some that trouble you, and would
pervert the gospel of Christ" (Gal. 1:6-7). How could Paul have written those
words if it had not been clear what the Gospel was? How can you say that
another person's teaching is wrong if you do not know what the true teaching is? If the Gospel is just some wonderful feeling inside, or some marvelous
sensation resulting from hopes and speculations and desires, or if it is a great

thrilling quest for truth—if that is the Gospel, then how can you say that any teaching is wrong, that it is "another gospel"?

But Paul goes further. He says:

> *Though we, or an angel from heaven, preach any other gospel unto you than that which we have preached unto you, let him be accursed. As we said before, so say I now again, If any man preach any other gospel unto you than that ye have received, let him be accursed. For do I now persuade men, or God? or do I seek to please men? for if I yet pleased men, I should not be the servant of Christ. But I certify you, brethren, that the gospel which was preached of me is not after man. For I neither received it of man, neither was I taught it, but by the revelation of Jesus Christ.*
>
> *Gal. 1:8-12*

Paul knew what the Gospel was because it was not his own conjecture. He was given it; he was told exactly what it was and was given the command, "Go!" ". . . delivering thee from the people, and from the Gentiles, unto whom now I send thee" (Acts 26:17).

So Paul not only knew what he was preaching—he could say that anything that contradicted it was wrong. Later on he wrote to Timothy, "Remember that Jesus Christ of the seed of David was raised from the dead according to my gospel" (2 Tim. 2:8). And his Gospel, I repeat, was the same Gospel as that preached by all the other apostles.

Can you not see that these things follow by a logical necessity? It is God's Gospel. It is therefore unchanging and clearly defined. So anything that is vague and loose and uncertain, anything that is only developing and trying to arrive at truth, is not the Gospel. And because we know what the Gospel is, we can say that nothing else is the Gospel. With the apostle John, we can speak of "antichrists." We can denounce error and say it is not Christianity.

But I want to emphasize something else. "Go, and speak in the temple to the people all the words of this life," said the angel. I want to stress the word "all." The Gospel is comprehensive and many-sided—"*all* the words of this life." I read an article by a learned philosopher who is an elder in his church, and in this article he attacks the orthodox faith; he attacks the Gospel as preached by the apostles.

This philosopher says, "These orthodox people, these fundamentalists," as he calls them, "they talk about the wrath of God and about the absolute necessity of the death of the Son of God. They have their Communion services, broken body, poured out blood, and they say that the Son of God had to bear the punishment of sins. How terribly wrong this is, how tragically wrong! That has been the trouble. People have been held under that sort of legalism for all the centuries. But now we are beginning to see through that sort of thing and we know it is all wrong."

And this is how that philosopher proves his assertion. He says: "Where do you find all that in the parable of the prodigal son? That fundamentalist teaching libels God. God is like the father of the prodigal son. The boy makes a fool of himself, wakes up to the realization of that in the far country, and then goes home and says to his father, 'Father, I'm sorry.' But the father does not say to him, 'It's all right for you to be sorry, but I cannot forgive you like that. Some atonement must be made. Some sort of sacrifice is needed. In order for this to be put right, the law must be satisfied.' No, it was nothing like that. The father embraced his son. Indeed, he ran to meet him and before the boy began to say anything, his father was kissing him and surrounding him with his love. That is the Christian message."

Now that is an argument you hear so often; there is nothing new about it. I have heard it and read it many, many times. We are asked to believe that the whole message of the Gospel is summed up in the parable of the prodigal son and nothing else needs to be added.

Others tell us that the whole Christian message is given in the Sermon on the Mount. None of your doctrine or your dogma, none of this theological teaching about atonement, and so on: Christianity is a moral, ethical code teaching people how to live.

But the command the angel gave to these men was, "Go, stand and speak in the temple to the people all the words of this life." And when Peter began to speak, he talked about the one "whom ye slew and hanged on a tree." And he said, "Him hath God exalted with his right hand to be a Prince and a Saviour, for to give repentance to Israel, and forgiveness of sins" (Acts 5:30-31). We shall not consider those words in detail now, because at this point I am concerned about a totally wrong attitude to the Gospel—the failure to realize how big and comprehensive it is. It cannot be summed up in the parable of the prodigal son.

The one who uttered the parable of the prodigal son also said, "The Son of man came not to be ministered unto, but to minister, and to give his life a ransom for many" (Matt. 20:28). He said, "Except a corn of wheat fall into the ground and die, it abideth alone: but if it die, it bringeth forth much fruit" (John 12:24). Also, "And I, if I be lifted up from the earth"—He is referring to His death—"will draw all men unto me" (John 12:32). "As Moses lifted up the serpent in the wilderness, even so must the Son of man be lifted up: that whosoever believeth in him should not perish, but have eternal life" (John 3:14-15).

You see how monstrous and how tragic it is to insist that the whole Gospel is in the parable of the prodigal son, and that any teaching that is not there is false! No; we are commanded to preach *"all* the words of this life." This means that there is a sense in which the Gospel is simple, but there is also a sense in which it is the most profound message that has ever come into this world. There is a sense in which you and I, in our weakness and help-lessness and hopelessness, simply believe. But you do not stop at that. And to me, one of the most marvelous things about the Gospel is its comprehen-siveness, its largeness, its greatness, its many-sidedness.

The Gospel is a great body of truth, a great body of doctrine; it is a great theology, a marvelous, biblical, systematic theology. "God, who at sundry times and in divers manners spake in time past unto the fathers . . ." (Heb. 1:1). He did it in parts and portions. He revealed this, then that, and on it went, this great comprehensive truth, this corpus of truth, this marvelous truth of God.

What is the Gospel? It is the whole message of the Bible, and that is where the world has gone wrong. The world does not believe the Bible but trusts to human thought and speculation and theorizing. But Peter and John had been given "all the words of this life." This is a message that goes back to cre-ation—the creation of the world and of human beings.

At the risk of being misunderstood, let me say that many intelligent men and women have been kept outside the Gospel because true believers have sometimes failed to present the message correctly. The Gospel is not just a plea to "come to Jesus." It ends there, but it does not start there. That is not the beginning and the end of the message. "Emotionalism!" Is it? No, no! If you are to present "all the words of this life," you must start by asking ques-tions: What is the world? Where has it come from? What is man? Why is he as he is? That is a part of this message. It starts with the whole creation, the whole cosmos. "All the words of this life" includes the Old Testament as well as the New. I know moderns do not like the God of the Old Testament. They like the God and Father of our Lord Jesus Christ. But our Lord believed the Old Testament!

The tragedy we are in is that men and women no longer have any author-ity to turn to. It is part of the "quest for truth" to say things at random, the last thing that has been thought of, as it were. But where does that leave you? What do you have to live on? "In the beginning God" (Gen. 1:1). Creation!

Another vital part of gospel preaching is the fall of man. That is a part of "all the words of this life." Why do we need salvation? What is the matter with us? Why are we as we are? Now the Gospel must deal with that, and it does—it tells us why things are as they are; it tells us about man disobeying, rebelling, falling, getting into trouble. And then it teaches the judgment of God upon that, and it tells us that the world is as it is chiefly because of human sin and God's judgment on that sin.

Then the Gospel introduces a grand redemption. Listen to these resounding phrases: "But of him are ye in Christ Jesus, who of God is made unto us wisdom, and righteousness, and sanctification, and redemption" (1 Cor. 1:30). Do you know what that means? This is a part of "all the words of this life," this full-orbed, complete Gospel.

Let me give you another great statement of this grand redemption, and if this does not do you good, there is something wrong with your mind, let alone your heart! "We know that all things work together for good to them that love God, to them who are the called according to his purpose" (Rom. 8:28). "The called"! Do you know anything about the doctrine of the call of God? Paul speaks about the effectual call in 1 Thessalonians 2:13: "which effectually worketh also in you that believe."

And then in Romans Paul goes on to say, "For whom he did foreknow, he also did predestinate to be conformed to the image of his Son, that he might be the firstborn among many brethren. Moreover whom he did predestinate, them he also called: and whom he called, them he also justified: and whom he justified, them he also glorified" (Rom. 8:29-30). "What shall we then say to these things?" asks the apostle (v. 31). My answer is: This is glorious! Marvelous! Worthy of God and of Him alone! This complete, comprehensive, glorious salvation!

And then, of course, there is the final judgment, the coming again of the Son of God into this world to judge it in righteousness and to pronounce the eternal verdict—on those who have believed this message, blessing; on those who have rejected it, eternal perdition outside the life of God.

But the gospel message does not stop at judgment—there is restoration, the whole universe renovated, redeemed; the great regeneration when the Son of God shall come again out of heaven back into this world and shall restore this fallen creation to its original perfection and even heighten its glory.

All that is something of the content of "all the words of this life." And I close with this word: All and every part is essential to the Gospel. You and I are not to choose; we are not to take out what we like and reject what we do not like. It is not for us to approve or disapprove any part of the

Gospel. It is altogether of God, and therefore we are to believe it and to accept it as it is. I always tell people that they must read the whole Bible and try to do so once a year at least. Not just your favorite passages. You do not select—it is all the Word of God. Read it all; you fail to do so at your peril.

And the preacher must preach "all the words of this life." He does not choose. Paul puts it wonderfully in preaching to the Christians in Thessalonica. He reminds them that preachers who want to please people omit certain teachings because they are unpopular. But Paul says that he does not do that: "But as we were allowed of God to be put in trust with the gospel, even so we speak; not as pleasing men, but God, which trieth our hearts. For neither at any time used we flattering words, as ye know, nor a cloak of covetousness; God is witness: nor of men sought we glory" (1 Thess. 2:4-6).

The apostle Paul never tried to wheedle his congregation; he never tried to get around them and tell them emotional stories; he never threw in a joke or two in order to humor them and put them on his side. He never tried to show off. He did the exact opposite of all that. He preached the unvarnished truth, unpleasant though it is to fallen human nature.

But today people subtract from the Gospel, do they not? They say, "We can no longer believe the early chapters of Genesis; science proves that they're not true." Actually it does not, of course.

"But," people say, "evolution disproves Genesis."

But what is evolution? It is just a theory. It has never been proved, and it never will be. But why am I concerned about this? It is because the Gospel is a unit, a whole, and if you reject any part of it, you will be in trouble with all the rest.

You might say, "I think man has evolved out of the animals, but I am still a Christian—I still believe in the doctrine of salvation." But how can you? What do men and women need to be saved from? Why do they need to be saved? Have they ever been perfect? Has there been a fall or not? How many people fell if there was a fall? The whole of the Gospel hangs together.

And then people say they cannot possibly accept the teaching in the Bible about the wrath of God. But Paul says to the Romans, "The wrath of God is revealed from heaven against all ungodliness and unrighteousness of men, who hold the truth in unrighteousness" (1:18).

"Of course," they reply, "he would say that—he was a Jew and had been brought up as a Pharisee. He believed in the God of Sinai, the God of the Old Testament. He didn't know the God and Father of our Lord Jesus Christ, the

God of Jesus. The parable of the prodigal son proves that there's no such thing as wrath in God."

But if you take out the wrath of God, why did the Son ever die? Why did He "stedfastly set his face to go to Jerusalem" (Luke 9:51)? Why did He say He had to die? Why did these apostles preach that His death was essential? You must be careful. I say again that if you subtract from this Gospel at any point you will always be in trouble because the message will no longer be consistent.

Let me add this on the other side: You must preach "all the words of this life." You do not take from it, but you do not add to it either. It is all here. It was all given to these first apostles. The Roman Catholic Church claims that she has made discoveries since the time of the apostles. She claims, indeed, that new truths have been revealed to her. But there is only one answer to that, and let us be clear about this in days when men and women are thinking so loosely about these matters.

Jude says, "Beloved, when I gave all diligence to write unto you of the common salvation, it was needful for me to write unto you, and exhort you that ye should earnestly contend for the faith which was once [and forever] delivered unto the saints" (Jude 3). It was all given to these first apostles, and there never has been and never can be any addition to it. Mary is not a "co-redemptrix"! We do not need the help of the saints who are in glory. We do not need and must not be utterly dependent upon the ministrations of priests. You are not saved by being baptized. You are not saved by taking Communion or by the absolution pronounced by a priest.

The test that the early church applied to any book that was put forward for inclusion in the canon of the New Testament was the test of apostolicity. If a letter or book could not be traced to the apostles, it was not included. The message that saved the first Christians is the only message that can save anyone. And every part is essential in the perfect mosaic of God's plan of redemption.

We preach "all the words of this life" because of the glory of the whole. Paul, in the third chapter of his letter to the Ephesians, refers to the Gospel as "the manifold wisdom of God" (v. 10). That is the message. The world in sin and shame, the failure of civilization, the problem of men and women and their need for deliverance—it seems hopeless; nothing can be done. But here comes the "manifold," variegated wisdom of God, and how glorious it is, seen in its completeness in the face of Jesus Christ.

That is why I tremble to leave out anything. That is why I always try to give the whole Gospel. It is all in Christ. "For in him dwelleth all the fulness of the Godhead bodily" (Col. 2:9). "In whom are hid all the treasures of wisdom and knowledge" (Col. 2:3), and all God's power and everything else.

That is the Gospel; that is the message: "all the words of this life"! Do you know them? Do you believe them? Are you rejoicing in them? May God deliver us all from the thralldom, the fetters of modern thought and knowledge, which is blinding humanity to the manifold, comprehensive, all-inclusive wisdom of God in Jesus Christ our Lord.

3

THE CONTENT OF THE MESSAGE

Then Peter and the other apostles answered and said, We ought to obey God rather than men. The God of our fathers raised up Jesus, whom ye slew and hanged on a tree. Him hath God exalted with his right hand to be a Prince and a Saviour, for to give repentance to Israel, and forgiveness of sins. And we are his witnesses of these things; and so is also the Holy Ghost, whom God hath given to them that obey him.

—Acts 5:29-32

We have considered the general character of the message that was preached at the beginning by the apostles, and now we move on to consider the message itself. Obviously, within the limits of one sermon I can only begin to approach such a theme. But what is the content of this message? What is the Christian church to preach? What am I commissioned to preach?

The answer is that I am to preach the great message that is known as the message of salvation. And clearly, as the whole of the New Testament indicates to us, it is the message that is concentrated particularly in the person of our Lord and Savior Jesus Christ: "The God of our fathers raised up Jesus. . . . Him hath God exalted with his right hand to be a Prince and a Saviour, for to give repentance to Israel, and forgiveness of sins."

Now Peter and John were in trouble because they were preaching "Jesus"—Jesus and the resurrection (Acts 4:2). That was all they preached. When they worked a miracle and people were ready to fall down at their feet and worship them, they said, "Don't do that. We've not healed the man. His healing is not because of any power or godliness in us, but is because of 'his name through faith in his name' (Acts 3:16); the one whom you rejected and crucified has made the lame man walk."

And when the apostles were set free from prison, Peter put the same message to the authorities with his customary boldness and bluntness. In his sermon, he reminded them of the tragic fact that they had rejected the Lord Jesus Christ and all that He had come to do for the human race. Peter put it quite plainly: "The God of our fathers raised up Jesus, whom ye slew and hanged on a tree. Him hath God exalted with his right hand to be a Prince and a Saviour."

Peter presented the gospel message in terms of a contrast: salvation through Christ Jesus or rejection of this person and all that He stood for. He again pressed upon the Jewish authorities the tragedy of their rejection of Christ, and it is this that I am anxious to draw to your attention, for it is still the great tragedy of the human race. There are many other and lesser tragedies—the world is increasingly a tragic place—but the rejection of the Lord Jesus Christ is the tragedy of tragedies. Indeed, it is this tragedy that accounts for all the others because here humanity is rejecting its one and only way of salvation.

The world in its unhappiness, with its problems and perplexities, is seeking deliverance; it is desperately looking for an answer to its problems, searching for it in every possible way; and yet when a solution is offered, the world rejects it, rejecting the only thing that really can give the satisfaction for which it longs. It is this tragedy that is pinpointed in the words of the apostles to the Sanhedrin. In these words we have a summary of human history; this is what has been happening throughout the centuries, and it confronts us today.

But why does the world reject the Gospel? The answer is shown very clearly in this incident in Acts 5. The reasons do not change. Of course, we like to assure ourselves that our reasons for rejecting the Gospel are new, but that is where we are completely wrong. Men and women reject the Gospel for all the old reasons.

The world is in trouble: It has a problem with the Gospel. But what is the cause of this trouble? It is due to the fact that the world's ideas of salvation and redemption are all wrong. Here in the Bible I find a wonderful contrast in the true teaching about the Redeemer and redemption. Let me put it to you in a number of propositions.

The first proposition is that according to apostolic preaching, according to the true message of the Christian church, the Lord Jesus Christ is God's way of salvation. Notice the emphasis: He is *God's* way of salvation. I am compelled to say that because of the words that are used: "The God of our father raised up Jesus" (v. 30). It is God who has done this.

Here we come immediately to the first great contrast. The world seeks redemption, but always in its own way. The world looks to human beings for emancipation. And so the writers of biographies and the historians say, "Suddenly a genius appeared," or "This outstanding and gifted man came upon the scene." That is the outlook of the world. It looks for saviors who display its own wisdom, education, training, and knowledge. It has always believed this is the way to find salvation. This is what it means when it talks about "civilization."

Civilization is the attempt of the human race to get out of its difficulties and problems. It is always hoping that it will produce a wise man, that out of all this striving and effort and thought and philosophizing suddenly some outstanding genius will appear who will utter the magic formula that will solve all the world's problems. Of course, each generation has its variations and changes. We say, absolutely rightly, that we are now living in the days of small men, that there are no longer any great people, and the world is waiting for them.

Oh, how confident they were in the nineteenth century that the twentieth century really would bring about worldwide peace and happiness: the parliament of man, the federation of the world. We would be "beating our swords into plowshares" in the next century, the golden century, the twentieth century, the crowning century of all civilization. And though we now tend to be more cynical, we still persist in the hope that somehow or another, as the result of all our efforts and organization, we will produce someone who will lead us to the salvation for which we long. The world is always looking to the future, always hoping that the solution will come. What a fallacy all this is! The world has to realize that there is only one who can save it and deal with its problems, and that is God.

Here is the message of the Bible: "The God of our fathers raised up Jesus." Now some people tend to misinterpret that statement. They think that it refers to the resurrection, but that comes later, in verse 31: "Him hath God exalted with his right hand." No; the words "raised up" are used in the Old Testament sense of God raising up a leader or a prophet (I shall shortly be looking at Moses' prophecy of the leader whom God would raise up). So the apostles were saying to the Jewish authorities, This Jesus, whom you slew and hanged on a tree, was not just a man; He was not just a phenomenon who suddenly appeared among the Jewish people but was the one who was sent by God. It was God who put Him among us. It was entirely the action of God.

Now this statement, "The God of our fathers raised up Jesus," is one of the fundamental statements of the whole Christian faith. The Christian faith does not start with the Lord Jesus Christ; it starts with God the Father. So many of our troubles are due to the fact that we have forgotten that the gospel message begins with the great story of the Old Testament. That is why Peter, with a touch of sarcasm in his words and, I imagine, in his voice, brought this home to these Jewish authorities. Do not forget that he was addressing the Pharisees and scribes, the Sadducees and chief priests, the religious leaders of the nation, and he drove his point right home to them. Peter said: "The God of your fathers . . ."

Peter was saying in effect, "It is astonishing that you should have rejected Jesus. You ought to know who He is. He is the fulfillment of all that God has planned for the salvation of humanity. It is God who raised the fathers in the past; indeed, it is God who raised Abraham."

Here they were, Jews and proud of it; proud that they were the descendants of Abraham. But where did Abraham come from, and why had he ever come? The answer is that God had raised him. Abraham had been born a pagan, in Ur of the Chaldees. And there he would have remained, and there would never have been a nation of the Jews at all if God had not said, "Come out, Abraham; go where I will send you." God had raised up Abraham in order that through him God might produce the Jewish nation. So Abraham was the great father of the Jews.

But why did God ever do this? What is the meaning, the explanation, of the Jew in history? And this is the great message of the Bible: It is God's way of saving the human race. Men and women had got themselves into trouble because they had disobeyed God, because they had rebelled against Him, because they had followed their own wisdom. They are still in trouble and cannot do anything to help themselves. But God in His infinite kindness and compassion planned a way of salvation before the very foundation of the world and has been putting it into operation.

In the Old Testament you get the beginnings, the adumbrations, the suggestions, the prophecies. Indeed, we are told that the moment Adam and Eve sinned, God came down into the Garden. He addressed the man and woman and told them they would bear the punishment of their sins, but then He gave them a promise. He said, "Because you have listened to the tempter, you have become his slaves, and this slavery will be the story of your life and of civilization. There will be war between the seed of the woman and the seed of the serpent. But I give you this promise: 'I will put enmity between thee and the woman, and between thy seed and her seed; it shall bruise thy head, and thou shalt bruise his heel' (Gen. 3:15)." That is the first promise we are given in the Bible that God will send the Savior—a deliverer for the world.

And then the story goes on. Moses made an exact prophecy: "The LORD thy God will raise up unto thee a Prophet from the midst of thee, of thy brethren, like unto me; unto him ye shall hearken" (Deut. 18:15). Moses' words "raise up" are used by the apostles in Acts 5. They are saying that God has done it. He has fulfilled the promise He made through Moses. The Lord Jesus is the Prophet of whom Moses spoke of old.

All the Old Testament prophecies point to the Savior: "Shiloh" would make his appearance (Gen. 49:10); "a man of sorrows" would be led "as a lamb to the slaughter," stricken for the sins of His people (Isa. 53). The ceremony and ritual of the temple also point forward to the Savior. Why was a lamb offered as a sacrifice morning and evening? Why did the priests have their burnt offerings and sacrifices? Well, these were all foreshadowings. They were saying: This is temporary. A day is coming when God will provide His own Lamb who will be the sin-bearer. The whole of the Old Testament looks forward to the great act of God, to the Deliverer, the one God will raise up. God raised up kings, He raised up prophets, and they all taught about the King who was to come.

There is perhaps no more eloquent statement of the salvation planned by God than the words recorded in the famous fortieth chapter of the book of Isaiah: "Comfort ye, comfort ye my people, saith your God" (v. 1). Why? Someone is going to come. "Make straight in the desert a highway for our God," says Isaiah. "Every valley shall be exalted, and every mountain and hill shall be made low: and the crooked shall be made straight, and the rough places plain . . . and all flesh shall see it together" (vv. 3-5).

You do not understand the Old Testament unless you see it in terms of a preparation for the coming of the Savior. It was "when the fulness of the time was come" (Gal. 4:4) that the baby was born in a stable in Bethlehem. He was called "Jesus," a word that means, "the Lord saves." Why? The angel gave the reason: "Thou shalt call his name JESUS: for he shall save his people from their sins" (Matt. 1:21). Here He is: He appears, He grows up, He works as a carpenter. Suddenly, at the age of thirty, He begins to preach and to teach, and He is a phenomenon. The authorities look on and say, "How knoweth this man letters, having never learned?" (John 7:15). He does not belong to any of the schools; He is an artisan, a common man.

"Who is this fellow?" the authorities ask. "Who is this person who assumes such authority and arrogates such powers and privileges to himself?" So they listen to Him and are confused and confounded.

But it is what this carpenter says that is important. He says, "The Son of man is come to seek and to save that which was lost" (Luke 19:10). He looks at people and says, "Follow me." He says, "If any man will come after me, let him deny himself . . ." (Matt. 16:24). This is His teaching. He says, "The Son of man came not to be ministered unto, but to minister, and to give his life a ransom for many" (Matt. 20:28). He is there before them as the Savior, the one who has come to take His stand with them. He submits to baptism, though He does not need it, and though John remonstrates with Him and does not want to baptize Him. He identifies Himself with sinful humanity and goes through it all. "Come unto me," he says (Matt. 11:28). Here He is, standing before the people and offering Himself as the Savior in His teaching, in His actions, in everything He is.

So Peter and the apostles say, "This is the one whom God, 'the God of your fathers,' has raised up. This is the focal point of God's plan of redemption, the very center of all history. This is something that divides all history. Here is the one in whom everything meets. Here is God acting for the salvation of humanity."

And if you want that in other language, you find it in John 3:16: "God so loved the world, that he gave his only begotten Son, that whosoever believeth in him should not perish, but have everlasting life." The world in its busyness is looking for saviors. It is seeking them among men, using its own methods, but God has raised His Savior. That is the first principle that I find in Peter's words here.

As we turn to the second principle, I again focus attention on the tragedy of the world. The world and its rulers rejected Christ: "The God of our fathers raised up Jesus, whom ye slew, and hanged on a tree." That is what the world did with Him. John puts it in a pregnant, tragic phrase in the prologue of his Gospel: "He came unto his own, and his own received him not" (1:11). Rulers and people—they all rejected Him. These rulers complained to the apostles and said, "Ye have filled Jerusalem with your doctrine, and intend to bring this man's blood upon us" (Acts 5:28). They had forgotten that a few weeks before they themselves had said in their arrogant boastfulness, "His blood be on us, and on our children" (Matt. 27:25). That was the reply they had given to Pilate. Then they did not care. But later they were frightened because of the power of God working through the apostles. But the point is that the world rejected Him. "He is despised and rejected of men" (Isa. 53:3).

The authorities slew the one who had come to save them, and they did it by hanging Him on a tree. To the Jew, that was a terrible thing to do—it was impossible to heap a greater insult upon anybody. Only those who were beyond the pale, who were "accursed," were given that treatment. "He that is hanged is accursed of God," said their own Scriptures (Deut. 21:23). They made a curse of Him. The rulers incited the people, and the people were ready to respond; they cried out, saying, "Away with him, away with him, crucify him" (John 19:15). Pilate tried to avoid making this terrible judgment and said, "Can I not release someone else to you? Here is a man called Barabbas, a thief and a robber." "No, no," they said. "Away with this man, and release unto us Barabbas" (Luke 23:18).

That is what the authorities did when our Lord was here in the flesh, that is what the Jewish authorities are doing here in Acts with His representatives, and that is what the world is still doing today. The world is still rejecting Him; it still regards Him as irrelevant. The vast majority of people in this country regard faith in Him and church attendance as the height of folly. "Christianity?" they ask. "Preaching Jesus? What has that got to do with the modern world? Look at the problems—Ghana, Nigeria. Look at the whole continent of Africa and the problems all over the world, and you are preaching that old story about Jesus. Away with Him!"

That is the tragedy, and that is why the world is as it is. But why does it reject its Savior? There are many explanations, but I will suggest some of the more important ones. First, the world does not know its real need. It has not yet awakened to the depth of the problem. That, I suppose, is the ultimate diagnosis. The world still thinks that its basic need is political.

Now do not misunderstand me. I am not here to say that there are no political problems. Of course there are. The political, social, and moral problems facing us today are almost endless in number, and it would be sheer folly to say that they are of no account. No; I am saying that the world is mistaken when it thinks the political problem is the preeminent problem.

The world has always been politically minded. It has to be, because of the problems created by its own sin, though it does not recognize sin as the cause. The Jews themselves were highly political. In the eighth chapter of John's Gospel, we read that our Lord was preaching one afternoon with great power and authority. We know this because we are told, "As he spake these words, many believed on him" (v. 30). So he looked at the people and said, "If ye continue in my word, then are ye my disciples indeed; and ye shall know the truth, and the truth shall make you free." And their response was this: "We be Abraham's seed, and were never in bondage to any man: how sayest thou, Ye shall be made free?" (vv. 31-33). They said in effect, "You are insulting us; You are offering us freedom when we don't need it." Actually they were lying. At that very time they were in bondage to the Roman Empire, but do you see the political pride? "We were never in bondage to any man": political freedom! The world always tends to think that this is its one and only need—"Give us political freedom and we will have everything."

Others think that society is to be blamed for the problems we are facing. Some seem to think that the one great need is money: "Give us a large sum of money and we'll have no problems." If you are financially well off, you can have plenty of food, plenty of drink, plenty of sex, plenty of entertainment. Money is the one universal solvent, and the great need is for the equal distribution of wealth, together with political and social equality—a solution taught by Marxism.

Others put all their emphasis upon culture and upon knowledge, as if that will solve our ills. So the first reason for the world's rejection of its Savior is that it does not know its real need.

The second explanation is ignorance. As I have already shown you, Peter brought this home to the Jewish authorities when he said, "The God of our fathers." "Where," he said in effect, "is your knowledge? Where is your memory? Don't you know the Scriptures? You are always talking about them. You are the expounders and the expositors; you are the teachers. So why on earth don't you begin to understand the Scriptures? Here is the fulfillment of all your Scriptures."

And the world is still ignorant of the truth, is it not? It was Hegel who said that history teaches us that history teaches us nothing. And how true that is! In every age and generation, men and women go on repeating the same old errors. They still cling to the same old fallacies and vain hopes. Throughout the centuries the world has tried the very things that we are pinning our faith to today. People have never succeeded; yet in their ignorance they still go on believing in them and trying them out.

What, then, is the real, the supreme, need of the world? It is the need to know God. Try as we will to make a happy world without God, we cannot do it. More than ever before, the world today is proving the truth of Isaiah's words: "There is no peace, saith the LORD, unto the wicked" (Isa. 48:22). Do what you like—become prosperous, influential, garner all knowledge, have all information at your fingertips, you will find that does not give you peace, that does not give you final satisfaction and rest. Humanity's need is the blessing of God, and without it the world ever turns into chaos. There is nothing but unhappiness and disappointment and frustration without Him.

Men and women need the salvation of their souls, the salvation of the biggest and the central part of their beings. They are concentrating on symptoms on the periphery of their lives without realizing that there is a deep, a profound need within them, without realizing that they were made in the image of God and that nothing and no one can ever satisfy them but God.

"Thou hast made us for Thyself, and our hearts are restless until they find their rest in Thee," said Augustine. Men and women need reconciliation with God. They need forgiveness of sins. They need to be restored to the favor of God, who is the source and the fount of every blessing. They also need to be delivered from the forces that are captivating them and making them slaves and serfs—the world, the flesh, and the devil, or, in other words, Satan and sin.

Oh, the ugliness and foulness that is in our perverted natures as the result of the Fall! You can put us in new houses, but they do not change our natures, and we may turn our homes into pig sties. You can give us learning and knowledge, but that does not stop this rot that is in the soul. You can give us wealth, but it does not make us into new people. Each of us needs a new life, a new heart, and a new and profound satisfaction. But the world does not know its need; so it rejects Christ. "[Him] ye slew and hanged upon a tree."

Third, the world turns away from the Savior because it does not recognize His glory and the glory of His salvation. This is where the folly of humanity and its vain boasting of its knowledge and its understanding are finally exposed. It is here that you see the blindness of the human race. It looks at Him and sees nothing but a nuisance who must be gotten rid of: "Away with Him! Crucify Him!" The world always glories in the false and always rejects the true. That is a summary of the story of the human race since the Fall.

> *Truth for ever on the scaffold,*
> *Wrong for ever on the throne.*
> James Russell Lowell

That is the story of the world's vaunted civilization, of its boasting, of its understanding and sophistication.

The world is always ready to believe in saviors; it is always ready to believe in emancipators and liberators and redeemers. Rome was ready to believe in the Caesars, France in Napoleon, Italy in Mussolini, Germany in Hitler, Russia in Stalin. And this is still as true today as it has ever been. I have mentioned other nations, but let us not forget that we ourselves have behaved in the same way. Even in recent history, we have tended to turn men into gods. We have been ready to accept leaders at their own valuation.

This is not a text that I have picked at random to suit the current situation. Only this week we have had a great illustration of the world's readiness to believe in human saviors: Nkrumah [prime minister and then president of Ghana in the 1950s and 1960s], who calls himself "the savior of Ghana and its people." The world is eager to bow down before such men, and while it does, it is rejecting the one whom God has raised up to be the one and only Savior.

Shall I show you the contrast? Shall I expose to you the folly of human wisdom? Look at the one whom the world rejects. Then look at those it is ready to worship, praise, and follow. What do you find about them? First of all, they always exalt themselves. Listen to their arrogant boasting; look at the attitudes they strike as they address the populace. Our Lord put this perfectly: "I am come in my Father's name, and ye receive me not: if another shall come in his own name, him ye will receive" (John 5:43).

False saviors exalt themselves; they give themselves titles; they set themselves up on pedestals and build monuments and statues to themselves and write on them, as Nkrumah did: "Redeemer"! They plaster cities and walls with their photographs. You cannot get away from them.

Second, look at the pomp and the show with which these human saviors surround themselves. They have their "cheerleaders" to organize applause, to tell people when to cheer and when to stop. Fancy fooling themselves to that extent! This is the mentality of the world.

Another interesting characteristic I always notice about these self-styled deliverers with all their pomp and show and claims to authority is the craven fear in their hearts. Look at the way they protect themselves; look at the fear in which they live.

Then listen to what these leaders offer. They offer everything. But what do they give, what do they produce, these saviors of the people? The people acclaim them and shout their glory. Yet they always give nothing but tyranny and slavery; they rule over police states. They fetter people; they keep them down and rob them.

And, finally, human messiahs always go out in disgrace and defeat. All their pomp and show and greatness and power always ends in nothing. God always makes it laughable.

But now look again at the Savior whom the world rejects. What a contrast! This is the curse of humanity; this is the blindness that comes as a result of sin, this failure to recognize the lineaments of the true Savior when He appears. What are his characteristics? Well, thank God, He is the exact opposite of all human saviors.

The first thing I read about this one is this: "Who, being in the form of God, thought it not robbery to be equal with God . . . he humbled himself" (Phil. 2:6, 8). "He humbled himself"! He came down! He was born in a stable. He lived in poverty and worked with His hands as a carpenter. He has been described as "the meek and lowly Jesus." He did not talk about His rights and demands; He did not spend millions of pounds [or dollars] on palaces and statues and monuments to Himself. On the contrary, He quite deliberately "took upon him the form of a servant" (Phil. 2:7). He mixed with the common people, and they "heard him gladly" (Mark 12:37). The charge the authorities brought against Him was that He was "a man gluttonous, and a winebibber, a friend of publicans and sinners" (Matt. 11:19). We read, "A bruised reed shall he not break, and smoking flax shall he not quench" (Matt. 12:20).

Instead of speaking in boastful language, He did not lift up His voice in the street (Matt. 12:19) but lived quietly and unobtrusively. He tried to get away from the crowds. He went about doing good and relieving suffering, showing His love and mercy and compassion. He touched the outcasts, the untouchables; these were the people for whom He had come. "[He] endured such contradiction of sinners against himself" (Heb. 12:3). Can you not see that at every point He was the complete antithesis of human saviors and self-designated redeemers, the people the world acclaims while they are rejecting this Christ? That is why they do not see His glory.

But, finally, far from seeking His own aggrandizement and His own greatness and pleasure and comfort, here is one who set His face steadfastly to go to Jerusalem. Here is one who went deliberately to death. Here is one who not only humbled Himself by taking the form of a servant but "became obedient unto death, even the death of the cross" (Phil. 2:8). When He faced this end, He prayed, "What shall I say? Father, save me from this hour?" No! "For this cause came I unto this hour" (John 12:27). He came into the world to save.

How does this one save? Is it at the expense of others? No; He saves at the expense of Himself, of His own life. He came "to give his life a ransom for many" (Matt. 20.28). He took the position of the felon, the guilty, the vile! He took our sins upon Himself: "Who his own self bare our sins in his own body on the tree, that we, being dead to sins, should live unto righteousness: by whose stripes ye were healed" (1 Pet. 2:24). Here He is, the eternal antithesis to the world's leaders, and the world does not recognize Him but gets rid of Him and says He is irrelevant and worships its human saviors and redeemers.

Oh, the tragic folly and blindness and ignorance of men and women in sin! Yes, and as in the first century, it is the most learned, the most sophisticated, who are the leaders in the rejection of the Savior of the world.

Look further at the one who is rejected. He has been raised from the dead! In the words of the apostles before the Sanhedrin: "Him hath God exalted with his right hand to be a Prince and a Saviour, for to give repentance to Israel, and forgiveness of sins" (Acts 5:32). He takes away our sins; He introduces us to God and reconciles us to Him. God adopts us into His family; we become His children. We are set free from the things that put us down; we are given inner peace and independence from the world and its wealth and its pomp; we are given a quiet, restful mind and heart and spirit. Seeing a new purpose in life in this world, we are ready to live to His glory, knowing that we have nothing to fear in death because to die is "to be with Christ; which is far better" (Phil. 1:23); it is to be in the presence of God. He gives us all the satisfactions that our hearts are crying out for. And He has purchased all this at the cost of giving His own life for us, and dying our death, and being buried in our grave, and then rising again to justify us.

But the world does not see the glory of His great salvation. It prefers a life of ease—food, drink, and sex. It prefers all that to the blessings that Christ alone can give.

But, lastly, the world rejects Him because it does not realize that in rejecting Him it is opposing God and His eternal power. "The God of our fathers raised up Jesus, whom ye slew and hanged on a tree. Him *hath God exalted with his right hand to be a Prince and a Saviour.*" You treated Him with sarcasm and scorn and ignominy and shame; you spat upon Him; you reviled Him; you regarded Him as a curse. In your cleverness you thought you had finished with Him. But God, with His mighty power, raised Him and exalted Him and set Him at His own right hand.

The apostle Paul expresses it all in the second chapter of Philippians:

Wherefore God also hath highly exalted him, and given him a name which is above every name: that at the name of Jesus every knee should bow, of things in heaven, and things in earth, and things under the earth; and that every tongue should confess that Jesus Christ is Lord, to the glory of God the Father.

—*vv. 9-11*

He has been made the Prince and the Governor. God has raised Him! Whatever man may do, God raises Him and by the resurrection proves that He is the Savior. So if you reject this Christ, you are rejecting the power of God.

His kingdom cannot fail;
He rules o'er earth and heaven;
The keys of death and hell
Are to our Jesus given.

He sits at God's right hand,
Till all his foes submit,
And bow to his command,
And fall beneath his feet;
Lift up your heart, lift up your voice,
Rejoice, again I say, rejoice.

Charles Wesley

Oh, the tragedy of a world that does not realize it is pitting itself against God and His great plan and purpose. Our Lord Himself said, "Did ye never read in the scriptures, The stone which the builders rejected, the same is become the head of the corner: this is the Lord's doing, and it is marvelous in our eyes? Therefore I say unto you"—He is addressing these same rulers— "The kingdom of God shall be taken from you, and given to a nation bringing forth the fruits thereof"—that is the Christian church—"And whosoever shall fall on this stone"—this is Christ—"shall be broken: but on whomsoever it shall fall, it will grind him to powder" (Matt. 21:42-44).

I have already referred to that poor man Nkrumah who elevated himself on a pedestal, built a statue, a monument to himself, and on it described himself as "Redeemer." Have you heard the news? That monument has been smashed and reduced to powder. The monument is already gone, and the same will be true of the man himself, unless by the grace of God he is brought to repentance, unless he humbles himself and falls at the feet of the only one who is entitled to use the designation "Redeemer."

Have we learned the lesson of this old incident in the Acts of the Apostles? Cannot you see the whole history of humanity epitomized in these stories? When Christ arises, He will shake the kingdoms of this world until there is not a rock left behind. But:

Jesus shall reign where'er the sun
Doth his successive journeys run;
His kingdom stretch from shore to shore,
Till moons shall wax and wane no more.
                                    Isaac Watts

So if you have rejected the Lord Jesus Christ until now, wake up to the folly of your action and, while there is still time, repent and believe. Ask God to forgive you, and I assure you that He will.

4

MAN'S GREAT PROBLEM

Then Peter and the other apostles answered and said, We ought to obey God rather than men. The God of our fathers raised up Jesus, whom ye slew and hanged on a tree. Him hath God exalted with his right hand to be a Prince and a Saviour, for to give repentance to Israel, and forgiveness of sins. And we are his witnesses of these things; and so is also the Holy Ghost, whom God hath given to them that obey him.

—Acts 5:29-32

In this passage in Acts 5, the apostles are in the same position as the blind man who was healed by our Lord (John 9). Like the apostles, the blind man was examined by the authorities in Jerusalem. They were very annoyed that he had been healed and asked him to explain how it was that he was able to see. The man gave the only answer he could give: "One thing I know, that, whereas I was blind, now I see" (v. 25). I did nothing: it was this man. And the apostles are virtually saying the same thing here, and in doing so, of course, they give us a perfect summary of the Christian message.

We are in the process of considering together why it is that men and women still object to the Gospel and reject such an amazing offer of deliverance. We have seen that one of the problems is that their idea of a savior is altogether wrong; so they cannot see the glory of the only true Savior. But now I want to show you another reason for their rejection of the Gospel: They are equally wrong in all their thinking about salvation. The two wrong ideas, of course, belong together and interact upon each other. An erroneous view of the Savior must obviously be based upon an erroneous view of the salvation—the deliverance—that is needed.

As we have already seen, men and women today are no different from the members of the Sanhedrin at Jerusalem: They all reject the notion that God alone can provide them with salvation. This rejection is because, to put it generally, they fail to realize the depth of their problem—they never see their real need. But let us work out the details as we find them put to us in this statement of the apostles to the Sanhedrin.

My first principle under this heading is that *men and women persistently fail to realize that their greatest need is the need to be reconciled to God—* the need for forgiveness. You see how the apostle brings it out: "Him hath God exalted with his right hand to be a Prince and a Saviour, for to give repentance to Israel, and *forgiveness of sins.*" But they do not think they need to be forgiven, and so they oppose this message. Indeed, they regard it as insulting.

Today people are looking for solutions to their problems, and political parties are competing with one another to offer their remedies. But it is only when there is an election[5] that we tend to think they are offering anything new. The strange thing about the world is that it makes fun of the Gospel. "Tell me the *old, old* story!" it mocks, as if politicians do not repeat *their* old stories! Because they change a little of the terminology, they convince themselves and others that they have something new; but there is nothing new under the sun. Politicians merely play variations on the one theme—the same theme, no matter what the party. The differences are not worth considering when you view the problem of human beings and of human nature in the light of the biblical teaching.

And here we come to the essential difference between political manifestos and the teaching of the Gospel. The primary difference, and the profoundest error, is that men and women will persist in forgetting God, or if they believe in Him, they have a wrong attitude toward Him. They persist in thinking that their problem belongs entirely to this world. They vary in their emphases. Some say the causes are political, others that they are social or economic— you know the variations; but all are agreed in thinking that the problem is purely a problem of men and women in their relationships with this world. Never a thought is given to the fact that the real problem is, as some put it, the vertical relationship to God.

I throw this out as a challenge. Start with the human situation as it is. Consider the whole story of civilization and its obvious failure to solve its problems, and ask, Why is this? What led to this?

There is only one adequate answer: Man himself produced his own chaos. The world was not meant to be like this. It is as it is because way back at the very beginning man went wrong in his attitude to God. The very warp and woof of biblical teaching is that man's initial sin, his original error, was breaking his relationship with God. That was what brought chaos into life, and you always have to go back to that. Peter pinpoints this, saying in effect, "You throw us into prison as if we were proponents of some new view of life or some new philosophy. But we are preaching about what the God of our fathers has done; we are not rivals to you in any sense."

So I repeat that fundamental to every other consideration is the question of our relationship to God. Only in the light of that can we understand ourselves. We go wrong because we forget that we are created by God. We did not create ourselves. God put into us the power of sex and of generation, but that does not mean that man has ever created man. We are created *by* God, and we are also created *for* God, to have a relationship with Him. God made us with certain basic laws in our nature, and because we do not recognize this, we are frustrated and live in constant misery.

We must also realize that we are entirely dependent upon God. We cannot escape Him. Throughout the centuries, people have done their best to avoid Him, but they cannot—and this is because God *is*, because our ways and our times and everything are in His hands. God ever breaks in upon our little arrangements and ideas.

And not only that, we are under God in the sense that we are under the laws of God. Though we may not believe in them and may fight against them, that does not make the slightest difference. They are there, and whenever anything works against the law of its own nature, there is bound to be conflict and trouble. This is the essence of our whole predicament and misunderstanding of ourselves and all our misery. We think we are liberating ourselves, but what we are really doing is fighting against ourselves.

The result is that we have become totally estranged from God. This is the teaching that you will find everywhere in the New Testament, particularly in the expositions given by the apostle Paul. In memorable words in his letter to the Ephesians, he writes:

> This I say therefore, and testify in the Lord, that ye henceforth walk not as other Gentiles walk, in the vanity of their mind, having the understanding darkened, being alienated from the life of God through the ignorance that is in them, because of the blindness of their heart: who being past feeling have given themselves over unto lasciviousness, to work all uncleanness with greediness.
>
> —Eph. 4:17-19

Now if you can give me a better analysis of modern life at its most sophisticated and intellectual, then let me know where I can find it! Here is the perfect analysis.

Why do people live lives of lasciviousness? Why the perversions? Why the amorality? Why the confusion? It is ultimately due to wrong thinking, because thinking determines practice. As a man thinks, so he is; and the trouble is, as the apostle points out in that passage in Ephesians, men and women are alienated from God in their ways of thinking and in their whole attitude. If they think of God at all, they think that He is against them, that He is some kind of monster waiting to crush them. So they fight against Him, stand up to Him, as they think. They deliberately break His laws and defy everything that is sacred.

Now the biblical teaching is—and this is the point made by the apostles before the Sanhedrin—that the whole trouble arises because men and women are guilty before God. That is the real trouble. They look at circumstances and conditions but never go deep enough to discover that the underlying cause is that they have displeased and offended God, and that, therefore, their first and greatest need is for forgiveness: "for to give repentance to Israel, and forgiveness of sins."

So the biblical message cuts right across all other types of thinking. They all come to a common denominator, and they all stop short of pointing to our need for forgiveness. But the Gospel says to us, What you really need is not more money or shorter working hours or better houses or further education. What you need is to be forgiven, and this just means that you need to be reconciled to God. You are as you are and your world is as it is because you are under the wrath of God. God is not smiling upon you. You are alienated. You are living at cross-purposes. You are not only fighting the law of your own being; you are fighting your Maker, the only one who can really bless you. Blessing, happiness, and peace all ultimately depend upon your relationship to God.

I remember once reading a clever man's criticism of that verse in Charles Wesley's hymn:

> *Just and holy is thy name,*
> *I am all unrighteousness;*
> *Vile and full of sin I am,*
> *Thou art full of truth and grace.*
> Charles Wesley

This man said, "Fancy a man applying for a job and going to a prospective employer and saying that about himself! It's ridiculous!"

But Charles Wesley says that you need forgiveness for your vileness and sinfulness. That is summed up in Peter's words: "Him hath God exalted with his right hand to be a Prince and a Saviour, for to give repentance to Israel, and forgiveness of sins." That is the first principle.

The second principle here is that people are completely helpless at their point of greatest need. Where do I find that teaching? It is here in Peter's statement: "for to *give* repentance to Israel, and forgiveness of sins." The repentance and forgiveness are given, and that means that men and women can do nothing about it. Now this is a great source of trouble. The popular thinking is: Believe in yourself. If you want a job, well, don't go cringing; stand up and say, "There's nothing I can't do. Yes, I'll tackle any job. I'm the one." People are self-confident and self-assertive; they have been brought up on the psychological teaching that tells them, "Trust yourself; express yourself; show the greatest that is in you."

People are always convinced that they can put things right. When they believe in God, they are convinced that they can even put themselves right with Him. They think that by living a good life, by not doing certain things, and by starting to do other things, they can satisfy God. They believe that nothing further is demanded. They have willpower, which they can and will exercise.

"But," you say to them, "what about the teaching of Jesus Christ?"

"Oh, yes," they reply. "Jesus"—as they call him—"came and instructed us, and that's where He's of great value. He gave us incomparable teaching on moral living. And He not only gave us instructions, He gave us a wonderful example." And so they praise "Jesus and His teaching." "We have our ideas," they say, "but His are the highest; so we must set out to follow Him and imitate His example. He helps us tremendously by giving us a living illustration of how life based on these exalted principles is to be lived and can be lived."

So these people set out on the imitation of "Jesus," confident that they can do it and that they can save themselves. In other words, they do not realize that there is any problem in this matter of salvation. On their side, they think they can accomplish it, and they are unaware that there is any problem on God's side. God has no difficulty at all.

It is thought that if anyone goes to God and says, "I'm sorry," then God says, "Of course I forgive you. I had forgiven you before you asked Me." God forgives everybody, they say. God is love, and therefore He cannot refrain from forgiving the whole world. The popular teaching that passes for Christianity says that the whole business of preaching is just to tell everybody that God loves them. They are all going to heaven, whether or not they believe the Gospel. These preachers have their own gospel: It is that God loves the world and has forgiven it in spite of its rebellion and opposition to Him. Even those who do not believe in heaven will arrive there. God is love, and all is well.

So now I want to show you from this apostolic statement that the modern understanding is completely wrong in both respects—wrong from man's side, wrong from God's side. It is wrong from man's side because the apostle says here, "Him hath God exalted with his right hand to be a Prince and a Saviour, for to give repentance to Israel, and forgiveness of sins." *He* gives it. Men and women can do nothing because, according to this Gospel, they are dead in trespasses and sins—spiritually dead. And of course they prove it by their thoughts and activities.

By nature, human beings are entirely lacking in spiritual understanding; that is why they do not believe in God. The psalmist said, "The fool hath said in his heart, There is no God" (Ps. 14:1). It is not surprising that the fool should say that; I do not expect anything else. I do not expect fallen men and women to believe these spiritual truths; they cannot—they are blind. "The natural man," says Paul, "receiveth not the things of the Spirit of God: for they are foolishness unto him: neither can he know them, because they are spiritually discerned" (1 Cor. 2:14). Man lost his spiritual understanding when he broke his relationship with God.

Way back in Genesis 6 there is a powerful description of human beings before the Flood: "Every imagination of the thoughts of his heart was only evil continually" (v. 5). And the world is still like that today. We are like that by nature; we cannot help it; that is the nature we have received. So we are incapable of pleasing God. We cannot keep the commandments. What is the use of pretending that we can? We have all broken them. You might say, "But I have never committed adultery." But remember what our Lord said: "Whosoever looketh on a woman to lust after her hath committed adultery with her already in his heart" (Matt. 5:28). We are all adulterers.

So we cannot keep the commandments. Not only that, all our actions are finally useless. This is the great teaching of the Bible: "All our righteousnesses," says the prophet Isaiah, "are as filthy rags" (Isa. 64:6). And then there is the great statement by the apostle Paul. Looking back at his old life as Saul of Tarsus, a life of religious observance and morality in which he surpassed everybody else in his knowledge and practice of the law, Paul wrote,

"What things were gain to me, those I counted loss for Christ. Yea doubtless, and I count all things but loss for the excellency of the knowledge of Christ Jesus my Lord . . . and do count them but dung, that I may win Christ" (Phil. 3:7-8). He sees that in the sight of God his righteousness is utterly useless.

All men and women are in an utterly helpless position. They are so bad that they cannot even feel sorrow for sin. Can they repent when they want to? Have you ever tried? Can you make yourself feel sorry for sin? You cannot. You can say it, but you cannot make yourself feel it. You are as dead as that.

But above all—and here is the real crux of the problem—you cannot find God. You can improve your life, you can decide to be more moral, and you may feel a sense of satisfaction that you are doing very well, but that is not the problem. No; the problem is how to know God, how to have fellowship with Him, how to be blessed by Him, and to live in harmony with Him and with the laws of your own being. And that means finding God. But how can you find God? As the author of the book of Job put it so long ago, "Canst thou by searching find out God?" (11:7). Paul says, "The world by wisdom knew not God" (1 Cor. 1:21), and remember that "wisdom" there means the wisdom taught by the great Greek philosophers during the flowering of Greek philosophy.

Men and women can never find God. They have been trying throughout the centuries, but they cannot. That is the difficulty from the human side, and all our modern self-confidence is ridiculous at this point. Why not look at the chaos of the world and face the facts?

But look at the difficulty from God's side, and here you see the truth that the apostles preached before everything else: "Him hath God exalted with his right hand to be a Prince and a Saviour, for to give repentance to Israel, and forgiveness of sins." Why did God do this? The biblical message, and the only answer, is that God sent the Savior because only He could save us. Man cannot produce a savior who is able to save, but God has done it.

But why is the modern teaching wrong—this teaching that God loves everybody, that everybody is automatically forgiven and nobody is going to be punished? It is wrong because it is a blank contradiction of the historical events concerning Jesus Christ, especially His death upon the cross. It is because of Christ's death that there is all this great doctrine in the New Testament. It is because of His death that we have Communion and talk about broken body and shed blood.

The problem of forgiveness, of reconciling men and women to God, is the greatest problem the universe has ever known or ever will know. This, I say with reverence, is the greatest problem of all even to Almighty God, and none other but He could solve it.

The problem arises because of the character of God. How can God forgive men and women? You will find that the greatest theological writings throughout the centuries have dealt with this question. A notable example was Anselm who wrote a book called *Why God Man?* That is another way of putting the same problem. Why this Jesus? Why that cross? Why the resurrection? It is all because of the great problem of how God can forgive man. People think that forgiveness is easy for God, but I want to show you that it is more difficult than anything else. And this is where we see God's wisdom shining out in the greatest glory.

The apostle Paul put this problem for us once and forever in his letter to the Romans:

> *Being justified freely by his grace through the redemption that is in Christ Jesus: whom God hath set forth [before the whole world] to be a propitiation through faith in his blood, to declare his righteousness for the remission of sins that are past, through the forbearance of God; to declare, I say, at this time his [God's] righteousness: that he [God] might be just, and [at the same time] the justifier of him which believeth in Jesus.*
>
> —Rom. 3:24-26

How can God remain just and righteous and holy and yet forgive sin? Have you ever thought of that?

"Ah," you say, "but God is love."

I know, but God is also holy, and He cannot change. He is of such a pure countenance that He cannot even look upon sin. How can this just God forgive a single sinner? God cannot go back upon His own laws and upon His own nature. He had taught the ancient people of Israel that "without shedding of blood is no remission [of sin]" (Heb. 9:22); and that is where these Jews whom Peter was addressing in the Sanhedrin had gone so terribly wrong.

Peter was saying in effect, "You do not know your own Scriptures. You do not understand the problem. You are trusting your temple and its ceremonial, your burnt offerings and sacrifices and lambs, the blood of bulls and goats and the ashes of heifers. You think these sacrifices are enough. Can you not see that they are but shadows and types, but prophecies of what God was going to do? Now he has done it, and you do not see. You are holding on to the shadows and the semblances and missing the reality itself." That is what Peter was saying, and that is what we need to say to this modern world.

It is part of my duty and my commission as a preacher to say that God, in His justice, cannot forgive men and women simply by saying so. I have ample grounds for making that statement. If God could so easily forgive people, He would have done it. But that is not what He did. As we have seen, the whole of the Old Testament tells how God prepared His people for the coming of the Savior. He commanded the children of Israel to build the tabernacle and the temple, and He gave minute instructions both for their construction and for the sacrifices and festivals that were to be held. He told the priests to kill a lamb every morning and evening. What does it all mean if God has already forgiven everybody? What is the point of it all?

But let me ask the great question: What was the point of the life, death, resurrection, and ascension of Christ? And the only answer to that question is that this was made necessary by the awful problem of human sin and helplessness and the nature and being of God. There was no other way. And so the message of the apostles is just this: "Him hath God exalted with his right hand to be a Prince and a Saviour, for to give repentance to Israel, and forgiveness of sins." Unless God himself had raised a Savior and provided a way of salvation and given it to us as a free gift, we would all have been undone.

If you and I are to be reconciled to God, some fundamental needs must be met. First, we need someone to represent us before God. We cannot get there in our own strength, as we have seen. We cannot lift ourselves up and reason with God and plead with him. When we try, we immediately say with Thomas Binney:

> *Eternal Light! Eternal light!*
> *How pure the soul must be,*
> *When, placed within thy searching sight,*
> *It shrinks not, but with calm delight*
> *Can live and look on thee!*
>
> Thomas Binney

Have you ever thought of standing in the presence of God? I know it is easy to talk about God in theological arguments and disputations. Yes, we discuss God, but can you imagine yourself in the presence of the living God, in holiness indescribable? We shrink into nothing. We need somebody to represent us. No human being can do it because everyone is sinful, and yet we must be represented by a man. We must be represented by someone who knows us and shares our nature, someone who can plead for us as our representative. Here is the first requirement.

But, second, that representative must be perfect. If he is to represent us, then he himself must be without fault, without sin; he must keep the law of God. If he does not, then he will have to spend the whole of his time pleading for himself, and in any case he cannot because he is a sinner before God. So he must be a man, and he must be a perfect man. He must know God. He must know the way into the presence of God, and he must have a right of entry. He must have access to God, and he must not be afraid to speak to Him.

Then, third, and above all, he must be able to bear our sins and their punishment. It is not sufficient merely to be able to speak on our behalf. Our sins are facts; they have been committed, and God has made it abundantly clear that sin must be punished, not because God is against us, but because—I say it with reverence—God has no choice in the matter. He is holy. His whole character is behind this and is involved. God is just, and He cannot act in an unjust manner. So our sins must be dealt with. We are all guilty: "For all have sinned, and come short of the glory of God" (Rom. 3:23); "There is none righteous, no, not one" (Rom. 3:10). So this one who is to represent us must be able to take our sins upon himself and bear their punishment and still go on living.

That is the problem, and it is no less than that, and only God can do something about it. That is why Peter and the apostles said, "The God of our father raised up Jesus." They said to the Sanhedrin, who were the experts in the Old Testament Scriptures, "You ought to know this. God has been saying throughout the centuries that He is going to produce a Messiah, He is going to send a deliverer. There will be a Lamb of God. Don't you know your Scriptures? But we are here to tell you that God has acted, and this Jesus is the one whom God has raised up."

The Lord Jesus Christ is the only one who answers these needs and meets these criteria. He is man, born of the virgin Mary. That is the whole message of the Incarnation and the virgin birth. He is truly man. He is of the seed of Abraham. But He is not only man, He is also God. And this is an absolute necessity. This message that was preached here by the apostles to the Sanhedrin is not only true—it *must* be true. This is the only way in which the problem can be solved. That is why the apostles say here, "We must obey God rather than men." They said in effect, "We would sooner die than refuse to preach this message. This is good news! It is the only message that can save a single soul. We must go on preaching it. God has done this. He has raised up a man, and this man is His own Son."

Because all others had failed, God had to make a new man. There had to be a new beginning, a new humanity. There had to be a new representative, one who could be "touched with the feeling of our infirmities" (Heb. 4:15), one who could sympathize with us and bear with us and succor us. Yes, but there is more. He had to be sinless and perfect. He had to know God and have access to Him and stand and plead for us.

And He does it. The Lord Jesus Christ is God and man. In His life on earth He rendered a perfect obedience to God's holy laws. But oh, above and beyond that, as Peter puts it in those resounding words in his first epistle, He was the one "who his own self bare our sins in his own body on the tree, that we, being dead to sins, should live unto righteousness: by whose stripes ye were healed" (2:24). That is the teaching that Peter put in embryo as he stood before the Sanhedrin and spoke for the other apostles. Our Lord was the only one who could satisfy God's holy nature. God punished our sins in Him, and therefore He offers us free pardon and forgiveness.

And, of course, the wonderful thing about it all is that it is *God* who did it: "The God of our fathers hath raised up Jesus." The God against whom we have rebelled, the God whom we have offended, the God upon whom we—as it were—have spat. It is He who did it all. As Paul says, "[God] was in Christ, reconciling the world unto himself, not imputing their trespasses unto them" (2 Cor. 5:19). That is how God reconciled humanity to Himself.

God planned it. Human beings could never have thought of it—they reject it when they are even told it. It was God's plan. "God sent forth his Son, made of a woman, made under the law" (Gal. 4:4). "God so loved the world, that he gave his only begotten Son, that whosoever believeth in him should not perish, but have everlasting life" (John 3:16).

It was God who sent His Son into the world, and it was God who sent Him to the cross. Peter said to the Sanhedrin, ". . . whom ye slew and hanged on a tree," but in his sermon on the Day of Pentecost he explained that this was "by the determinate counsel and foreknowledge of God" (Acts 2:23). Paul wrote, "[God] delivered him up for us all" (Rom. 8:32), and centuries earlier the prophet Isaiah wrote, "the LORD hath laid on him the iniquity of us all" (Isa. 53:6). "We did esteem him stricken, smitten of God" (Isa. 53:4). It was God who brought about this great transaction between Father and Son. God solved His own problem. He remains "just, and the justifier of him which believeth in Jesus" (Rom. 3:26). As a result, "There is therefore now no condemnation to them which are in Christ Jesus" (Rom. 8:1).

This is God's way of salvation. But it was not easy. God sent His only Son from the glory of heaven into the sin and shame and squalor of this world. That is what it cost Him. And consider what it meant to the Son to come from the purity and the glory of eternity into a world like this with all its sin and shame and foulness. Yet He came, and He became a friend of publicans and sinners. And not only that—He went to the cross, and there His Father averted His face from Him. His soul became an offering for sin, and separation came between the Father and the Son, so that the Son cried out in agony, "My God, my God, why hast thou forsaken me?" (Matt. 27:46).

What a message and what a Gospel! And what a world that refuses it, what a mad world. The world has never realized the cause of its troubles or its deepest need. It goes on trusting itself and its failing powers and abilities, and it rejects this free offer of forgiveness: "By grace are ye saved through faith; and that not of yourselves: it is the gift of God" (Eph. 2:8).

God gives repentance and forgiveness of sins to all who believe in Christ Jesus His Son—that is the message. Do you believe it? Do you accept the Savior and His great and only salvation? God raised Him up. God has done it all, and He gives it to us freely. Oh, the madness of rejecting Him!

5

REPENTANCE—THE DOOR TO FORGIVENESS

Then Peter and the other apostles answered and said, We ought to obey God rather than men. The God of our fathers raised up Jesus, whom ye slew and hanged on a tree. Him hath God exalted with his right hand to be a Prince and a Saviour, for to give repentance to Israel, and forgiveness of sins. And we are his witnesses of these things; and so is also the Holy Ghost, whom God hath given to them that obey him.

—Acts 5:29-32

We are in the process of looking at the interplay between the gospel message preached by Peter and the apostles and the Jerusalem authorities who rejected that message. This not only gives us a picture of what the message was but shows us why it was rejected. Here it is before us, presented in a very dramatic and pictorial manner, and easy for us all, therefore, to remember.

We have seen that men and women reject the message of the Gospel because they are totally ignorant of the character of the Savior. Furthermore, they do not see their need for forgiveness. That leads us to the subject we must now consider, which is the message concerning repentance. "Him hath God exalted with his right hand to be a Prince and a Saviour, *for to give repentance* to Israel, and forgiveness of sins."

The need for repentance is another fundamental postulate of the Christian faith, and it is also one of the truths that people most resent. Teaching about repentance utterly infuriates people today, as it did these rulers in Jerusalem. There is no difference whatsoever in this respect between the first and the twentieth centuries. The fact that the message of repentance is regarded as a very great insult is further proof of that fatal self-righteousness that is always the greatest hindrance to acceptance of the gospel message. The rejection of the Gospel because of self-righteousness is the astounding fact that is put before us here in this picture in Acts 5.

So we turn to the need for repentance. What does the gospel message tell us? First of all, it tells us that repentance always comes first: "Him hath God exalted to his right hand to be a Prince and a Saviour, for to give repentance to Israel, and forgiveness of sins."

"So," somebody may say, "why, in your last exposition, did you speak about forgiveness and are only now dealing with repentance?"

It was for one reason only: to show people's need. But now we are looking at the way in which men and women are able to enter into the provision that God has made for that need. The need is for forgiveness, but the door to it is repentance. So I must emphasize that repentance always comes first. And I say again that nothing shows more clearly the antagonism of the natural, unregenerate heart to the Gospel of Jesus Christ our Lord than this instinctive dislike of the teaching concerning the necessity for repentance.

Now there are many reasons for this antipathy to teaching about the need for repentance. First, there is the climate of thinking at the present time. The world sits in criticism of other people: Mistakes are always because of someone else's failure; national and international troubles are always the fault of the government, regardless of the party in power. We sit in judgment on the political parties, and we say there is very little to choose between them. They are all wrong, we say, while in their turn each one claims that it alone is right. The leaders of each political party say that all would be well if only people had the sense to see what *they* see and do what they say should be done. It is all based on an innate self-confidence and self-righteousness.

Politics thrives on self-confidence. Politicians never make mistakes, they never break their promises, they can explain everything—they are all doing it at the present time.[6] But we are all like this. Politicians are merely ordinary men and women who happen to be in places where they get the publicity and who have some control over the sources of power. The same spirit is in the whole of the human race.

Is there anything more difficult than to admit that we are wrong? We are prepared to say that we will do something in a different way next time, but there is a big difference between saying that and admitting that we were wrong this time! We are all experts at rationalizing our sins; we can always explain them away—our own, that is, not other people's! We condemn the sins of other people, but of ours we always say, "If only people knew the full story, they wouldn't blame us."

We will do anything rather than admit that we have been wrong. That is part of our nature as the result of the Fall, and it is one of the marks of today's non-Christian outlook. But I am sorry to say that in this century [1900s] this mentality has even been allowed to enter the Christian church. All this modern preaching on the fact that God is love is an indication of the same attitude and spirit. We are told today that the old sermons that preached the law and talked about conviction of sin and called people to repentance were all wrong because they were legalistic. It is said that preachers had unfortunately been led astray by that man Paul who, having a Pharisee's legalistic brain, had foisted all this legalism, this Pharisaism, upon the simple, delightful Gospel of Jesus, which simply told everybody that God is love.

So it is said that we must return to the message of Jesus. We must get rid of all our theology, our argumentation and doctrine—it is all unnecessary. The business of preaching is to tell people that God is love. It does not matter what they are, or what they have been, or what they have done, or what they may do—God loves them. Nobody will ever be punished. There is no law; so there is no retribution and no hell.

So, this argument continues, we should not call upon people to repent in order to be forgiven because God has already forgiven them, whatever they may have done. He would not be God if He had not, for God is only love. You must therefore not talk about righteousness and justice and law and punishment and condemnation—all that is wrong. Love! Dignitaries in the church tell us that what we need is a "religionless Christianity." One of them has written a book in which he says that if you really want to find God, do not go to places of worship. He says that he has found more of God in the brothels and beer parlors of Algeria than he has ever found in a church. Kindness, love for one another—that, we are told, is the message. This is all just a very clever, modern, sophisticated, philosophical way of saying, No repentance!

But to be quite fair, this failure to teach repentance is sometimes found even among evangelical people and in evangelistic preaching. I have known many an evangelist who has said, in sermons and in writing, that you need not bother about repentance. What people should do is come to Jesus and take Him as their personal Savior. Repentance will come later. You need not bother about it at first. This, too, is another manifestation of this antipathy in the human heart to the whole notion of repentance.

But according to biblical teaching, repentance always comes first. As the apostles say here, "Him hath God exalted at his right hand to be a Prince and a Saviour, for to give repentance to Israel, and forgiveness of sins." And if you go through your Bible, you will find that is the invariable teaching.

That great line of prophets that God raised up in Israel always preached a message of repentance. They said, "All your troubles are due to your wrong relationship to God—you must turn." "For why will ye die, O house of Israel? . . . wherefore turn yourselves, and live ye" (Ezek. 18:31-32).

Then when you come to the New Testament, you find the same message. The first preacher in the New Testament is John, the son of Zechariah—we know him as John the Baptist. After the days of the prophet Malachi, there had been a great silence for four hundred years when there had been no word from the Lord. But then suddenly John appeared. We read: "Now in the fifteenth year of the reign of Tiberius Caesar, Pontius Pilate being governor of Judaea . . . the word of God came unto John the son of Zechariah in the wilderness" (Luke 3:1-2).

What was the word that came to John? What did he preach? It was "the baptism of repentance for the remission of sins" (Luke 3:3) You cannot have remission of sins without the baptism of repentance. The first message of the first preacher in the New Testament is the message of repentance.

And if you continue reading and move on to the ministry of our Lord, who is the second preacher to appear before us in the four Gospels, you will find exactly the same teaching. This is stated in many places. It is there in the first chapter of Mark's Gospel: "Now after that John was put in prison, Jesus came into Galilee, preaching the gospel of the kingdom of God, and saying, The time is fulfilled, and the kingdom of God is at hand: repent ye, and believe the gospel" (vv. 14-15). Notice the priority, the order in which our Lord put these things at the beginning of His ministry. But at the end of His ministry, you find the same message. After His resurrection He appeared to the disciples in the upper room, and we read:

> *Then opened he their understanding, that they might understand the scriptures, and said unto them, Thus it is written, and thus it behoved Christ to suffer, and to rise from the dead the third day: and that repentance and remission of sins should be preached in his name among all nations, beginning at Jerusalem.*
>
> —Luke 24:45-47

So the apostles were simply obeying our Lord's command when they put repentance before remission of sin. That is always the order.

When we come to the church herself and the great baptism with the Spirit on the Day of Pentecost and Peter's sermon to the people of Jerusalem, this is what we read: "Now when they heard this, they were pricked in their heart, and said unto Peter and to the rest of the apostles"—here is the first great preaching under the auspices of the church, and the audience is moved, convicted by the Spirit, and now for the first time this question is asked—"Men and brethren, what shall we do?" (Acts 2:37). Then Peter says, "Repent, and be baptized every one of you in the name of Jesus Christ for the remission of sins, and ye shall receive the gift of the Holy Ghost" (v. 38).

And the apostle Paul preached exactly the same message. There he was one afternoon in the famous city of Athens—the mecca of all philosophers—at the headquarters of all the schools of philosophy. He was there among them, standing before the Council of the Areopagus on Mars Hill. He knew all about their learning and their ability and all their philosophies, and what did he preach to them? He preached about God, but he brought his teaching to a point and said, "Forasmuch then as we are the offspring of God, we ought not to think that the Godhead is like unto gold, or silver, or stone, graven by art and man's device" (Acts 17:29).

Here were these great philosophers, worshiping idols, things made of stone and precious metals. The place was cluttered with their various temples and altars. But Paul said, "The times of this ignorance God winked at; but now commandeth all men every where to repent: because he hath appointed a day, in the which he will judge the world in righteousness by that man whom he hath ordained; whereof he hath given assurance unto all men, in that he hath raised him from the dead" (vv. 30-31).

Then further on in Acts you find Paul bidding farewell to the elders of the church at Ephesus. He tells them that they will not see him again, and he reminds them of the message he has always preached to them: "serving the Lord with all humility of mind, and with many tears, and temptations, which befell me by the lying in wait of the Jews: and how I kept back nothing that was profitable unto you, but have showed you, and have taught you publicly, and from house to house, testifying both to the Jews, and also to the Greeks"—what?—"repentance toward God, and faith toward our Lord Jesus Christ" (Acts 20:19-21).

This is the message throughout the New Testament. So here is the question that confronts us: Why must repentance have this priority? Why must we always start with it, when the world hates it and instinctively rebels against it and rejects it and regards it as insulting? Why is it an absolute essential?

If you know the message of the Bible at all, you will be in no difficulty about answering this question. Repentance is essential to salvation. There is no salvation without it. It is no use saying, "You can come to Christ now and repent later"; you cannot. Our Lord Himself says that repentance leads to remission of sins (Luke 24:47).

But why is repentance essential?

Here is one answer. Why did God ever send this great salvation into the world? Why did the Son of God ever come and live and die and rise again? What is the object of salvation? And the answer is that it is not merely so that our sins might be forgiven. People have that impression, and, of course, it is included, but that is certainly not the ultimate object; it is not even the main object.

No, the ultimate object of salvation is to deliver us from our sins. "Who gave himself for us," says Paul to Titus, "that he might redeem [deliver] us from all iniquity, and purify unto himself a peculiar people, zealous of good works" (Titus 2:14). The main object of salvation is the production of a new race of people, God's people, a new kingdom—the kingdom of light and the kingdom of glory, the kingdom of God and of His dear Son. In Mark 1 we are given a summary of our Lord's preaching: "The time is fulfilled, and the kingdom of God is at hand" (v. 15). It is a kingdom of righteousness, a kingdom of holiness. This is the object of our Lord's coming to this world, and this alone is a sufficient answer to the question of why repentance is necessary.

But there are other answers. What do you mean by saying that Christ is your Savior? How does He save? What does He save you from? All these things fit together, do they not? If you say you need a Savior, it must be because you realize that the life you have been living is wrong and sinful, that it deserves the judgment and punishment of God and of hell. What do you mean by *Savior* if you do not mean that He saves you from the consequences of your evil actions? But if you realize that is why you need salvation, then you must have a new idea about your past life and your past actions—and that is repentance. So you can either say, "I repent" meaninglessly, as some sort of incantation, and I am afraid that many have done that, or, if you really believe in Christ as Savior, with all the content of the gospel teaching, then you can use these words in an admission that your actions were wrong and you are a guilty sinner. It is thus impossible truly to believe in Christ as Savior without repenting.

Or to put it another way, the object of that death upon the cross was to reconcile us to God. It is a personal reconciliation. Christ's death does not just put us right with a law—it puts us right with a person. And because we enter into a personal relationship, because God is who He is, because, as John says, "[He] is light, and in him is no darkness at all" (1 John 1:5), we must realize at once that to have this relationship, this communion and fellowship with God, we must be like Him. We see that we must be righteous, for there is no communion between light and darkness—that is impossible, and therefore we must be delivered from all that is wrong and evil. That is repentance.

So, as we see very plainly here in Acts, the first part of the gospel message is the call to repentance. But what does repentance include? What is its connotation? And again there is no difficulty. The very words explain the New Testament teaching. The English word *repent* comes from a Latin word meaning "think again." And that is the first call of the Gospel—it is a call to men and women to think.

Let us get rid of the notion that Christianity is some sort of sob stuff, some sort of anesthetic, the "opium of the people" that paralyzes thought and wafts us up into some psychological or even psychic condition in which we have ceased to use our intelligence and are living in the realm of subjective feelings. It is quite the opposite. Let me say it once more: If the preaching of the Gospel does not make you think, and think as you have never thought in your life before, it is very bad preaching.

The tragedy of the world is that it does not think. With all due respect to the politicians, they do not provoke much thought. They are appealing to something else in us. Their speeches are bribes in some shape or form. They praise us, but do they really try to get us to think for ourselves? No; people do not think, and as a result they are committing a kind of suicide. In everything they do, they are governed by their feelings and prejudices. But here is a message that causes us to stop, to think for all we are worth, and then to think again—to repent.

The call to repentance is a call to think about our lives. Before I come to the conclusion that all I need is more money, I ought to ask myself, What am I? Am I a creature that can really be satisfied with more money and less work? Better houses, better education, more amusements, more cars—is that what we really need? Well now, says the Gospel, stop and think before you begin to listen to the rival parties arguing as to whether you are going to get some extra money or whatever. They tell us this is what really matters, and we all get so excited!

The Gospel says, "Stop a moment!" And it is the only voice that is saying this to this country today. It asks, What are you? What is a human being? What is this world we are in? What is life? What is the object of it all?

Think! Think again! Don't, don't, don't just accept what you read in the papers. Newspaper editors are not interested in the truth and in what is normal, but only in the abnormal and the sensational. Think! Ask yourself these fundamental questions. Think again, for unless you do, you will get nowhere. You will simply continue to be carried along by your prejudices and impulses, your passions and desires. "No," says the Gospel, "stop and think. What is death? What lies beyond? Think about all these things, and think about God."

But there is a second meaning to the word *repentance*, a meaning that is expressed in the Greek word for repentance—*metanoia*—which may be translated "a change of mind." It is very wonderful that these two languages give us the full content of repentance. Yes, you must think, and you must think seriously and hard, but you have not repented merely because you have thought. Thought may be sterile, or it may merely confirm you in your prejudices. We are all very clever at rationalizing our prejudices and supporting them with brilliant arguments. So repentance also means that, having considered all the evidence, especially the evidence given in the Bible, as against all the information that is purveyed to us in abundance day by day, we then change our minds. But about what?

First of all, we change our minds about God. The "natural man" is a God-hater. The newspapers are a wonderful illustration of his thinking. They always report stories against God, and they report the most fantastic claims of pseudo-scientists, anything that attempts to prove there is no God. They always ridicule the truth. Listen to these satirists—if they are even worthy of that name—as they sneer at God. All this is because people think that God is against them, that He is a monster. You must change your mind about God; you must see that your thinking about Him has been wrong.

We do not know God: "No man hath seen God at any time; the only begotten Son, which is in the bosom of the Father, he hath declared him" (John 1:18). That is why Christ came. He came to reveal God to us, and He said, "He that hath seen me hath seen the Father" (John 14:9). Is your idea of God something like Jesus Christ, in His humility, in His compassion, in His mercy and His love? "[He] went about doing good" (Acts 10:38). What is your thinking about God? Do you think you are being clever if you are always arguing against Him and saying, "If God is this, then why that?" Repentance means to change your mind about God.

And then repentance means to change your mind about yourself. Oh, that God would make humanity think correctly about itself! Do you not object to this notion that you are just an animal, and that the whole business of life is to eat and drink and have sex? That is what we are being taught, is it not? That is what is shouted at us day by day by all the media. But is that what a human being is? In the name of God, think again, change your mind! You need to know that you are made in the image and likeness of God, that you are meant to be the companion of God. Repentance is when you come to a true understanding of yourself and your own nature.

Repentance also tells you to think again about your life and your death. Is death the end? That is what the world thinks, is it not? It cannot prove it, but it convinces itself that death is the end, that when you die you are finished, and there is no more. No, no; think again, change your mind! There is the unseen, the eternal, the spiritual realm, the realm of God, and there is the judgment of God when every one of us will stand before Him. Paul writes, "For we must all appear before the judgment seat of Christ; that every one may receive the things done in his body" (2 Cor. 5:10).

The world needs to be reminded of judgment. This country [England] is becoming lawless—all countries are—and it is no use trying to solve the problem by passing acts of Parliament—you cannot do it. I agree with those who say that you cannot deal with the problem of labor and of capital by legislation. Of course you cannot; you need to change human nature. The trouble is in the human heart, on both sides of industry. Because people have no idea of the judgment of God, they ultimately have no sense of responsibility. Every man is out for himself, trying to get the best for himself. This is folly and tragedy, even on the political level, and how much more on the level of the judgment of God.

The world needs to know that it is rushing in the direction of final judgment. Only the prospect of judgment can sober it and bring it to its senses, and it is the business of the preaching of the Gospel to tell the world that, and not to say that God loves everybody and therefore everybody is going to heaven. Our Lord preached judgment, as we have seen; that is the sole explanation of why He died.

And then you must change your mind about the Lord Jesus Christ. He is not just a man, not just the "pale Galilean" (Swinburne), not just the carpenter, not a political agitator or a pacifist. He is the Lord of glory, who came into the world to save men and women, to take their sins upon Himself and to bear the punishment of those sins in His own body on the cross. What is your view of Jesus Christ? Think again before you dismiss Him as just one of the philosophers or one of the great men of the world. Think again; change your mind; acknowledge Him. Do what Thomas did—fall at His feet and say, "My Lord and my God" (John 20:28).

And then think again about your way of life. Do not go on regarding life as just something to shuffle through. Regard it as a royal pilgrimage, a preparation for heaven and for everlasting and eternal glory.

So repentance means thinking again and changing your mind, but I want to emphasize that it is not only a mental activity. You must repent with your heart. There must be real sorrow as the result of this thinking. The prophet Joel preached a great word when he addressed his contemporaries at a time very similar to the age in which you and I are living. He said, "Rend your heart, and not your garments" (Joel 2:13).

We are all ready at certain times to rend our garments, are we not? When a war comes, we make great sacrifices and we do wonderful things; but when the war ends we revert to where we were. There was no repentance in the last war.[7] It was a terrible time, and we were near disaster, but the country never repented. After the war we went back to the same old ways, eating and drinking without any thought of God, and the same old competitiveness. It is all back again. Why? Well, we only rended our garments.

In repentance the whole person is involved; the heart is involved. "Ye that love the LORD, hate evil" (Ps. 97:10). That is the mark of true repentance. William Cowper wrote:

> *I hate the sins that made thee mourn*
> *And drove thee from my breast.*

We do not merely contemplate our sin intellectually and say, "Well, on the whole I see that I have not thought as I should have done; so I must change my philosophy." No, no; repentance drives us to put on sackcloth and ashes; it humbles us to the dust and makes us see that we are fools. We hate ourselves and revile ourselves for what we have been and for our unutterable folly. Our hearts as well as our heads, the whole personality, is involved in the repentance.

And even that does not end repentance. We think again, and change our minds and feel sorrow for what we have been and done, but the next step is that we acknowledge it—and that is the difficulty. But when we see the depth of our sin, we have no trouble in acknowledging it. We rush to God and say, "Against thee, thee only, have I sinned, and done this evil in thy sight" (Ps. 51:4). Like the publican in our Lord's parable, we say, "God be merciful to me a sinner" (Luke 18:13). That is it. We confess our sin to God. We no longer care for our own reputation; we say, "I'm a fool." What is the point of comparing and contrasting ourselves with others? "All have sinned, and come short of the glory of God" (Rom. 3:23). "I have played the fool," as Saul, the first king of Israel, said to David (1 Sam. 26:21). I am ready to admit it.

But there is yet more. There is a final step. Repentance means that you act upon what you have now come to believe. Having seen that your life was wrong, you leave it and start living in exactly the opposite way. The apostle Paul brings this out very clearly in his first letter to the Thessalonians, probably the first epistle that he ever wrote. Here is a wonderful summary of the whole message of the Gospel: "They themselves show of us what manner of entering in we had unto you, and how ye turned to God from idols to serve the living and true God" (1:9). That is the ultimate step in repentance.

The road to hell is paved with good intentions. A man gets convinced, listening to a sermon perhaps, and he says, "Yes, I can see I'm wrong. I really must do something about it." But if he does not, he has not repented. Repentance includes rising up and forsaking the idols. As Paul wrote: "Ye turned to God *from* idols."

So the call to repentance means that you turn away from a life of opposition to God that is based upon lusts and desires and follows the way of the world and seeks its glittering prizes. You renounce that, and you turn to God. You seek His face and begin to worship Him. You try to serve the only true and living God. That is the very essence of repentance. It is a complete change in thought, in feeling, in action. It involves the heart, the mind, the will, the whole person. There is a total change away from the world and its evil, to God and His way of life in Christ Jesus. And that is what the apostles put in the forefront of their message. That always comes first.

But, finally, what leads to repentance? What brings it about? First, notice that it is a command. When the people cried out to Peter on the Day of Pentecost, "Men and brethren, what shall we do?" (Acts 2:37), he said to them, "Repent." Paul said to the people of Athens, "[God] commandeth all men every where to repent" (Acts 17:30).

But though it is a command, men and women cannot repent. Here is the depth of human iniquity. Here is the measure of the problem. People cannot repent; they are as bad as that. Why is this? Paul gives the answer: "Because the carnal mind is enmity against God: for it is not subject to the law of God, neither indeed can be. So then they that are in the flesh cannot please God" (Rom. 8:7-8). Men and women cannot sit down and decide that they have to change their opinion and their feelings about all these matters that I have been putting before you. Their whole nature is against it. I have simply been describing what happens when they do repent, but not what makes them change. "They that are in the flesh"—men and women as they are as the result of sin—"cannot please God," and they do not even want to.

So what can be done? We are commanded to repent, and yet we cannot. And the answer is in Peter's words in Acts 5: "Him hath God exalted with his right hand"—by His mighty power—"to be a Prince and a Saviour, *for to give repentance* . . ." Our only hope lies in the grace and the kindness and the goodness of God. And that is why He sent His Son into this world; it was in order to give us repentance.

Paul writes, "Or despisest thou the riches of his goodness and forbearance and long-suffering; not knowing that the goodness of God leadeth thee to repentance?" (Rom. 2:4). God's goodness is our only hope. No one ever repents until he has come under the influence of the Holy Spirit of God. Why did those people cry out on the Day of Pentecost, "Men and brethren, what shall we do?" They were the people who had cried out a few weeks earlier, "Away with Him! Crucify Him!" Why had they changed their minds? They had been so confident and proud of their actions in getting rid of this person. So why were they now in trouble? What had happened to them? There is only one answer: The people had been convicted by the power of the Holy Spirit. Nothing can ever make us think straight except the power of the Holy Spirit. He can and He will convict us "of sin, and of righteousness, and of judgment" (John 16:8). He can open blind eyes. He can give us an understanding of the truth.

Look at Paul himself, Saul of Tarsus, that proud, self-satisfied Pharisee, convinced that he was righteous before God. He knew his law; he could argue; he was proud of the religious things he did. But he underwent a complete change. Why? Oh, the Spirit convicted him. He suddenly understood the meaning of the law—he had thought he knew, but he had not. He had thought that the law was a matter of external actions. That was the trouble with the Pharisees, as with all these people who were opposing Peter and John. Because they had never actually killed a man, they said, "We have never committed murder." But our Lord had said, "Whosoever shall say to his brother . . . Thou fool, shall be in danger of hell fire" (Matt. 5:22). You can murder a man in your heart and in your spirit; we are all murderers, are we not? The law is spiritual, searching motives and desires. But the religious authorities had never seen that, and there is nothing that can enable anyone to see these things but the Spirit of God.

Peter said, "Him hath God exalted with his right hand to be a Prince and a Saviour"—why?—"for to give repentance." He sent His Spirit to give repentance on the Day of Pentecost, and the Spirit is here today. Have you been made to think again? Are you beginning to see these things? Are you troubled, disturbed, anxious about yourself? Are you crying out in your heart, "What shall I do?" If you are, the Spirit of God is leading you to repentance. Let Him lead you. Listen to Him.

> *Let not conscience make you linger,*
> *Nor of fitness fondly dream;*
> *All the fitness he requireth,*
> *Is to feel your need of him:*
> *This he gives you;*
> *'Tis the Spirit's rising beam.*
>
> Joseph Hart

Is this primary, essential message clear to you? Have you seen that all your thinking about yourself and about your life, about this world and about death, about the next world and about God and eternity is all wrong? Have you seen that the mentality of the world as represented in the newspapers and the sophisticated journals is all wrong? This alone is the truth: Men and women, though made in the image of God, are lost because of their rebellion; but God sent His Son into the world to save them, to redeem them, to purchase their pardon, to reconcile them to God, to give them a new nature and a new birth, and to prepare them for everlasting joy and bliss in the presence of God for all eternity. Have you seen this? "The goodness of God leadeth thee to repentance" (Rom. 2:4).

6

THE SAVIOR

Then Peter and the other apostles answered and said, We ought to obey God rather than men. The God of our fathers raised up Jesus, whom ye slew and hanged on a tree. Him hath God exalted with his right hand to be a Prince and a Saviour, for to give repentance to Israel, and forgiveness of sins. And we are his witnesses of these things; and so is also the Holy Ghost, whom God hath given to them that obey him.

—Acts 5:29-32

The term that we must now consider in the apostles' great defense to the Sanhedrin is the word "Saviour": "Him hath God exalted . . . to be a Prince and a Saviour." That is why the apostles said, "We must obey God rather than men" and why they insisted on preaching Him, whatever the Sanhedrin might say. It is this Savior and His great salvation that men and women are rejecting.

We have seen that one reason for this rejection is that the world has such a false idea of what a savior should be like. In this century we have seen the adulation of mere men, the tendency to turn men almost into gods. That is how the world thinks of saviors. Moreover, we have seen that though the world thinks it knows what it needs, it is ignorant of its need for forgiveness. Every political party and every individual belonging to every party need God's forgiveness.

And we have gone on to see that the first thing we are called upon to do is to repent, to acknowledge our sin. We must not argue that we are better than somebody else, that we are right and they are wrong, when all the time we are behaving just like them. We all need to repent, to acknowledge our unrighteousness, our iniquity, our selfishness. If only everybody in this country did that, what a difference it would make. Then we really would have a new start. Most of our problems would be resolved if both employers and employees acknowledged their selfishness, their self-centeredness, and especially if all of us did this together, under God. That is what the Gospel says are the absolute essentials. There is no hope for us at all until we repent.

The apostles put this teaching in a summarized form before the people. But that is not enough; these are only the first steps. Forgiveness is an absolute necessity, but we cannot stop there because the term *Savior* includes much more than that. My greatest need is not to come face to face with a law, but to come face to face with God, with a person. Reconciliation is something that takes place between persons. So forgiveness can never be enough for me, because what I really need is to be able to stand in the presence of God, to be able to approach Him and have free communion and fellowship with Him.

Then, looking beyond this life and this world, I anticipate what in the Bible is called "heaven." Heaven means spending eternity in the presence of God and of the holy angels. There are many descriptions of heaven in the Scriptures. In the book of Revelation, John the apostle writes of the vision he had of God and of how he saw exalted beings bowing their heads before Him and crying day and night, "Holy, holy, holy, Lord God Almighty" (Rev. 4:8). Heaven!

Now if I say that our desire is the vision of God, to see Him and to spend eternity with Him, then I must see at once that forgiveness is not enough. Indeed, forgiveness, in a sense, makes me feel yet more hopeless. If God in His grace and compassion has forgiven the guilt of my sins because He has laid them on His own Son and punished Him instead of me, then that makes me feel more like a worm than I ever felt before. How can I therefore stand in the presence of God? How can I have communion with God? How can I dwell with Him and spend eternity in His presence?

So here we are introduced to further elements in the work of our Lord Jesus Christ as our Savior. He is a complete Savior. He has come to save us from all the consequences of the Fall. Our estrangement from God and all our troubles, problems, and sufferings are the direct outcome of the Fall. As John summarizes it, "For this purpose the Son of God was manifested, that he might destroy the works of the devil" (1 John 3:8), and it was the devil who brought about the Fall.

Our Lord came to restore us to the full fellowship that Adam and Eve enjoyed at the beginning and that humanity was meant to enjoy. "So," says Peter here, "you are telling us not to preach or teach anymore in the name of this Jesus, but we must. Why? Because God has appointed Him to be a Savior." Peter has already said that there is no other Savior: "There is none other name under heaven given among men, whereby we must be saved" (Acts 4:12). Our Lord is the complete, the full, the perfect Savior; there is nothing that we need but that He has already done it.

Now the New Testament gives many summaries of how our Lord achieves salvation and what this means. In 1 Corinthians 1:30 the apostle Paul says, "But of him are ye in Christ Jesus, who of God is made unto us wisdom . . ." Do you want wisdom? Here it is; it is all in Christ. There is ultimately no wisdom apart from Him; there is only an apparent wisdom. No human teaching can truly deal with the totality of my problems, with my whole situation. But Christ is God's wisdom, and this wisdom, says Paul in this verse, "is righteousness, and sanctification, and redemption."

We have considered the wisdom of God in salvation as it is revealed in general, but now let us go on to consider specific aspects. First, justification.

"But," says somebody, "modern men and women do not understand the meaning of that word."

I have only one reply to make to that comment. Of course they do not— that is why they are in trouble. If they did understand the word, they would not be as they are. But it is the business of preaching to explain the terms. The meaning of justification cannot be expressed simply by a different word. Recent translations of the New Testament attempt to do this, but they empty the term of some of its most glorious aspects. No; the preacher must expound the Word.

Now Paul tells us in 1 Corinthians 1:30 that Christ is made unto us righteousness: That is, He is our justification, and we are justified in Him. And when Paul was preaching in Antioch in Pisidia, he made exactly the same point. Indeed, there is nothing else to preach. This is the message: "By him all that believe are justified from all things, from which ye could not be justified by the law of Moses" (Acts 13:39). I know that I need forgiveness, and if God does not forgive me, I have nothing, and it is no use going any further. But God has forgiven me.

Yes, but I am still in trouble. I am now aware of my sinfulness; I have repented; I have seen the ugliness and the vileness of my own inner nature; I have seen my smallness face to face with God. So merely to be told that I am forgiven is to make me feel like running away and hiding. I cannot face God; I cannot stand in His presence; I cannot have communion with Him because

I feel I am such a worm. As Isaiah put it to his own generation, "From the sole of the foot even unto the head there is no soundness in it; but wounds, and bruises, and putrefying sores" (Isa. 1:6). The moment I am convicted by the Spirit, I come to see that is the literal truth about myself.

To use a simple illustration, imagine a man living in the rough who has not washed for weeks, perhaps months and who is suddenly invited to take part in a banquet in Buckingham Palace. How would he feel? Now that is the position of the sinner before God, and that is why I say that forgiveness is not enough. It is essential, but it is not enough for me. Forgiveness, in a sense, is negative. I am told I cannot be punished for my sins. Yes, but though I am not punished, I may be banished from God's presence. I deserve to be executed. The great King may say, "I forgive you, and you will not be put to death." But I am still an outsider. I am faraway somewhere. There has been no restoration of communion. That is the great problem that arises.

Before I can enjoy fellowship and communion with God, I must be positively righteous. Why? Because God is righteous. This is an argument that you will find running right through the Bible. "Can two walk together, except they be agreed?" asks Amos (Amos 3:3). Paul says, "What communion hath light with darkness? and what concord hath Christ with Belial?" (2 Cor. 6:14-15). And in the Sermon on the Mount our Lord says, "Ye cannot serve God and mammon" (Matt. 6:24).

Before there can be fellowship there must be likeness, there must be similarity. This is the great problem confronting the human race, and this is where superficial ideas of the love of God and of forgiveness and modern objections to terms like *justification* are a sheer display of the fact that men and women have really never seen the problem.

So thank God for this great term *justification*. It means that Christ is my righteousness because He has not only purchased my forgiveness by dying on the cross on Calvary's hill and bearing my punishment, but He also does something else that, in a sense, is yet more glorious—He gives me His righteousness. My sins were placed upon Him—that is where I get my forgiveness; but I am justified, I receive righteousness, because His rightness, His holiness, His obedience to God's law, everything that He was, is put on my account. There is a great transference here, a great transaction, and the Bible is full of it.

When Paul writes to the Corinthians, he refers to himself as an ambassador for Christ. Now the business of an ambassador is to bear a message, and Paul gives the message. This is how he puts it:

God was in Christ, reconciling the world unto himself, not imputing their trespasses unto them. . . . Now then we are ambassadors for Christ, as though God did beseech you by us: we pray you in Christ's stead, be ye reconciled to God. For he hath made him to be sin for us, who knew no sin; that we might be made the righteousness of God in him.

—*2 Cor. 5:19-21*

It is because so many people today have never understood this tremendous transaction that they do not rejoice as they should. What is this great message of salvation that the apostles insisted they had to go on preaching? It is Christ the Savior, and it is the proclamation of the transaction that took place between the Father and the Son on the cross: "[God] hath made him to be sin for us." God took our trespasses and laid them on His Son. Think of it in terms of ledgers. Here is the list of my debts, my trespasses, my transgressions against God. They are taken out of my record and are put on Christ's record. My guilt is transferred to His account, and He pays the bill. He bears the punishment.

Yes, that is all right, that part of my account is cleared; but now I am in a neutral position. What was against me is taken out, and my debts are paid, but I have nothing, and I cannot go on like that. I must have something; I must be in a relationship with God. And there it is: "[God] hath made him to be sin for us, who knew no sin; that we might be made the righteousness of God in him," that we might be made righteous in the presence of God through Him and by Him. That is the meaning of justification. As God takes my sins and puts them on Christ, so He takes Christ's righteousness and holiness and puts it on me.

The doctrine of justification thrilled the apostle Paul; he never tired of referring to it. This is what revolutionized his life. There he was, a Pharisee, and he held the typical pharisaical view of these matters. The Pharisees believed—and their modern counterparts still believe—that as long as people live good lives, as long as they are religious and moral, as long as they do their best, they satisfy God. Saul of Tarsus believed that absolutely. He says, ". . . touching the righteousness which is in the law, [I thought I was] blameless" (Phil. 3:6). And, of course, he compared himself with other people. He compared himself with other Pharisees, and he knew that he was ahead of them. He was an abler man. He always beat them in the examinations, and he made greater sacrifices. So he could look at others and thank God that he was so much better than they were.

He was proud of this amazing righteousness that he by his efforts had worked out, and he had no doubt at all but that God was very pleased with him.

Then one afternoon he found himself looking into the face of absolute righteousness. On the road to Damascus, he looked into the face of the risen Lord Jesus. He saw the holiness and the purity and the love and the compassion streaming out of that blessed face, and he felt that all his righteousnesses had become like filthy rags. Let the apostle say it for himself in his tremendous statement in the third chapter of Philippians:

> *But what things were gain to me, those I counted loss for Christ. Yea doubtless, and I count all things but loss for the excellency of the knowledge of Christ Jesus my Lord: for whom I have suffered the loss of all things, and do count them but dung, that I may win Christ, and be found in him, not having mine own righteousness, which is of the law, but that which is through the faith of Christ, the righteousness which is of God by faith.*
>
> —*vv. 7-9*

Paul's own righteousness could not stand the gaze of heaven and of God and of Christ; it became rags and dung and refuse, and he saw himself in his utterly hopeless state. But now he realized this great statement concerning justification by faith only. He saw that God has taken the righteousness of His own Son and credited it to our account.

Justification is the most glorious aspect of the gospel message, and yet this is what people do not seem able to grasp. The trouble with men and women has always been their pride—and what they hate about the Gospel is that it is a free gift. Each person says, "But I want to make myself fit to stand before God, and I can do it! Show me the law, and I will keep it." Thus they reject this free gift of God.

To take a further illustration, justification has often been explained in this way: Here am I, in my filthy rags, and in His grace God has taken all my guilt from me. Then He takes my rags from me and puts on me the robe of the righteousness of His own dear Son. This understanding is what led to the great evangelical awakening two hundred years ago. It started with the Moravian brethren in what is now part of Germany and Czechoslovakia, and it influenced the early Methodists in this country. Count Zinzendorf, the leader of the Moravians, has expressed it in a glorious hymn, translated into English by John Wesley:

Jesus, thy blood and righteousness
My beauty are, my glorious dress;
'Midst flaming worlds, in these arrayed,
With joy shall I lift up my head.

I am unfit and unworthy—I am not dressed in an adequate manner to enter the banqueting chamber of the King; but He provides clothing for me. Our Lord said it all in a parable—the parable of a king who invited guests to a wedding feast. On the day of the wedding, the king saw that one of the guests was not wearing the wedding clothes he had provided, and no one could enter the feast without being clothed in the wedding robe.

This is the great message of salvation. John, in his vision in the book of Revelation, gives us the same picture. He sees certain people, but he does not understand them. He says:

I beheld, and, lo, a great multitude, which no man could number, of all nations, and kindreds, and people, and tongues, stood before the throne, and before the Lamb, clothed with white robes, and palms in their hands; and cried with a loud voice, saying, Salvation to our God which sitteth upon the throne, and unto the Lamb. And all the angels stood round about the throne, and about the elders and the four beasts, and fell before the throne on their faces, and worshipped God, saying, Amen: Blessing, and glory, and wisdom, and thanksgiving, and honour, and power, and might, be unto our God for ever and ever. Amen. And one of the elders answered, saying unto me, What are these which are arrayed in white robes? and whence came they? And I said unto him, Sir, thou knowest.

—7:9-14

John did not know. Who were these people in their white robes in all this glory and magnificence and wonder?

And he said to me, These are they which came out of the great tribulation, and have washed their robes, and made them white in the blood of the Lamb.

—v. 14

That is another way of saying that multitude was justified by faith. This is the robe of righteousness that is given to us freely in and through the blessed

Savior. So it comes to this: The teaching of justification by faith is diametrically opposed to justification by your own works. Nor is it justification by
the Roman Catholic sacraments—by baptism or by the Lord's Supper; you
are not saved or made righteous by the church or by the Virgin Mary. No,
no; our righteousness is in Christ, and it is in Him by faith and by faith alone.
You do nothing, nobody else does anything—He has done it all.

If you believe this message—that you are a vile, damned sinner, that Christ
the Son of God has borne your sins and your punishment and has died for you
and risen again—if you believe that, then God pronounces you righteous. It is
a legal pronouncement. "There is therefore now no condemnation to them
which are in Christ Jesus" (Rom. 8:1). "Being justified by faith, we have peace
with God through our Lord Jesus Christ" (Rom. 5:1). He is the Savior.

But this great salvation does not even stop at justification. When the angel
set the apostles free from the prison, he commanded them, "Go, stand and speak
in the temple to the people all the words of this life" (Acts 5:20). "This *life*"!
Christianity is not morality; it is not a philosophy; it is not merely a number of
rules and regulations; it is not a message telling you to stop doing this and to
start doing that. No, no; it is *life*. Our blessed Lord said, "I am come that they
might have life, and that they might have it more abundantly" (John 10:10).

The trouble with the human race is that we are all dead in trespasses and
sins, unaware of God in the soul, unaware of the spiritual realm and the most
glorious truths about humanity and eternity. We are dead, and what we need
is life—"the words of this life." When Adam and Eve sinned, they died; they
died spiritually immediately, and later they died physically. But men and
women need never have died at all; death came in because of sin.

All the problems come from the Fall, do they not? Not only the problems being discussed by the politicians today—they only see the surface—but
the moral problems that they cannot touch. And at the back of all of them,
the final consequence of man's rebellion is death—spiritual death. But Christ
is our Savior, and that means, in part, that He can give us life.

Forgiveness I need, yes, and righteousness too. But I also need life. How
can I live in the presence of God? How can I enjoy God?

> *O! how shall I, whose native sphere*
> *Is dark, whose mind is dim,*
> *Before the Ineffable appear,*
> *And on my naked spirit bear*
> *That uncreated beam?*
>   Thomas Binney

How can men and women enjoy God? Take someone who lives for food and drink and sex and bingo and all these other things. If you put that person into heaven, he would say it felt like hell. So how can one enjoy heaven? How can one enjoy the society of God? There is nothing twisted or perverted or ugly or suggestive in God's conversation; yet those are the very things that give pleasure to sinful human nature. Before we can enjoy the things of God, we need new life.

"All right," I say, "I've been given a wonderful robe, a spotless robe, a white robe washed in the blood of the Lamb. Yet I feel unclean within." I say, "Look at my robe! It's been given me by the Judge, by the King. I'm free!" Yes, but what of how I am within myself? Oh, I know the plague of my own heart, and it is darkness.

But the Gospel tells me that Christ as the Savior has come to give me new life. If He had not come to do this, His salvation would not be complete. But He has! The new life given by Christ is the great doctrine that is expounded so frequently in the Scriptures. We see it especially perhaps in Romans 6, where the apostle Paul teaches about our union with Christ. It comes to this: By nature we are all what the Bible calls the "old man," the "old self"; that is, we are "in Adam." We have all inherited the Adamic nature. We have all been born as sinners. We all prefer the wrong to the right, the darkness to the light. We all prefer that which belongs to the flesh and the devil rather than to God. And the amazing message of the Gospel is that we are made one with Christ, so that when He died on that cross, that old self that was in us died with Him: "Knowing this, that our old man is crucified with him [Christ]" (Rom. 6:6).

The death of the old self is the negative aspect of this work of Christ; on the positive side, Paul goes on to say:

> *Now if we be dead with Christ, we believe that we shall also live with him: knowing that Christ being raised from the dead dieth no more; death hath no more dominion over him. For in that he died he died unto sin once; but in that he liveth, he liveth unto God. Likewise reckon ye also yourselves to be dead indeed unto sin, but alive unto God through Jesus Christ our Lord.*

—vv. 8-11

"Alive unto God"—alive to the fact that we are children of God and that God is looking on us and blessing us and that we are going to share His life.

*Let not sin therefore reign in your mortal body, that ye should obey
it in the lusts thereof. Neither yield ye your members as instruments
of unrighteousness unto sin: but yield yourselves unto God, as those
that are alive from the dead, and your members as instruments of
righteousness unto God.*

—*vv. 12-13*

What we are offered here is the death of the old man, the birth of the
new man, union with Christ, being born again, receiving a new start, being
given a new nature, a new heart, a new outlook, a new orientation, new
desires. "If any man be in Christ, he is a new creature [a new creation]: old
things are passed away; behold, all things are become new" (2 Cor. 5:17).

So the purpose of the Gospel is not to tell people how to change the
world—that is what politics is about, trying to "change the face of Britain,"
as they say. But they never will. They may put on a new coat of paint or a bit
of varnish here or there, but it will be the same old Britain—the same old sinful Britain—no worse than the other nations, but equally bad. This nonsense
that one nation is inherently better than another—what utter folly that is! No,
no; you only make little differences and changes on the surface, but what people need, individually and collectively, is a new nature. They need a new
understanding of everything.

"Go out," says the angel to the apostles in prison, "go back to the temple, stand there, speak boldly 'all the words of this life,' life in Christ, life that
is life indeed, life more abundant."

So if you are not a Christian, do you not realize that you are refusing the
very thing you need—to be "alive unto God"? You are refusing the possibility of knowing Him, the possibility of having fellowship with Him, the possibility of receiving gracious blessings from His hand day by day, no longer
a stranger and a foreigner, no longer "far off," but "made nigh" (Eph. 2:13),
introduced into the family. You are refusing the possibility of becoming a citizen of God's kingdom—yes, but also of becoming a member of God's household, of becoming a child of God, and because a child, an heir of God and a
joint-heir with Christ (Rom. 8:15-17). That is a part of this great salvation,
and that is why the apostles felt they must preach it. They could not be
restrained; they had to tell everybody.

But it does not stop even there! I believe, I am a child of God, I go to God
as my Father, but I am still aware of this pollution within. I am still aware of
this ugliness and vileness. I have come to the point of knowing that Charles
Wesley was not just writing wonderful lines of poetry when he said:

Just and holy is thy name;
I am all unrighteousness;
Vile and full of sin I am.

The politicians do not say that about themselves, do they? They say that about one another, but the Bible says it about every one of them and about you and me with them. "Vile and full of sin I am"—and if you know yourself, you know that is nothing but the truth. We are all under the dominion of sin. That is the contradiction that is in us: desiring the better but doing the worse; this downward tug and pull, this bias, this fatal "law . . . in my members" that Paul speaks of (Rom. 7:23). How can I get rid of this pollution? I know I am forgiven—thank God. I have the robe of righteousness upon me, this spotless white robe. Thank God, I know I have a new nature, a new life, a new beginning, a new and a clean heart, but still the pollution remains. We cannot get rid of it, but Christ the Savior can.

Christ is the Savior! He has been exalted by God to be a Prince and a Savior (Acts 5:31), and because He is a complete Savior, He deals with this pollution. That is what the Bible calls sanctification. The actual word does not matter, though I defy you to think of a better one, but that is the scriptural term. Sanctification means not only being set apart for God, but being set apart from the sin that is in us. It is a process of purification. He starts it the moment we are born again, the moment the seed of new life is put into us. We have been made "partakers of the divine nature" (2 Pet. 1:4), and now He sends His Spirit into us. What for? In order to tend this seed and to foster it, to encourage its growth: "Christ in you, the hope of glory" (Col. 1:27).

Oh, do not worry because you cannot understand this! Who can understand it? This is a fact that you will go on trying to understand for the rest of your days if you are a Christian, and on through eternity. The miracle of God's way of salvation is that somehow or another He puts something of this life of Christ into us, and it begins to grow and develop and bear fruit. "Sanctify them," our Lord says in His last prayer to His Father: "Sanctify them through thy truth: thy word is truth" (John 17:17).

If you have come to see this truth, make sure that you continue to learn more about sanctification. Meet together with other Christians to hear these great doctrines expounded, and you will see how you can be delivered from the pollution and the power of sin. This is what people have cried out for.

> *Rock of Ages, cleft for me,*
> *Let me hide myself in thee!*
> *Let the water and the blood,*
> *From thy riven side which flowed*
> *Be of sin the double cure . . .*

The double cure, I need two cures.

> *Cleanse me from its guilt . . .*

He has died, His body is broken, His blood is shed; the guilt is gone. But, oh . . .

> *Cleanse me from its guilt and power.*
> Augustus Toplady

Christ is a complete Savior, and He can cleanse you from this evil, dominating power. That is what is meant by sanctification.

But I am still not finished. This will never be finished; we only begin with these things in this world of time. In eternity we will still be working out this theme, still glorying in it, still wondering at it, still praising Him on account of it. So let me give you some further thoughts to work out for yourselves.

Listen to this: Christ as your Savior will lead you while you are still in this world. We need His leadership, do we not? And it is a part of His great salvation that He does lead us. The author of the letter to the Hebrews puts it like this: "We see Jesus"—and we are going to follow Him—". . . for it became him, for whom are all things, and by whom are all things"—that is God—"in bringing many sons unto glory"—those who believe this message—"to make the captain of their salvation perfect through sufferings" (Heb. 2:9-10). "The captain of their salvation"! A great leader is going ahead of us. I am forgiven, given a robe of righteousness, given a new nature, aware of the process of sanctification, but I am still left in this world. Here I am, confronted by the world, the flesh, and the devil, and it is difficult to see my way through.

How can I go on? How can I arrive at the city? Here is the answer: "the captain of their salvation," the leader, none other than this blessed Jesus, the Son of God.

For both he that sanctifieth and they who are sanctified are all of one: for which cause he is not ashamed to call them brethren, saying, I will declare thy name unto my brethren, in the midst of the church will I sing praise unto thee.

Then listen:

Forasmuch then as the children are partakers of flesh and blood, he also himself likewise took part of the same; that through death he might destroy him that had the power of death, that is, the devil.
—vv. 11-12, 14

Here I am. I know I am a child of God, but everywhere I see the devil in his various forms, enticing, attacking. I know his power, and who am I to withstand him? But here is one who has beaten him, and this one is my captain, the leader of my salvation. He leads me on, and I follow Him. You find the same picture in Hebrews 12: "Looking unto Jesus the author and finisher of our faith" (v. 2). We are called upon to follow Him, and we are told that He will never leave us or forsake us.

Our Lord also promises to help us. There are days when we feel almost overwhelmed, when all hell seems to be let loose against us, and temptation comes in all its subtlety from every quarter at the same time. What can we do? Here is the answer:

Wherefore in all things it behoved him to be made like unto his brethren, that he might be a merciful and faithful high priest in things pertaining to God, to make reconciliation for the sins of the people. For in that he himself hath suffered being tempted, he is able to succour them that are tempted.
—Heb. 2:17-18

Are you having a difficult time? Do you feel that temptation is mastering you and getting you down and that you are hopeless? Listen:

For we have not an high priest which cannot be touched with the feeling of our infirmities; but was in all points tempted like as we are, yet without sin. Let us therefore come boldly unto the throne of grace, that we may obtain mercy, and find grace to help in time of need.
—Heb. 4:15-16

This perfect Savior provides you with everything you need, and even when He has given it all to you, including the new nature, He knows the struggle. He has been in the world. He has felt the force and the power of the devil and of temptation—"in all points tempted like as we are, yet without sin." He is with you, and He will sympathize with you and will hold you and help you. You can turn to Him at your most hopeless moment and say:

> *I need thee every hour,*
> *Stay thou nearby;*
> *Temptations lose their power*
> *When thou art nigh.*
>   Annie Sherwood Hawks

He will make you strong and give you victory. What a Savior! What a perfect salvation! And then we are told by Paul that "[He] also maketh intercession for us" (Rom. 8:34). We are given the same teaching in that great Epistle to the Hebrews. We have a high priest who represents us before God and will present our case. Indeed, the writer puts it in a yet more glorious way. Because they were persecuted and having a hard time, some of these poor Hebrew Christians who had believed the Gospel were beginning to ask, "Were we right to believe in Christ? Shouldn't we go back to the temple and our burnt offerings and sacrifices?" In the same way, many people today are tempted to go back to Mary and the priesthood, to some *ex opere operato* belief in the grace that is inherent in bread and wine, in water and baptism. Fancy going back to things like that, to beggarly elements! Like the Hebrew Christians, some go back to human priests. Why? Because they have never understood that those are only temporary, but that this high priest whom God has appointed lives forever.

> *They truly were many priests, because they were not suffered to continue by reason of death: but this man, because he continueth ever, hath an unchangeable priesthood. Wherefore he is able also to save them to the uttermost [to the very end] that come unto God by him, seeing he ever liveth to make intercession for them.*
>   —Heb. 7:23-25

He is there, and He is there forever.

We have seen that Christ our Savior caters for our every need, that He undoes all the works of the devil. To complete this wonderful picture, we ask:

What is the last of the devil's works? It is death itself, and Christ has dealt with that, He has conquered it. He has defeated the last enemy. Christ will present all who believe in Him to the Father absolutely perfect. All the pollution will have gone. We will be as clean inside as we are outside, having wisdom, righteousness, sanctification, redemption, glorification, the very body changed and delivered, sin entirely exterminated. The Savior said at the end of His earthly life:

> *Let not your heart be troubled: ye believe in God, believe also in me. In my Father's house are many mansions: if it were not so, I would have told you. I go to prepare a place for you. And if I go and prepare a place for you, I will come again, and receive you unto myself; that where I am, there ye may be also.*
>
> —*John 14:1-3*

Jude in his epistle puts it like this: "Now unto him that is able to keep you from falling"—while we are here—"and to present you faultless before the presence of his glory with exceeding joy, to the only wise God our Saviour, be glory and majesty, dominion and power, both now and ever. Amen" (vv. 24-25).

What else can one say? Amen. "Blessing, and honour, and glory, and power, be unto him that sitteth upon the throne, and unto the Lamb" (Rev. 5:13)—the Lamb who was slain and has redeemed us to God. Do you know Him, this Savior whose followers the Jewish Council tried to silence? Have you believed in Him? Are you ready to defy the whole world and face even death rather than cease to believe in Him? ". . . who of God is made unto us wisdom, and righteousness, and sanctification, and [complete] redemption" (1 Cor. 1:30).

7

A PRINCE

Then Peter and the other apostles answered and said, We ought to obey God rather than men. The God of our fathers raised up Jesus, whom ye slew and hanged on a tree. Him hath God exalted with his right hand to be a Prince and a Saviour, for to give repentance to Israel, and forgiveness of sins. And we are his witnesses of these things; and so is also the Holy Ghost, whom God hath given to them that obey him.

—Acts 5:29-32

I want in particular to deal now with the first part of that thirty-first verse: "Him hath God exalted with his right hand to be a Prince"—a Prince!—"and a Saviour." Here, let me remind you, we see the apostles confronted by earthly, human, worldly authority and power; and this authority is trying to prohibit the preaching of the Christian message. The apostles say in reply, "We cannot promise to stop; we must go on preaching this message. 'We ought to obey God rather than men.'" And they say this because God has raised up this Jesus and appointed him as Prince and Savior. So we have here a picture of two different types of government, two ideas of the government of the world: the human and temporal, and the divine and eternal.

We have been looking at this great message, and so far we have been concentrating on the personal aspect—Christ as the Savior, as the one who delivers us from our individual predicaments. It is always right that we should start with that, but it is very wrong indeed to stop there and to think that is the whole of the Gospel. It is not, as we are reminded here. Christ is not only the Savior—He is the Prince, the Governor, the Ruler—and in this wonderful way we are given the contrast. Here is a little summary of the whole of human history—human governors and the Prince who governs the universe.

There are many people who think the Gospel only has a personal message. Indeed, many are not Christians because they take that view. They say, "In a sense we're all in trouble, and there are some people who seem to be helped by Christianity. It gives them comfort and a little bit of happiness, it gives them fellowship, and that's all right. If they get help from that sort of thing, let them have it—they're welcome to it. But, of course, that has nothing to do with us. We get our relief and help and happiness in other ways."

People who speak in that way are not interested in Christianity. Their view is that we are all born with a certain type of temperament, we are all different psychological types, including the religious type, and they have no quarrel with that. They maintain that they are not the religious type, and therefore the Gospel does not concern them. They dismiss it because they regard it as something purely personal that has nothing to say to the world at large. They think it is some sort of aid to survival for that little group of people who are interested in Christianity, some 10 percent only in this country [England]—I use figures because we are living in times of statistics and polls! It is said that of course this percentage will quickly get smaller as humanity grows up and becomes more educated, and in the end Christianity will vanish altogether.

Now unfortunately there are certain Christian people who very wrongly give a good deal of credibility to that view. Let us be honest and admit this. There are Christian people who do seem to confine the Christian message to a personal matter of salvation—Jesus Christ, the Savior. They are interested in it because of what it does for them, and they are always looking at themselves and their own experiences and wants.

Thank God that our Lord is the Savior. The first need of every one of us is for salvation. But if you confine the Christian faith to a matter of personal salvation, then you are not only encouraging other people to go wrong in their thinking, you are putting a very grievous limit upon the glory of this great Gospel. This is a Gospel for the universe. It starts with personal salvation, but it does not end with it. The Gospel is a proclamation that God has exalted His Son to be a Prince. It is concerned about the whole world, whether people realize it or not, and not only does it deliver us as individuals from this present world, but it will eventually deliver the whole universe from all the ravages and consequences of sin.

Has the Gospel anything to say on this particular Sunday night therefore, a pre-election Sunday night?[8] Has this Gospel any relevance to the conditions in this country at this very moment? It has a very relevant message indeed, a message that is needed more than all the other messages that are being delivered at this present time. Christ is the Prince as well as the Savior—Prince of the world and of the universe.

The Bible states this great message in many ways. One of the best, perhaps, is a statement made by the apostle Paul in the first chapter of Ephesians. This, he says, is the will of God:

> *Having made known unto us the mystery of his will, according to his good pleasure which he hath purposed in himself: that in the dispensation of the fulness of times he might gather together in one all things in Christ, both which are in heaven, and which are on earth; even in him.*

—*vv. 9-10*

That is God's great purpose in Christ with respect to this universe. It is an essential part of the preaching of the Gospel and is exactly what the apostles Peter and John meant. They turned to the earthly rulers and said in effect, "You are trying to stop us from preaching this Gospel, and you think that you are exercising your rights when you tell us not to preach about this person. You think you are doing what you should be doing as governors who are here to maintain law and order. But you are not only ignorant as to who He is, you are also ignorant as to what He has come to do in this world. He is the Governor! He is the only one who can govern. He is the ruler of the universe, the only one who can do successfully what you are trying and failing to do." That is why they could not keep silent. "Him hath God exalted with his right hand to be a Prince and [as well as] a Saviour." Now this is the message that the earthly powers have always opposed, and that is the great problem of today—the two powers, the two attempts at government. And I want to show you that it is all here in the apostles' words in Acts 5.

There is only one way whereby we really can grasp the message that Christ is Prince over the universe, and that is by taking a kind of bird's-eye view of the teaching of the whole of the Bible. This is a convenient opportunity for doing that; our text makes us do it. It says that he is "a Prince," and I want to show you that in terms of the present situation—the general election.

"Well, we must have a government," you say.

But why must we? That is the question that is raised. My argument is that you cannot understand the history of the human race, the past, the present, nor the future, except in the light of the teaching of this book that we call the Bible. But we must take it as a whole. It is not enough to say, "Christ can do this, that, and the other for me." He will; but there is so much more. Look at Him—this blessed Prince—let Him speak for Himself! Look at Him in the glory and the greatness of His power; see it here and in the whole of the Bible.

The apostles said, "The God of our fathers raised up Jesus." In other words, they were immediately correcting the thinking of the authorities. They said, "You are looking at Jesus, that man who walked about this city and other places and who did all that He did. You are just starting with Him as He appeared before you, as you crucified Him and as He was dead and buried. But your views are too small; you do not have the context—'the God of our fathers.' If you want to understand Him, go back into history."

And that is the trouble with so many today: Their views are foreshortened, and everything is oversimplified. The problems of the world are profound, and there is only one way to understand them. We must have this great context. So much of what we are so frequently hearing at this present time is so trivial. It is not surprising that the country and the world are in a muddle. People do not know how to take their problems and put them into the setting of eternity, and that is why they always fail.

Let me show you what I mean. I can summarize the message of the Bible—the message for today and tomorrow and every day until election day on Thursday and after that and always—in these terms. You must go back to the beginning, to creation. You must start with the world itself, what it is and where it has come from. You must start with the origin of the human race. It is no use trying to decide what you are going to do for men and women until you know what a human being is, and that is where all the politicians in all the parties are so insulting to us. They think that we can be bought with money or with bread and butter, with handouts. They compete in attempts to bribe us. This is, I repeat, an insult to us. The problems of humanity are not dealt with at that level. You must stop to consider what the whole universe is, what men and women are, and where they have come from.

Then you go on to face this question: Why is the world as it is? I ask again: Why do you need government? Why do you need magistrates? Why do you need swords? Why do you need laws? Why do you need punishment? Why do you need prisons? Here are the questions that the Bible alone deals with. Government officials will argue as to whether you should provide new beds for the prisoners and give them psychotherapy, but they never ask why there is ever a need for prisons at all. They never face up to that question.

Why are there any troubles in the world? And there is only one answer—the answer that is provided here. It is that man has fallen; it is that he who had been made perfect, in the image of God, rebelled against God and thereby brought down chaos and punishment upon himself. It is humans who have brought trouble and confusion into the world.

So we start as the Bible starts. Now Scripture does not spend much time in giving us all the details about creation. What it does do, there in the first two chapters of Genesis, is give us the background and the setting, and it tells us that everything comes from God. What the Bible is really interested in is the state of the world as it is now. And in chapter 3 of Genesis we are told about the fall of man, the resulting trouble and confusion, man earning his bread by the sweat of his brow. And the Bible shows us that the trouble went on increasing. Indeed, in the early chapters of Genesis we read accounts of the condition of the world that could have been written today.

From Genesis 3 onward, we are confronted by two great lines or two types of history. There is human history, and there is God's history. This is the way to understand life and all its attendant circumstances and problems. Whether we know it or not, you and I are involved in both types of history, and it is the business of preaching to make us aware of that and to give us instruction about it.

It is the essence of the tragedy of the world that it only knows about human history. A general election. The possibility of a change of government. Governments deciding to declare war. Secular history books are about men and women, great and small, making history. The world reads its Sunday papers, and it thinks it knows and understands what is happening. But it is completely blind to God's history, to the amazing story of what God is bringing to pass.

Let me give you the most notable example of human ignorance. Take the accounts that we are given of the birth of our Lord and Savior. I am thinking particularly of the account we are given in the second chapter of Luke. Surely even in these days everybody remembers this story:

> And it came to pass in those days, that there went out a decree from Caesar Augustus, that all the world should be taxed. (And this taxing was first made when Cyrenius was governor of Syria.) And all went to be taxed, every one into his own city.

That is human history. That is what men and women are interested in. Then we are told:

And Joseph also went up from Galilee, out of the city of Nazareth,
into Judaea, unto the city of David, which is called Bethlehem;
(because he was of the house and lineage of David;) . . .

A taxing was a notable occasion, something like a general election. It did
not have the same purpose, but everybody was involved and everybody had
to go and register.

. . . to be taxed with Mary his espoused wife, being great with child.
                                                              —Luke 2:1-5

And you remember what happened. Mary was on the verge of giving
birth to her child, but all the rooms in the inn were taken—"there was no
room for them in the inn" (v. 7). So Mary and Joseph had to go to a stable,
and it was in the stable that the child was born.

You can see what was happening, can you not? Have a look at the inns
of Bethlehem; can you not see them all crowded, the bars particularly, everybody drinking? What are they talking about? Politics! Taxation! Taxes might
be put up: is it right or wrong? Should they not make a protest; should they
not do something? This is the important matter. This is what everybody
should be interested in and arguing about. This census for the purpose of taxation is the big event. The fact that a child is born in a stable and his little
body placed in a manger—well, it is too trivial to notice. Pay attention to
that? What nonsense!

But that is God's history. That event, according to human history, seemed
unimportant, but it has turned the world upside-down. That thing that did
not matter makes us call this year 1966. Now this is the message of the Gospel
to us and to our world today. What God does is ignored and forgotten;
nobody sees anything in it, and yet that is the history that really matters.

I must hold these two histories before you. There is the Sanhedrin, the
worldly authority, the worldly government, that says to a preacher of the
Gospel, "Stop doing that! Don't mention this name. We don't want to hear
anything about it. It's creating a disturbance. It's not helping law and order.
It's irrelevant, but at the same time it's a nuisance, and you must stop it. 'Did
we not straitly command you that ye should not teach in this name?'"

And there is only one answer to be given to that, the answer of the apostles, and I am privileged to repeat it now: "We ought to obey God rather than
men." Why? Because we are preaching about the one who is the Prince of the
universe, the only one who can govern, who has a right to govern, the only

one who will govern. But there is a conflict because the world does not accept this and has to be convinced and convicted. So let us proceed by looking at human history, this history that is made chiefly by men and women.

The first thing we must say about even human history is that it is God who brought it into being. The problem is that humanity has rebelled and fallen; the world is in trouble. What can be done about it? God, in His infinite wisdom and through what is called His common grace, determined to produce a certain order that was to be arranged and kept going by men and women. This order is human government.

There are many statements in the Scriptures on the subject of human government. In Paul's address to the Stoics and Epicureans in Athens, for instance, we are told that God ordered the bounds of the habitation of all the peoples of the earth, dividing up the world into nations (Acts 17:26). But above and beyond that, as Romans 13:1 tells us, "The powers that be are ordained of God." In order to keep the effects of sin within bounds, God ordained that there should be governors, magistrates, kings, princes, and other officials. He laid down the principles of government and then, as it were, handed it over to men and women. In addition, God gave them gifts: abilities, intelligence, authority, political understanding, and so on.

So that was the origin of human government. But what we need to ask at a time like this is: What are its characteristics? And it is quite clear, in the Bible and in subsequent history, that this very order of government that has been ordained by God for our good has been abused. Human leaders reject God and take power into their own hands. They think they are able to order their own affairs without looking to God for help. They say:

I am the master of my fate;
I am the captain of my soul.
W. E. Henley

And what have governments done? From the beginning they have attempted to produce what is called *civilization*. They have tried to produce systems, order, and control. They have tried to regulate and manage human affairs. By means of farming and trading, by building cities and communities, by fostering interest in culture, art, music, and literature, they have attempted to deal with their own predicament, to improve their lot, to give themselves peace and rest and contentment. And above all, they have tried politics. All this in an attempt to reduce the chaos to order.

And, of course, the authorities that govern and control us are divided.

There are rival schools and parties in art and literature, music and politics. Their aims, however, are exactly the same, the only difference being a difference of method. They all offer us the same bribes, and they all say they are interested in our good. In spite of their differences and distinctions, they are all out to produce a civilized and ordered society.

But what happens? What does it lead to? Well, the world is a very old place, and we know something of what has been happening. In spite of all the efforts, the jungle is always encroaching. People try to make order out of the jungle. They cultivate it, and they work hard, they sweat and travail; but there are always setbacks, there are always threats of trouble, discord, and lawlessness. Strife is always ready to insinuate itself. Sometimes it has been thought necessary to impose a police state. There have been dictatorships, wars, suffering, theft, moral muddle, and unhappiness. That has been the long story of the human race.

Looking back across it all, we see that human history is no more than a perpetual cycle. There are times when things seem to be improving. That was more or less true in the Victorian era, and people thought they were on the verge of perfection and the Millennium and the golden age. But just when society seems to be at the top, it begins to go down the other side, and there is a period of regression. The history of humanity's endeavor to govern and to bring order can be summed up like this: rise—decline—fall.

It is amazing to see this very cycle in the history of the great empires of the world. It makes a fascinating study. From practically nothing, able and diligent men and women work and achieve success. Their small community grows and prospers. It rises, gains power, gets to the top, and dominates other communities and states. Then it declines and falls. You see this to perfection in the Roman Empire. That is the story of the human race as it attempts to make its own history, to control the world and bring order out of chaos. But there, at the back of it all, is God, and, as the Bible makes so plain and clear, God is allowing it and is controlling it. If a dictatorship arises and seems to threaten the whole world, God strikes. The Bible, the Old Testament in particular, is full of great illustrations of this. The Nebuchadnezzars who exalt themselves to the heavens are smitten and made fools of before the whole populace; down they are brought by God. He allows their power, and yet He controls it, never allowing it to advance beyond a certain limit.

But why, in spite of all our efforts and endeavors and great advances, is the world still in trouble? Why is every advance followed by regression, every rise by a decline and fall? Why do our attempts to govern the world end in disaster? What is the matter? And there is only one answer. It is due to the fact that men and women have sinful and fallen natures; it is due to their estrangement from God; and, more, it is due to God's wrath upon humanity in its sinfulness and arrogance. But the tragedy of the world is that it does not realize this.

I was reading again, only the other day, and it struck me forcibly, the explanation given by that great historian Edward Gibbon, who was not a Christian, for the decline and fall of the Roman Empire. And if his explanation is not also true of this country today, then I am completely ignorant! Here are the five reasons he gives:

1. The rapid increase of divorce and "the undermining of the dignity and sanctity of the home, which is the basis of human society." Now that is not being said by me, a little evangelical preacher—that is the great Edward Gibbon, and, of course, he is right. The home is the fundamental unit in society and once the home goes, everything will go, sooner or later.
2. "Higher and higher taxes and the spending of public monies on bread and circuses."
3. "The mad craze for pleasure and sport; sport becoming every year more and more exciting and brutal."
4. "The building of gigantic armaments when the real enemy is within—in the decadence of the people themselves."
5. "The decay of religious faith; faith fading into mere form which has lost all contact with reality."

The Roman Empire was a wonderful civilization. Those Romans were perhaps the greatest experts the world has ever known on local government and on legal systems. The Roman system—that was real civilization. Add to that the Greek civilization that had gone just before, and you had human endeavor almost at its highest point. But what happened to it? It was conquered by the Barbarians, the Goths, and the Vandals—the ignoramuses. How did they ever conquer this great civilization? Gibbon's answer is that internal rot in the civilization itself weakened and destroyed the Roman Empire. And that, I repeat, is the story of human civilization.

All human systems fail because the trouble is within the people themselves, and external rules and laws and regulations cannot change them. It is not that we need better laws, but that we need better natures; not better instruction, but better spirits and better desires. And so all this human history comes to nothing. And yet these earthly authorities prohibit the preaching of the Gospel, the only thing that can save the situation.

But, thank God, in spite of human prohibitions the message goes on. God's purpose goes on. "We ought to obey God rather than men. The God of our fathers raised up Jesus, whom ye slew and hanged on a tree." You have always done that, said Peter. But "Him hath God exalted with his right hand to be a Prince and a Saviour, for to give repentance to Israel, and forgiveness of sins." That was why the apostles could not be silent. They had a message that held the only hope for the world.

So, I repeat, our need is not for better laws or better conditions. Men and women are fighting the devil and fighting evil that is both outside and inside them, and that is why they fail. But here is the message, and thank God for it. It is not left to them. There is another history, another purpose, another plan: God's plan.

"The God of our fathers . . ." What did Peter mean by those words? Let me answer by giving you a summary of the whole of this great message in the Scriptures. Adam and Eve fell and brought down the trouble upon themselves, but God, in His infinite kindness and mercy and compassion, came down and addressed them in the Garden, called them out from behind the tree where they were hiding in shame, and told them about the punishment they had brought upon themselves. Then God said that He was going to do something about this punishment, and He promised that the seed of the woman would bruise the serpent's head (Gen. 3:15).

God made a promise, and now as a result, in between, over and above, and roundabout this human history recorded in the Bible, we can read God's history, the story of what God was and is bringing to pass. We see this history in Abel as over against Cain, and in Noah as against the rest of the world. This is God! God producing His people, raising up a man called Abraham, promising that a great nation will descend from him, and giving him a son called Isaac in his old age. Then Isaac has a son called Jacob, and out of this man comes a nation, the children of Israel, the people of God.

This is it. God is introducing His own kingdom into the midst of the kingdoms of the world, and this is how He does it. God makes this nation for Himself, and He says, "Through this nation I will speak to the others."

So God deals with this nation in a very specific manner. He gives them revelations of Himself. He gives them truth concerning men and women and their nature and being and purpose in this world, truth that He gives to no other nation. He gives them laws by which to live and order their conduct and affairs—including the Ten Commandments. He shows them the way to be blessed and to enjoy a life of righteousness and peace. The apostle Paul sums that all up when he says that one of the greatest gifts that God ever gave to the Jews was "the oracles of God" (Rom. 3:2), this mighty revelation of God and of humanity in its relationship to God and God's purpose.

God carries His plan on throughout the centuries, in spite of the repeated failure and recalcitrance and unutterable folly even of His own people. God still sustains them with His great promise that the seed of the woman shall bruise the serpent's head. So they all keep looking forward. Things are bad at times, and they do not know what to do, but there is hope—someone is coming. And all the great prophets repeat this message. "Comfort ye, comfort ye my people, saith your God" (Isa. 40:1). There is one coming who will be the Prince, and this is the one who will achieve God's purpose. Here it is in most wonderful words written by the prophet Isaiah:

> *For unto us a child is born, unto us a son is given: and the government [the government!] shall be upon his shoulder: and his name shall be called Wonderful, Counselor, The mighty God, The Everlasting Father, The Prince of Peace. Of the increase of his government and peace there shall be no end, upon the throne of David, and upon his kingdom, to order it, and to establish it with judgment and with justice from henceforth even for ever.*
>
> *—Isa. 9:6-7*

A tremendous promise runs through the whole of the Old Testament. And then, after the writing of Malachi, centuries pass—four hundred years—when there seems to be no word from God, and then an extraordinary event takes place. There is a maiden, a virgin, whose name is Mary. Suddenly, unexpectedly, she finds herself visited by an archangel. Notice the way in which the Bible introduces God's history:

> *In the sixth month the angel Gabriel was sent from God unto a city of Galilee, named Nazareth, to a virgin espoused to a man whose name was Joseph, of the house of David; and the virgin's name was Mary. And the angel came in unto her, and said, Hail, thou that art highly favoured, the Lord is with thee: blessed art thou among women.*
>
> *—Luke 1:26-28*

Not a great governor or king, not some human notability, but an unknown maiden. No one has ever thought anything about her, but it is to her that the archangel comes.

This is God's history, always the reverse of man's. "God hath chosen the foolish things of the world to confound the wise" (1 Cor. 1:27). God ridicules human greatness. He takes the nobodies and exalts them. So the angel speaks to Mary, and we are told that when she sees him:

> *She was troubled at his saying, and cast in her mind what manner of salutation this should be. And the angel said unto her, Fear not, Mary: for thou hast found favour with God. And, behold, thou shalt conceive in thy womb, and bring forth a son, and shalt call his name JESUS. He shall be great, and shall be called the Son of the Highest: and the Lord God shall give unto him the throne of his father David: and he shall reign over the house of Jacob for ever; and of his kingdom there shall be no end.*
>
> —Luke 1:29-33

Here he is, this little babe put in the manger. But the wise men come from the east, and they worship Him, bringing their incense and their adoration. Who is He? This is "The Prince of Peace"; this is the promised Governor, the one on whose shoulders the government shall be placed.

But what has this Prince of Peace come to do? Now let us be clear about this. This is where so much goes wrong at the present time. He has not come to reform the world, nor to teach it how to reform itself. Of all the men and women in this country today who deny the Gospel, the most culpable are those who turn it into a political message of human reform, those who are trying to persuade men and women to practice the Sermon on the Mount. That is the greatest denial of all. I infinitely prefer the publican and the sinner, the harlot and the drunkard, the murderer and the thief! Christ has not come to reform the world. But why then?

He has come to set up His kingdom—and that is a very different thing from reform. Read His teaching and you will find that it is always about the kingdom. He says, "The time is fulfilled, and the kingdom of God is at hand: repent ye, and believe the gospel" (Mark 1:15). How does He bring the kingdom about? He does not lay down a program of reform and say, "Now commend that to the people. Tell them to put that into practice." One day some people try to take Him by force to make Him king. That is their idea of His purpose in the world. They can see that He is unusual, that He has exceptional abilities and understanding and power; so they try to make Him king. But He gets away from them and goes up a mountain by Himself.

What, then, has He come to do? He has come "to seek and to save that which was lost" (Luke 19:10). He has come first and foremost to bring salvation, to reconcile us one by one to God. He starts with individuals, unknown people generally. Look at His first followers—fishermen, ordinary people who cannot understand political theory and philosophy. He deals with them as souls, as sinners, and explains to them that He has come to save them. He says, "The Son of man came not to be ministered unto, but to minister, and to give his life a ransom for many" (Mark 10:45).

He washes His disciples' feet. He says that He alone can save them by dying for them. He tells them that He must be lifted up on a cross and die, and thereby He will save them. He will reconcile them to God by bearing the punishment of their sins in His own body, and then, having reconciled them, He separates them from the world. He gives each of them a new birth and a new nature. You see how different that is? The other theory says, "All you need is instruction and education and knowledge and acts of Parliament. We can legislate a perfect world." But it is a complete failure. As Rome was, so Britain is today. And so the world will always be.

Our Lord can give us a new birth, a new heart, a new mind, a new outlook, a new nature. This is why He alone has the right to be called "Prince." He works a miracle in the depths of the soul. The prophet Jeremiah puts it like this: "I will put my law in their inward parts, and write it in their hearts" (Jer. 31:33). Not on statute books in Westminster, not on tablets of stone, not published in newspapers—He writes his law within us, in our minds and on our hearts. The new nature makes us love the light and hate the darkness, instead of loving the darkness and hating the light. He reverses the whole procedure. This is *His* program.

Immediately after His baptism and temptation, our Lord begins His work of setting up His kingdom. He calls individual men and women to be His followers; He takes them out of "this present evil world" (Gal. 1:4) and sets them in a new kingdom that He calls the church. Our Lord is gathering a people for Himself out of the kingdoms of this world to form His own perfect kingdom of glory that is coming in the future. This is still going on, and it will continue through the centuries until His purpose is complete.

"Christ sitteth on the right hand of God" (Col. 3:1). He says, "All power is given unto me in heaven and in earth" (Matt. 28:18). The writer of Hebrews tells us, "When he had by himself purged our sins, [he] sat down on the right hand of the Majesty on high" (Heb. 1:3). What is He doing there? He is waiting until God makes His enemies His footstool (Heb. 1:13). While the world is busy and excited about its elections and its politics, its gatherings and all its cultures, while it is increasingly festering in iniquity, as our newspapers are showing us, there is this other history, the history that the world treats with disdain, as it did His birth and as it did when the apostles were before the Sanhedrin. But God is continuing to make history—His history—and nothing can prevent Him.

And then, in His own time, Christ will come back again into the world. There is a description in Revelation of a man riding a white horse, with a sword in His mouth (Rev. 19:15), "conquering, and to conquer" (Rev. 6:2). Who is He? Oh, He is the "King of kings, and Lord of lords" (Rev. 19:16). God's plan is unfolding, and nothing can stop it. Christ will return; He will destroy His every enemy. And, in the imagery of Revelation, these enemies, these beasts, these antagonists, these principles and powers of evil will be cast into a lake of fire and of destruction, and He will set up His glorious kingdom of righteousness and peace, of holiness and joy. And we shall hear the angel trumpeting, "The kingdoms of this world are become the kingdoms of our Lord, and of his Christ" (Rev. 11:15).

A day is coming when "at the name of Jesus every knee should bow, of things in heaven, and things in earth, and things under the earth; and that every tongue should confess that Jesus Christ is Lord"—Prince, Governor— "to the glory of God the Father" (Phil. 2:10-11). A day is coming—thank God for this—when all human political and social and cultural systems have finally failed, when we shall see peace "as a river" and "righteousness as the waves of the sea" (Isa. 48:18), and when "a king shall reign in righteousness" (Isa. 32:1). A day is coming when "the wolf also shall dwell with the lamb, and the leopard shall lie down with the kid; and the calf and the young lion and the fatling together; and a little child shall lead them. . . . They shall not hurt nor destroy in all my holy mountain: for the earth shall be full of the knowledge of the LORD, as the waters cover the sea" (Isa. 11:6, 9).

It is coming; God has started this. This is God's history. In spite of the opposition of men and nations, in spite of the failure and wretchedness of His own people, He has been carrying it on. "When the fulness of the time was come" (Gal. 4:4), Christ came. The world killed Him, but God raised Him. He is seated at God's right hand, and one day He will come again, "conquering, and to conquer." This is the ultimate consummation to which the whole creation is surely and steadily moving.

I say again that it is not my object to say that we do not need politics. We cannot remain indifferent to political issues. No, no; I have told you that God appointed governing authorities, and it is the business of every one of us to register our vote as honestly and as intelligently as we can. But at the same time, the fundamental problems will be left entirely unaffected—the problem of you and of everybody else in your personal lives, the problem that no acts of Parliament can ever solve because it is in the hearts and minds of men and women.

Oh, yes, render your vote! "Render therefore unto Caesar the things which are Caesar's." But in the name of God, I warn you, I plead with you, do not stop at that. "Render therefore unto Caesar the things which are Caesar's; and unto God the things that are God's" (Matt. 22:21). The really vital question for all of us is not which party we will vote for, but which kingdom we belong to. Do you only belong to the kingdoms of this world, or do you also belong to the kingdom of our God and of His Christ? This is a kingdom that cannot be shaken. The day is coming when Christ will put the whole cosmos in order. He will destroy evil and sin and all that belong to them, and if you do not belong to His kingdom, you will partake of that destruction and that eternal misery.

Here is the great question: Are you aware of God's history, of God's purpose, of God's kingdom? Are you being governed by God's Prince, the Prince of Peace, the King of righteousness? Are you looking forward to the day when "the earth"—the entire cosmos—"shall be filled with the knowledge of the glory of the LORD, as the waters cover the sea" (Hab. 2:14)?

"Him hath God exalted with his right hand to be a Prince"—*the* Prince, the one who governs the whole universe. Have you bowed at His name? Have you fallen at His feet in gratitude, praise, and thanksgiving for His ever having come into the world, for His ever having died for you and for your sins? Have you yielded yourself and your life to Him, and are you looking forward to the crowning day when He shall be crowned "Lord of all" (Acts 10:36)?

8

THE WITNESSES

Then Peter and the other apostles answered and said, We ought to obey God rather than men. The God of our fathers raised up Jesus, whom ye slew and hanged on a tree. Him hath God exalted with his right hand to be a Prince and a Saviour, for to give repentance to Israel, and forgiveness of sins. And we are his witnesses of these things; and so is also the Holy Ghost, whom God hath given to them that obey him.

—Acts 5:29-32

I now want to consider with you the statement at the beginning of the thirty-second verse: "We are his witnesses of these things." The apostles were on trial because they were preaching Jesus Christ crucified and risen as the Son of God and the only way of salvation. And they were ready even to face death rather than stop preaching this great and wonderful name.

But the fact that confronts us is that there are many people to whom Jesus Christ and His death mean nothing. They are not interested in Him at all. Indeed, some are bitterly opposed to Christianity and ridicule it, and the Jewish authorities here in Acts 5—astoundingly in the light of all that had just happened—belonged to that category. This is what should engage our attention. Why did the members of the Sanhedrin oppose the apostles and their message?

Not so long before, let me remind you, the Jewish authorities had rejected our blessed Lord Himself and all that He had said and done. Today is Palm Sunday [1966]. Think of all that happened between the first Palm Sunday and that death on the cross on Calvary's hill. Look at what our Lord had to endure, the sufferings He had to pass through. How do you account for the spite and malevolence of the Pharisees, the scribes, the Sadducees, the Herodian party, and everybody else? They all conspired against Him, and they persuaded the mob to shout out, "Away with Him! Crucify Him!" Now any intelligent person must at once want to ask, "Why was this? What was the matter with these people?" It must surely be the greatest tragedy in the whole story of the human race that this should ever have happened—indeed, that it should be still happening. What accounts for it?

It seems to me that there is only one fundamental answer to this question, and it is this: the refusal of these people to face the facts. That is what is so amazing about them when you look at them merely from a psychological standpoint. It is a perfect instance of men being confronted by facts and yet not seeing them—in a sense, not allowing themselves to see them. That is why the apostles replied as they did. They said, "Surely you cannot prohibit us from reporting these facts? We are witnesses."

The apostles' response—"We are his witnesses"—concentrates our attention on the fact that the authorities refused to face the facts. That was the essence of the problem. The trouble with the members of the Sanhedrin was that they were so governed by their prejudices that they did not see things as they were. The trouble with our Lord, as far as these Pharisees, scribes, and Sadducees were concerned, was that He did not fit into their pattern. He broke all the rules. He cut across everything that they had ever stood for and everything that they had always taught the people. And that is why they hated Him.

Now let us not forget our facts. These men who opposed the apostles were Jews; they were the teachers of the people and the experts in the Old Testament Scriptures. But they had misunderstood the Scriptures. The whole tragedy of men and women in sin is that their minds become twisted. The trouble with the Jewish leaders was that the prejudices to which they were victims blinded them to the truth of the facts that were staring them in the face. The very Scriptures that they taught proved that they were wrong. Our Lord said to them, "Search the scriptures; for in them ye think ye have eternal life: and they are they which testify of me" (John 5:39). But it was in the name of those Scriptures that they opposed Him and finally procured His crucifixion. Their blind prejudice is illustrated in the way they treated the apostles in spite of certain clear facts: the fact of our Lord Himself, the fact of the events on the Day of Pentecost, and the fact of what had happened to the apostles themselves.

Now our Lord had already said to the apostles, "If they have persecuted me, they will also persecute you" (John 15:20). He had warned them not to expect to be received with open arms—quite the contrary. He had said, "If they have called the master of the house Beelzebub, how much more shall they call them of his household?" (Matt. 10:25). And His words were proved true here in Acts 5.

Now we have already considered the opposition of the authorities in Jerusalem. They were frankly puzzled by the apostles; they could not understand them or explain them. We read in Acts 4:13, "Now when they saw the boldness of Peter and John, and perceived that they were unlearned and ignorant men, they marvelled." But they would not even consider the facts. Their argument was that these men must be wrong because they were not Pharisees or scribes. They were "unlearned and ignorant men," and therefore anything they said was wrong. It was inconceivable that they could be right. They must be wrong, and therefore they were wrong. That kind of argument is spoken by people who are blinded by prejudice.

Furthermore, not only were the religious leaders not facing the facts about our Lord Himself and about the events on the Day of Pentecost, they were not facing the fact that this lame man had been healed. Let me use legal jargon: There is an exhibit in court, and the exhibit is a man born lame, standing upright, his feet and ankle bones having received strength. That was a fact facing them, but they did not consider it at all. If they had, they would have had to change their opinion and their attitude because the fact of the healing demanded an explanation.

The authorities were also confronted by reports that these very men whom they were now charging and who had been put in jail the previous night had been set free by an angel. Now whether they believed in angels or not—and the Sadducees did not—they ought to have believed the evidence before their eyes and ears. The officers sent to collect the apostles from prison had reported that the prison doors were closed and the guards were standing outside the locked doors, but the cells were empty. Then a messenger had come with news that the prisoners were preaching in the temple court. So the soldiers had been sent to rearrest the apostles and bring them back again. And there they were, standing on trial. All these were sheer facts.

Now the Sanhedrin did not try to consider or explain the facts. They brushed them aside. Because the Sanhedrin said these men were wrong, they were wrong! That is how unbelief always argues. But the apostles said, "You told us not to preach, but we can't listen to you because we must obey God rather than men. We can't keep quiet. We are living witnesses, bearing testimony to something that we have seen and known and proved."

Now I draw your attention to the Sanhedrin's attitude because people are still the same. They are not interested in our Lord. That is why they are opposed to preaching. If they could, they would prohibit it. Modern men and women are annoyed by the Christian faith. That is why they jeer and sneer at it and make their clever jokes about it. They hate it for exactly the same reason as the Jewish authorities hated it, because they refuse to face facts.

Now I have shown you how the members of the Sanhedrin ignored the facts. Modern people reject them in what they would claim is a scholarly manner. They come to the New Testament, which is a record of these facts, with their modern knowledge, especially their scientific knowledge, and they start off by saying that they do not believe all the facts. In other words, instead of facing the facts, they sit in judgment upon them, deciding that some things are fact while others are not. And they do this, interestingly, on the basis of what they call historical and literary criticism, terms that come under the general heading of higher criticism. This is a most interesting process.

Let me quote from a well-known higher critic. He says that he rejects anything he reads in the Bible, including in the New Testament, even in the Gospels, that does not fit in with what he feels about Jesus and with what he thinks Jesus would do. That is his standard of judgment. Now I want to show you how this modern Sanhedrin man conducts himself and puts forward his arguments, how he evades the facts.

What does this man know about the Lord Jesus Christ? Well, he agrees that he knows only what he reads in the Bible. But he tells us that in reading the Bible he gathers an impression about Jesus; he feels he gets to know Him. He uses an illustration to explain what he means. He says that after having read *Treasure Island,* he feels he knows Long John Silver. He knows the sorts of things he would and would not say, the sorts of things he would and would not do. He says that if he came across something in *Treasure Island* that he feels is inconsistent with the Long John Silver he knows, he would not believe it. And, he tells us, he does exactly the same thing with the biblical account of Jesus! So when he finds that our Lord speaks about judgment and punishment, he says, "I don't believe it. He didn't say it. The Jesus I know couldn't possibly say a thing like that!" Half the facts in the Gospels are therefore immediately dismissed.

Most of the remaining facts are explained away according to various theories and according to the dictates of modern knowledge. Miracles, of course, are impossible, and therefore they did not happen.

"But," you say, "what about the accounts of miracles in the four Gospels?"

"Ah well," comes the reply, "we know now, by the study of psychology, that primitive people are always ready to believe in the magical. Even today there are people who believe in astrology and are ready to accept anything that is marvelous and wonderful. Now these early Christians were simple, primitive people, ignorant and unlearned; so of course they were ready to believe in miracles. We, however, know that science has proved that miracles cannot happen." That last statement is not true, of course—it cannot be proved. Nevertheless, out go miracles.

And so the facts are manipulated and twisted to fit what *you* think the Lord Jesus Christ was like, what *you* think He would have said, what *you* think He would have done, what *you* think was the cause of His death. And it just comes down to this: He was a very good man, ahead of His time, and misunderstood by the world, as most good men are. Though He was sentenced to a shameful, cruel death, He did not become bitter and sour but forgave the very people who were putting Him to death. His death was the supreme example of passive resistance, of pacifism, if you like. His teaching was that we should be good and kind and just and should go on loving people even when they hate us. We should do our best to cultivate a beautiful and a loving and a good spirit. And that, we are told, is Christianity.

Now let me just ask you some questions. Does that view of the Lord Jesus Christ explain the Christian story? Is that an adequate explanation of the origin and long history of the church? Would it ever have come into being if that had been the truth? How did the church begin, and what is her message? There is only one way to discover the answer to these questions, and that is to do the very thing we are doing—to study these early chapters of the Book of Acts. And as we read this book, we see that Christianity is not a mere teaching, it is not a philosophy or a point of view, nor is it merely an attitude to life. It is first and foremost something that happened in history.

The church came into being as the result of historical events. Look at the apostles. They are the men through whom the church was started and built up; nobody can deny that. So what did they preach and teach? They were ignorant and unlearned men. They were not men who could weave philosophical and political theories; they did not write poetry and have wonderful mystical experiences; they were fishermen, and what they did was report facts. "We are his witnesses of these things," they said. In a sense they had nothing to talk about except certain historical events and the meaning and significance of those events.

Let me borrow a phrase that Peter used when, as an old man on the verge of the grave, he wrote his last letter. He says, "While I am left in this world I am going to remind you of these things. You know them, but you keep on forgetting them" (see 2 Pet. 1:12).

> *Yea, I think it meet, as long as I am in this tabernacle, to stir you up by putting you in remembrance; knowing that shortly I must put off this my tabernacle, even as our Lord Jesus Christ hath showed me. Moreover I will endeavour that ye may be able after my decease to have these things always in remembrance. For we have not followed cunningly devised fables, when we made known unto you the power and coming of our Lord Jesus Christ, but were eyewitnesses of his majesty.*
>
> —*2 Pet. 1:13-16*

Now there it is in a phrase: "not . . . cunningly devised fables." These apostles did not preach fairy tales; they were not novelists with vivid imaginations who took a simple peasant and turned him into a great religious teacher. No; that is what the world does. They were incapable of doing that. They were reporters of facts. So here was Peter, at the end of his life, just saying what he had said right at the beginning of his career as an apostle: "We are his witnesses of these things; and so is also the Holy Ghost, whom God hath given to them that obey him."

So the Christian message, first and foremost, is a record of facts. Get rid of this notion that Christianity is just a point of view. The modern teaching is that it does not matter if all the facts are proved to be wrong. Bultmann, who is a teacher in Germany, talks about "demythologizing" the Scriptures. "It does not matter," he says, "if all your facts are gone"; indeed, he dismisses practically all of them except for the fact that a man called Jesus died on a cross. But he says that does not matter because the teaching remains. Now if there ever was a contradiction of the preaching of the apostles, it is that. If you take away the facts, there is no Christianity, there is no message. And that is what I am trying to remind you of. Our Lord rode into Jerusalem that Palm Sunday, mounted upon the foal of a donkey. That is a fact of history. It is as definite as the fact that this country [England] was conquered by Julius Caesar.

The apostles were very honest men. Later two of them, Matthew and

John, wrote their Gospels. The other two Gospels, the Gospels of Mark and Luke, are undoubtedly dependent upon the preaching of the apostles and upon what those men reported to the writers. Proof of their honesty is seen in the fact that they were prepared to tell us some not very flattering details about themselves. They tell us quite frankly that there was a time when they did not understand the things they were seeing. If you read the four Gospels, you find these apostles stumbling, grumbling, complaining, falling into all sorts of mistakes. They did not understand the facts until after the resurrection and especially after the events of the Day of Pentecost.

The apostles had thought that our Lord was only a man like everybody else, and we read in the Gospels that when He died upon the cross they were shattered. They were Jews and had hoped that their Messiah would be a great military figure who would deliver them from the tyranny and bondage of Rome and set up Israel again as a great military nation in the world. But He had not done that. When He had been crucified in weakness on a tree, they had not known where they were. They had all been in complete disarray. There is a wonderful picture in John 21 of a group of them just sitting together until Peter at last said, in his impulsive way, "Well, I'm going fishing." That was something he did understand, even if he could not understand anything else. All the claims and the teaching—but to end like that! They could not follow it. But as the result of our Lord's teaching after the resurrection, and after the baptism with the Spirit, they understood. They said, "Now we will tell you the facts and the meaning and relevance of the facts. 'We are his witnesses of these things.'"

What, then, are "these things"? What is Christianity? What are these facts on which the Christian message, the Christian truth, is based? Well, like the apostle Peter, I want to hold them before you. I make no apology. You have heard these things before, but do you believe them? Would you be as you are if you really believed these things? Do you react to our Lord as that hymn so beautifully puts it:

> *This is my friend,*
> *In whose sweet praise*
> *I all my days*
> *Could gladly spend.*
> Samuel Crossman

That is the test. If you do not react in that way, you have known the facts, but you have not realized their meaning and significance. You are not captivated and captured by them as these men were. Here were men who would sooner die than refrain from preaching the glory of the Son of God as the only Savior of the world.

So let me briefly look at the facts. First, the person of our blessed Lord Himself. "The God of our fathers raised up Jesus." That is Christianity. It is Christ. It is this "Jesus." And these apostles said that they were witnesses of Him. Think of them—Peter, James, John, and the others. They had been with Him and had felt from the very beginning that there was something strange and unusual about Him. They had felt His authority. They had felt some note of command. He had not come with all the learning of the law or the philosophy of the Greeks. He had not come from the academies or from among the students of the rabbis who met to study in the porches of the temple court. He had not been a great Roman dignitary, versed in law and government. No; he had just been an ordinary Galilean, a carpenter, the son of Joseph and Mary. Yet they never forgot how one day, as Peter and his brothers were mending their fishing nets in their boat, this strange Jesus had come along and said, "Follow me." And they had left their father and the boat and their nets and had gone after Him.

Then there was another man, Matthew, who had been a tax-collector. Remember, only the most mercenary of men became tax-collectors. No Jew should have been collecting taxes for the oppressor, the conqueror; yet some Jews demeaned and debased themselves to such an extent that they would even take on this job to make money and get on. Matthew the tax-collector had been sitting at the receipt of customs when Jesus passed by and said, "Follow me." And at once Matthew had left everything and had gone after Jesus.

Let me remind you of another occasion. One afternoon our Lord had singled Peter, James, and John out from the rest of the apostles and had asked them to come with Him to the top of a great mountain. At the summit He was suddenly transfigured before them. His face, His very clothing, began to shine. A radiance came out of Him, from His very presence, and His clothes were whiter and brighter than any bleach on earth could have made them. A bright cloud overshadowed them, and they heard a voice from the cloud saying, "This is my beloved Son, in whom I am well pleased; hear ye him" (Matt. 17:5). Much later, when he was an old man, Peter wrote, "And this voice which came from heaven we heard, when we were with him in the holy mount" (2 Pet. 1:18). And in effect the apostles were saying the same thing here in Acts. They had seen the Jesus whom they had known suddenly transformed and transfigured, and something of the radiance of eternal glory had come out of Him. They were witnesses of these things.

This is Christianity! Not what a clever man, whether he be bishop or anything else, thinks it is. No, no; it is this blessed person, the impact that He had upon these men through whom Christianity started. And there is a still more wonderful testimony to the power of His personality. We are told in John's Gospel that when He was about to be arrested, our Lord looked at Judas, who was leading armed soldiers to arrest Him, and said, "Whom seek ye?" And then we read the most astounding thing: "As soon then as he had said unto them, I am he, they went backward, and fell to the ground" (John 18:6). He did not have a sword, He was completely defenseless, and yet when these soldiers with their swords and staves came to arrest Him, as he spoke, they fell to the ground. What is this? Who is this? "We are his witnesses of these things."

And then, of course, there were our Lord's miracles. These extraordinary demonstrations of divine power—John calls them "signs"—were primarily intended to authenticate His person, to let the world know who He was. He used the argument Himself one afternoon when He was dealing with those Jews who did not believe in Him. He said to them, "Believe me that I am in the Father, and the Father in me: or else believe me for the very works' sake" (John 14:11). Face the facts! Look at them. But that is just what they would not do.

There was an occasion once when Peter and some of his companions had been fishing very hard throughout the night without catching a single fish. The next morning our Lord told them to go out into the lake and let down their nets. "Master," Peter said, "we have toiled all the night, and have taken nothing: nevertheless at thy word I will let down the net." The disciples threw the net into the water and caught so many fish that the net broke. What was the effect upon Peter? He was an expert fishermen and a daredevil, a courageous fellow, afraid of nobody. When he saw all those fish, he understood and said to our Lord, "Depart from me; for I am a sinful man, O Lord" (Luke 5:2-8).

Peter recognized unearthly power, power beyond the human, something divine. If you read the four Gospels, these are the sorts of phrases that you will find running throughout: "We have seen strange things to day" (Luke 5:26); "They marvelled, and glorified God, which had given such power unto men" (Matt. 9:8). The apostles were witnesses of these things, and now they were being told not to preach anymore in the name of this Jesus. They said, "But this is monstrous! We have seen the demonstration of His divine power."

And then there was our Lord's teaching. Here again, everybody was struck by His authority. We read at the end of the Sermon on the Mount that when He had finished preaching, the people acknowledged that "he taught them as one having authority, and not as the scribes" (Matt. 7:29). The Pharisees and scribes quoted authorities. In their cleverness they would say, "Gamaliel said this; Gamaliel said that." And writers today also quote one another—that is their sign of learning. But here was a man who spoke with His own authority, and they were all impressed. Soldiers were sent one day to arrest Him, but they went back without Him. "Where is the prisoner?" asked the rulers. "Why haven't you brought Him?" And they could only give one reply: "Never man spake like this man" (John 7:46).

Furthermore, this teacher made such astounding claims for Himself. He said, "I and my Father are one" (John 10:30); "Before Abraham was [born], I am" (John 8:58). Read the facts before you start talking. Christianity is not about your opinion. You are prejudiced, as I once was. Get at the facts, and they will begin to speak. Find out what He said about His awful death. Go back again to that Mount of Transfiguration, to the time when Moses and Elijah appeared and began to speak to Him. What did they speak to Him about? Is it not shocking, shameful, mad that people should argue about Christianity when they do not know the facts? Be honest. Do not be like the Sanhedrin. Do you know what Moses and Elijah spoke to Him about? "[They] spake of his decease which he should accomplish at Jerusalem" (Luke 9:31). There on the Mount of Transfiguration, they spoke to Him about His death.

And do you remember His teaching? When they were in Caesarea Philippi, our Lord asked these very apostles whose words we are studying in Acts 5, "Whom do men say that I the Son of man am?" They said, "Some say that thou art John the Baptist: some, Elias; and others, Jeremias, or one of the prophets." And our Lord said, "But whom say ye that I am?" Peter stood forward and said, "Thou art the Christ, the Son of the living God." And our Lord said to Peter, "Blessed art thou, Simon Bar-jona: for flesh and blood hath not revealed it unto thee, but my Father which is in heaven" (Matt. 16:13-17). And then He went on to talk about founding the church on the faith of this apostle and all others who had the same faith.

But then our Lord did something amazing. Immediately after Peter's great confession, we are told:

> *From that time forth began Jesus to show unto his disciples, how that he must go unto Jerusalem, and suffer many things of the elders and*

chief priests and scribes, and be killed, and be raised again the third day. Then Peter took him, and began to rebuke him, saying, Be it far from thee, Lord: this shall not be unto thee. But he turned, and said unto Peter, Get thee behind me, Satan: thou art an offence unto me: for thou savourest not the things that be of God, but those that be of men.

—Matt. 16:21-23

Our Lord frequently taught His followers about His death. He said, "For the Son of man is come to seek and to save that which was lost" (Luke 19:10); and, "For even the Son of man came not to be ministered unto, but to minister, and to give his life a ransom for many" (Mark 10:45). On one occasion some Greeks came to see Him. Talk about Him had spread, and these Greeks asked Philip if they could have an interview with Jesus. But our Lord would not see them; instead, He sent this answer: "The hour is come, that the Son of man should be glorified. Verily, verily, I say unto you, Except a corn of wheat fall into the ground and die, it abideth alone: but if it die, it bringeth forth much fruit" (John 12:23-24).

And our Lord went on to say: "Now is the judgment of this world: now shall the prince of this world be cast out. And I, if I be lifted up from the earth"—that is a reference to crucifixion—"will draw all men unto me" (John 12:31-32). And immediately before that He had prayed to His Father, "Now is my soul troubled; and what shall I say? Father, save me from this hour: but for this cause came I unto this hour. Father, glorify thy name" (vv. 27-28).

Now these apostles were with Jesus when He prayed this prayer, and they heard the voice from heaven saying in reply, "I have both glorified it, and will glorify it again." John tells us that the people around Jesus also heard the voice, and some said it had thundered, while others thought an angel had spoken to Him. But Jesus said, "This voice came not because of me, but for your sakes" (vv. 28-30).

On another occasion our Lord said, "And as Moses lifted up the serpent in the wilderness, even so must the Son of man be lifted up: that whosoever believeth in him should not perish, but have eternal life" (John 3:14-15). He said to the disciples when they were trying to defend Him at the end, "Don't resist. Put your sword away. Don't you realize that I could ask My Father for angels to rescue Me? 'But how then shall the scriptures be fulfilled, that thus it must be?'" (Matt. 26:52-54). And in His final prayer to His Father, which the disciples undoubtedly heard Him offering, He said, "[Father,] I have finished the work which thou gavest me to do" (John 17:4). And in that prayer He said, "And for their sakes I sanctify myself" (v. 19), by which He meant that He was ready to give Himself as a sacrifice to be offered to God's broken holy law.

When some Pharisees warned our Lord not to go up to Jerusalem because King Herod was waiting to kill Him, He said, "Go ye, and tell that fox, Behold, I cast out devils, and I do cures to day and to morrow, and the third day I shall be perfected" (Luke 13:32). Listen to Him saying, on one of the last days of His life on earth, as He was looking at the city of Jerusalem, "O Jerusalem, Jerusalem . . . how often would I have gathered thy children together, even as a hen gathereth her chickens under her wings, and ye would not! Behold, your house is left unto you desolate" (Matt. 23:37-38). That was His teaching, and these men had heard it. They had not understood it at the time, but it all came back to them after His death and resurrection.

The apostles had also witnessed the injustice of our Lord's trial. Peter had sneaked into the courtyard, you remember, because he wanted to find out what was happening, and yet he had denied his Master because he was afraid. But he never forgot the things he heard and was told. This carpenter had reasoned and argued with Pontius Pilate, talking to him about a kingdom that he called "my kingdom." Here was a representative of the Roman emperor, of the Roman Empire and its great system of government, but there before him stood this common man, as it were, who said, "My kingdom is not of this world" (John 18:36); "Thou couldest have no power at all against me, except it were given thee from above" (John 19:11). He knew what He was doing; He spoke with authority; He spoke as a king.

The apostles had heard something else too, something that was very germane to this argument here with this great council, the Sanhedrin. The authorities said to them, "Ye have filled Jerusalem with your doctrine, and intend to bring this man's blood upon us" (Acts 5:28). But the disciples had heard them saying something like that on another occasion. Pilate had reasoned with the religious leaders in an attempt to release Jesus, but they had refused to listen. So Pilate had washed his hands in front of them all and had said, "I am innocent of the blood of this just person." And they had replied, "His blood be on us, and on our children" (Matt. 27:24-25). So they had taken it upon themselves, and now they were objecting! Such is always the ridiculous character of unbelief.

And then, finally, the apostles had witnessed their Lord's death upon the cross. They knew this was not an accident. They knew that he had "stedfastly set his face to go to Jerusalem" (Luke 9:51). They had warned Him and had done everything they could to stop Him. But He had said He had to go. He had said, "For it cannot be that a prophet perish out of Jerusalem" (Luke 13:33). He had deliberately gone on. He had ridden toward death. And there in Jerusalem He had been nailed to a cross. But what do you hear Him say there? "My God, my God, why hast thou forsaken me?" (Matt. 27:46). That is a quotation from Psalm 22. Let me urge you to read that Psalm and then read any of the accounts of the death of the Lord Jesus Christ on the cross. You will find that our Lord's death was a literal fulfillment of the details described in Psalm 22.

And then our Lord's followers noticed the rapidity with which He died. Death by crucifixion was a very slow process. But when the soldiers came at three o'clock, they found Him already dead, and everyone was amazed that He had died so soon. One of the soldiers took a spear and thrust it into His side, and water and blood came out. He had already been dead for some time, and the blood had clotted. What does it mean? To me there is only one adequate explanation: He had literally died of a broken heart. Why? Because He was afraid of death? No, no! Because the sins of the human race were upon Him. Because God had "made him to be sin" (2 Cor. 5:21). Because His soul was made an offering for sin. Because He was enduring the vials of God's wrath in our place. He did not just swoon, He did not temporarily lose consciousness. The soldier proved that once and forever by piercing His side with his spear so that the blood and the water were seen. This is all historical evidence, exhibits in the court. This was a real death, and He was buried. Then He rose again, and the tomb was empty.

So the apostles continued to testify to these things. And they remembered how, after His resurrection, He had appeared among them in an upper room, filling them with astonishment. He had reprimanded them and had explained the Scriptures to them.

On the afternoon of the day our Lord had risen from the dead, two disciples were walking to a village called Emmaus. They had been very miserable because the one they had looked to as the Savior had died in weakness upon a cross. Then a stranger joined them and asked, "What is the matter with you? Why are you so downcast? What were you talking about?" They had looked at Him in astonishment and said, "Haven't you heard?" "Heard what?"

And Luke tells us that they replied:

Concerning Jesus of Nazareth, which was a prophet mighty in deed and word before God and all the people: and how the chief priests and our rulers delivered him to be condemned to death, and have crucified him. But we trusted that it had been he which should have redeemed Israel: and beside all this, to day is the third day since these things were done. Yea, and certain women also of our company made us astonished, which were early at the sepulchre; and when they found not his body, they came, saying, that they had also seen a vision of angels, which said that he was alive. And certain of them which were with us went to the sepulchre, and found it even so as the women had said: but him they saw not.

—Luke 24:19-24

And the stranger looked at them and said, "O fools, and slow of heart to believe all that the prophets have spoken: ought not Christ to have suffered these things, and to enter into his glory?" Then Luke adds: "And beginning at Moses and all the prophets, he expounded unto them in all the scriptures the things concerning himself" (vv. 25-27).

And later the two disciples said, "Did not our heart burn within us, while he talked with us by the way, and while he opened to us the scriptures?" (v. 32). But the Lord had reprimanded them for their blindness and for their lack of understanding.

Forty days later when our Lord's followers were with Him on Mount Olivet, He told them to stay in Jerusalem until they received power (Acts 1:4, 8). But then suddenly, while He was speaking to them, they saw Him ascending, and He disappeared into a cloud. Ten days later the Holy Spirit came, and they were filled with that promised power.

Just as in the second chapter of Acts, so here in Acts 5 the apostles say, "Don't you realize and understand that these facts to which we are bearing witness prove who He is? They are the fulfillment of the ancient prophecies. Go back and read your Scriptures. You cannot understand us. You say we are unlearned and ignorant men, and you are perfectly right. So how do you explain this? He is the only explanation. We are witnesses to the objective facts and events. We are living witnesses to the power and the truth of these things, and that is why we cannot accept your edict. That is why we propose to go on preaching."

So my simple question is this: These facts, these historical events about which I have been reminding you, what do they mean to you? You must come to some decision about them. You cannot get rid of them. They are the sole explanation of the origin and continuance of the Christian church.

This is the Christian message. This alone explains the saints of the centuries and the dynamic power of the Gospel. Have you ever really faced it? Can you not see the madness, the blindness, the prejudice of the members of this great Sanhedrin? Face the facts, and ask God by his Spirit to remove your prejudice and give you new life, new understanding, new power and make of you a living witness to the truth of these things and to the wonders of His grace.

9

THE RESURRECTION—GOD'S DECLARATION

Then Peter and the other apostles answered and said, We ought to obey God rather than men. The God of our fathers raised up Jesus, whom ye slew and hanged on a tree. Him hath God exalted with his right hand to be a Prince and a Saviour, for to give repentance to Israel, and forgiveness of sins. And we are his witnesses of these things; and so is also the Holy Ghost, whom God hath given to them that obey him.

—Acts 5:29-32

In an attempt to discover the true nature of the Christian church and the Christian message, we have been looking at the speech made by Peter and the apostles to the Sanhedrin, and I should now like to consider with you the witness of the apostles to the resurrection.[9]

Perhaps the best way of approaching this whole matter is to take this passage in its context. The apostles were on trial, having been arrested for preaching the Gospel, and Peter was explaining why they must continue to preach. Why did they speak as they did? Their lives were in jeopardy because their adversaries had authority—they were the great Sanhedrin, the highest court in the land. Those leaders were well connected to King Herod, well connected to the Roman governor. And here were these simple apostles—fishermen, artisans, "unlearned and ignorant men" (Acts 4:13)—daring to defy them and refusing to keep silent.

The apostles said they had to speak because of the character and nature of their message, which concerned Jesus, who had been exalted by God to be "a Prince and a Saviour." "We are his witnesses of these things," they said. Moreover, they were filled with a new life, with a new courage. Their lives had been revolutionized. They were entirely different people, filled with a joy and a happiness and peace that nothing could remove from them. They had to witness to this change that God had brought about in their lives, and nothing could silence them.

And I think the apostles had to go on preaching because of something further—namely, that they were animated by their desire to be of help to their fellow men and women. They knew that there was power in this Gospel to transform others as it had transformed them. Their very love for the souls of men and women, their very pity for those who were ignorant of "these things," impelled them to preach. They would defy any authority; they would die rather than refrain from preaching this glorious Gospel of the blessed God.

Those were the reasons for the apostles' defiance of the Sanhedrin. We have already considered some of the things of which they were witnesses. They were witnesses of our Lord's person and also of His incomparable teaching and His astonishing miracles for three years. They were witnesses of His teaching concerning His death, how He had prophesied it and indicated its meaning, and they had seen Him dying, nailed upon a cross.

But now we go beyond this. These men had been completely shattered by our Lord's death. As Jews, they had thought that He would deliver them in a political sense. They had pinned their hopes on Him, but He had been crucified in weakness, He had died and been buried. And the records show us that when this happened they had been completely disconsolate, utterly cast down. Never were men more hopeless than these apostles were after the death of our blessed Lord and Savior.

But then something had taken place that changed everything. What was it? It was Easter morning, the resurrection on the third day! Very early, even before daylight, some of the women had gone to the tomb with spices but had found it empty. They had come came rushing back with the news, but the disciples had not believed them.

Luke tells us that when the women came back and reported that He had risen, "their words seemed to them as idle tales" (Luke 24:11). The apostles thought the women were mad. Resurrection? Nonsense! Such things do not happen. But then they had become curious because the women seemed so certain. So Peter and John had run to the tomb together. John outran Peter and, peeping in, had seen the clothes. But he had not gone in. Peter, the more impulsive of the two, entered and saw the burial clothes lying in one place and the cloth for the head in another. And they had been filled with astonishment.

Then we read of our Lord's appearances to these very men. On the first Sunday evening, He suddenly came among them. They were very afraid, but He said, "What are you frightened of? I am not a ghost. 'A spirit hath not flesh and bones, as ye see me have'" (Luke 24:39). Then He asked, "Have you anything to eat?" And when they produced some broiled fish and honey, he ate it in front of them. Ghosts do not do things like that!

In John's Gospel, we read the story of Thomas—"doubting Thomas." Like all the disciples, Thomas had not taken in our Lord's teaching about His coming death and resurrection. The Gospels record with great frankness that they had never understood His teaching; they had their own ideas. That is the trouble with people who are sinners. As we have seen, they are prejudiced and blinded. Instead of listening to the teaching, they go on thinking their clever thoughts and miss the glory.

Now Thomas had not been with the disciples when our Lord appeared to them on that first Sunday night, and when they said to him, "We have seen the Lord," he said, "I will not believe it unless I can put my fingers into the imprint of the nails and thrust my hand into His side."

A week later Jesus again appeared among the disciples, and He looked at Thomas and said, "Thomas, reach hither thy finger, and behold my hands; and reach hither thy hand, and thrust it into my side: and be not faithless, but believing." And Thomas could only fall down at his feet and say, "My Lord and my God." And our Lord said to him, "Thomas, because thou hast seen me, thou hast believed: blessed are they that have not seen, and yet have believed" (John 20:24-29).

After the resurrection, the apostles were transformed. After observing their Lord on many occasions, and, still more, after listening to the instruction that He had given them—the way He had taken them through the Scriptures, showing how His death, His burial, and His resurrection had all been prophesied—they had been convinced. Then He gave them a commission. He said in effect, "Now I am leaving you. I am going back to heaven, to the glory I had with the Father before the foundation of the world. I am leaving you as My witnesses. I am sending you." It is all there at the end of Luke's Gospel. Luke writes:

Then opened he their understanding, that they might understand the scriptures, and said unto them, Thus it is written, and thus it behooved Christ to suffer, and to rise from the dead the third day:

and that repentance and remission of sins should be preached in his name among all nations, beginning at Jerusalem. And ye are witnesses of these things. And, behold, I send the promise of my Father upon you: but tarry ye in the city of Jerusalem, until ye be endued with power from on high.

—Luke 24:45-49

So our Lord had commissioned the apostles to do the very thing that the Sanhedrin now prohibited them from doing. Our Lord had said, "Wait until you get the power; then go and bear witness." That is why they defied the Sanhedrin and refused to keep silent. It is all because of the nature of these facts. Their meaning, their import, is summed up in Peter's statement: "Him hath God exalted with his right hand to be a Prince and a Saviour, for to give repentance to Israel, and forgiveness of sins." This Jesus, whom the Jews had rejected and slain upon a tree, is God's Prince, the Prince of the universe, the Savior of the world. He is the only Savior, and there is no salvation apart from Him. That is why the apostles had to defy the Sanhedrin's edict.

In order that we may understand what all this means, let us look at it in the light of the resurrection. Like Paul, the apostles preached "Jesus, and the resurrection" (Acts 17:18). But why did the apostles stress the resurrection in particular?

First of all, it is the resurrection that finally proves who our Lord is. It is the resurrection that finally establishes the point that this Jesus whom the Jewish leaders had despised—Jesus the carpenter, this fellow, this man who had learning, never having learned, this imposter, this blasphemer, this one who claimed equality with God—really was all He claimed to be. It is the final proof that He is none other than God's only begotten Son, the eternal Son of God; that though He was a man, He was not only a man.

"Ah," you say, "but what about the case of Lazarus? Didn't he also rise from the dead?"

Lazarus was merely restored to life, and he died again later on. Our Lord, by contrast, is "the first begotten of [from] the dead" (Rev. 1:5). He is the first person ever to have gone through death and come out the other side alive. And that is the proof of the fact that He is the Son of God. The apostle Paul, writing years later to the church at Rome, puts it in those very words. He says:

Paul, a servant of Jesus Christ, called to be an apostle, separated unto the Gospel of God, (Which he had promised afore by his prophets in the holy scriptures,) concerning his Son Jesus Christ our Lord, which was made of the seed of David according to the flesh; and declared to be the Son of God with power, according to the spirit of holiness, by the resurrection from the dead.

—*Rom. 1:1-4*

The resurrection was the final proof. And, as I have already indicated, it was the resurrection that finally convinced these apostles themselves. They had half believed in our Lord before. Peter had made that great confession at Caesarea Philippi, "Thou art the Christ, the Son of the living God" (Matt. 16:16), but he had not known what he was saying and went back on it later in disappointment. But after the resurrection there was no doubt.

Peter himself, preaching on the Day of Pentecost, worked through a wonderful piece of argumentation to demonstrate that the resurrection proved our Lord to be the Son of God. He reminded the people at Jerusalem of how they had crucified our Lord, and then he continued:

Whom God hath raised up, having loosed the pains of death: because it was not possible that he should be holden of it.

And then Peter quoted Psalm 16:

For David speaketh concerning him, I foresaw the Lord always before my face, for he is on my right hand, that I should not be moved: Therefore did my heart rejoice, and my tongue was glad; moreover also my flesh shall rest in hope: Because thou wilt not leave my soul in hell, neither wilt thou suffer thine Holy One to see corruption. Thou hast made known to me the ways of life; thou shalt make me full of joy with thy countenance.

And Peter expounds:

Men and brethren, let me freely speak unto you of the patriarch David, that he is both dead and buried, and his sepulchre is with us unto this day. Therefore being a prophet, and knowing that God had sworn with an oath to him, that of the fruit of his loins, according to the flesh, he would raise up Christ to sit on his throne; he seeing this before spake of the resurrection of Christ, that his soul was not left in hell, neither his flesh did see corruption. This Jesus hath God raised up, whereof we all are witnesses.

—*Acts 2:24-32*

David wrote that sixteenth Psalm, says Peter. But obviously he was not writing about himself because we know that David died and was buried. There is his sepulcher; you can go and visit it whenever you like. His body is rotting in that tomb still. David has not risen from the dead, but this one has. David was speaking as a prophet of one who would be descended from him, and Jesus was born of the seed of David. David's words indicate that the resurrection was prophesied in the Old Testament, and the Lord Jesus Christ fulfilled that prophecy. The resurrection is proof that Christ is the Son of God of whom David spoke.

So that is the first reason why the apostles emphasized the resurrection, and it is the most staggering thing that the world has ever heard or ever will hear—God has visited and redeemed His people. He had sent many prophets, many teachers, but they could not bring about salvation. Then He sent His own Son, His only begotten Son, and this is the message of the church to the world. We are not left to the mercy of men. God is concerned, and God's own Son entered into time. He lived, died, and rose again. God is saving the world, and He is doing it through His only begotten Son. And the resurrection establishes that these facts are true. The apostles were witnesses to this blessed person and to the truths concerning Him.

Then, second, the apostles emphasized the resurrection because it was God's declaration that He was satisfied with the work of His Son. This is the great argument that you find in so many places in the New Testament Scriptures, and it is absolutely vital to this message. The apostle Paul puts it like this in Romans 4:25: "Who was delivered for our offences, and was raised again for our justification." He has already been saying something similar in chapter 3: "Whom God hath set forth to be a propitiation through faith in his blood, to declare his righteousness for the remission of sins that are past, through the forbearance of God; to declare, I say, at this time his righteousness: that he might be just, and the justifier of him which believeth in Jesus" (vv. 25-26). And God, in raising His Son from the dead, was saying to the whole world, He has done the work that I sent Him to do.

What was that work? It was the work of fulfilling God's law. This is why none other than the Son of God could ever save us. God made man in His own image; He made him perfect and told him how he was to live. God told him that if he did not live like that, he would be punished, and that the punishment would be death: "The soul that sinneth, it shall die" (Ezek. 18:4); "The wages of sin is death" (Rom. 6:23).

God is holy and just. "God is light, and in him is no darkness at all" (1 John 1:5). He cannot play fast and loose with His own holiness, if I may so put it with reverence. He cannot pretend that He has not seen the sin. You and I do that. We are shams, we are frauds, we are liars; we are not true, and we are not just. All humanity is confronted by the law of God. If we do not keep it, we must bear the punishment; and the punishment is eternal death and banishment from the life of God.

The Lord Jesus Christ came to deliver us from that punishment. That was the direct object of His coming. And in the resurrection we have proof that He has done it. To quote the apostle Paul again:

> *Brethren, my heart's desire and prayer to God for Israel is, that they might be saved. For I bear them record that they have a zeal of God, but not according to knowledge. For they being ignorant of God's righteousness, and going about to establish their own righteousness, have not submitted themselves unto the righteousness of God. For Christ is the end of the law for righteousness to every one that believeth.*
>
> —Rom. 10:1-4

"There the Jews are," Paul says, "going about with all this sweating and effort and striving to keep the law and to justify themselves by observing the deeds of the law. Nobody can do it, but the tragedy is that nobody need any longer try to do it. God has sent His only Son, and He has done it. He is the end of the law. He fulfilled the law."

The same truth is stated again in that glorious chapter, one of the most eloquent passages in the whole realm of holy writ, 1 Corinthians 15. We hear it at funeral services, and people so rarely understand it because they are fascinated by the glory of the language. But let me show you what it means.

Paul says, "O death, where is thy sting? O grave, where is thy victory? The sting of death is sin; and the strength of sin is the law. But thanks be to God, which giveth us the victory through our Lord Jesus Christ" (1 Cor. 15:55-57). He is saying that sin is what makes us all afraid of death ("the sting of death is sin") because we know that at death comes judgment upon sin. Yes, and sin is made powerful by the law ("the strength of sin is the law"), because it is the law that pronounces the verdict that an action is sinful. The law shows how powerful sin is. Sin, and the law's judgment of death upon that sin, are the problems that confront us.

But, says Paul, the resurrection answers the question, "O death, where is thy sting?" and solves the problems. The fact that Christ has come again from the dead, that God Himself brought Him from the dead, means that

God's law is honored and absolutely satisfied ("Thanks be to God which giveth us the victory through our Lord Jesus Christ"). How? Well, He has fulfilled the law. During His life He actively observed the law's every demand, so that the law could not pronounce Him sinful; and in His death He passively bore its penalty upon our sins. Therefore the law is satisfied. It has nothing to say. Our Lord has fulfilled its every demand on behalf of all who believe in Him. And that is what the resurrection establishes.

If our Lord had not risen from the grave, it would have meant that the law had demanded such a penalty of Him that even He was killed by it, and that would have been the end. But He came through death. He will not die again. He has borne the full penalty—which is death—and yet He is alive. He has finished the work. He has satisfied all the demands of God's holy law both positively and negatively.

Now the fifteenth chapter of 1 Corinthians is a very long chapter of fifty-eight verses, but it only has one theme: the resurrection and the vital importance of believing in the physical resurrection of Christ. The apostle wrote that chapter because there were certain clever people in the first century—there were clever people in the first century; they were not all born in this century, as some people seem to think!—who denied the physical resurrection. So you are not being very novel if you deny it. These people were saying that the resurrection was past already and that there is no such thing as a literal, physical resurrection for anyone.

Isn't there? asks Paul. And he adds that if there is no physical resurrection of the dead, "Then is Christ not risen: and if Christ be not risen, then is our preaching vain, and your faith is also vain. . . . If Christ be not raised, your faith is vain; ye are yet in your sins" (vv. 13-14, 17), and "we are found false witnesses of God" (v. 15). This is absolutely vital; it is the resurrection alone that gives me assurance that God is satisfied, that the law has been honored and fulfilled and that

> *The terrors of law and of God,*
> *With me shall have nothing to do;*
> *My Saviour's obedience and blood,*
> *Hide all my transgressions from view.*
> Augustus Toplady

Third, the apostles gloried in the resurrection, and nothing stopped them from bearing witness to it and preaching it, because it is the proof that this same blessed Lord has conquered all our enemies. There are powers and forces

that are set against us. We know something about them, do we not? The world
and the flesh—here are our enemies. The world pollutes us. Peter talks about
the pollution that is in the world through sin, and we see it today. Look at the
Sunday papers—pollution. Look at the clever satirists, as they are called, on
your television screens. What is it? It is filth and mire. Peter describes it like
this: The man who returns to his sin is like "the sow that was washed [turned
again] to her wallowing in the mire" (2 Pet. 2:22). And what a perfect description
that is of the filth, the foulness, the uncleanness of the world.

With its suggestiveness and all its subtle attraction, all its glorying in the
illicit, the world pollutes us and robs us of all that is best and highest and
noblest in us. The world and the flesh, these enemies, defeat us all. There is
not a man or woman who has not sinned. We are all polluted and bespattered
by the mud of this evil world. We cannot conquer it. We have tried, and
the men and women of the Old Testament tried before us, and the world has
defeated us all. But here is one who was undefeated. The world never got Him
down. He never gave way to the flesh. He walked through this world perfect,
pure, separate from sin.

But not only that, the devil is our enemy. The world knows nothing about
Satan, the god of this world. The world thinks we are mad when we talk
about this subject. People say, "Fancy a man in the twentieth century still
believing in the devil!" But where does all the evil in the world come from?
Why are all the efforts of statesmen and others always frustrated? What is it
that dogs the footsteps of the human race and always robs it when it thinks
it is on the verge of gaining a victory? What is it? And the Bible has the complete
answer. It is the devil. "For," says Paul, "we wrestle not against flesh
and blood, but against principalities, against powers, against the rulers of the
darkness of this world, against spiritual wickedness in high places" (Eph.
6:12)—the devil, hell, evil spirits with a malign power who are ever surrounding
us. This world has known only one who has been able to defeat the
power of the devil and all his forces, and that is this selfsame Jesus. During
His life on earth He defeated the devil, routing him every time he tried to
tempt Him; but above all, He defeated him at the cross. It is there that our
Lord finally exposed the devil and made him look ridiculous to everyone in
the world with eyes to see.

The author of the letter to the Hebrews puts our Lord's victory over the
devil in very striking words in his second chapter:

*Forasmuch then as the children are partakers of flesh and blood, he
also himself likewise took part of the same; that through death he*

might destroy him that had the power of death, that is, the devil; and deliver them who through fear of death were all their lifetime subject to bondage.

—Heb. 2:14-15

By His death on the cross, and especially by the resurrection, our Lord robbed the devil of His power. Satan no longer controls death as He did before.

The marvelous thing about Easter is that it tells us that the last enemy that shall be conquered is death. You live in this world, you fight the world, the flesh, and the devil, but there, at the back of it all, is death and the grave. Here is the final enemy, and it gets everybody down.

> *The boast of heraldry, the pomp of pow'r,*
> *And all that beauty, all that wealth e'er gave,*
> *Await alike the inevitable hour,*
> *The paths of glory lead but to the grave.*
> Thomas Gray

Great men, great statesmen, great kings, great philosophers—they all die; everyone who lives is born to die. Yes, here is the final adversary, the last captain, who defeats everybody; all become his victims. There is only one who has conquered him, and that one is this same Jesus.

"The God of our fathers," said Peter to the Sanhedrin on behalf of his fellow apostles, "raised up Jesus, whom ye slew and hanged on a tree. Him hath God exalted with his right hand." The power of Almighty God took hold of Christ in the tomb and raised Him up, conquering even death and the grave. The last enemy has been conquered, and in the light of Christ we can again repeat these words: "So when this corruptible shall have put on incorruption, and this mortal shall have put on immortality, then shall be brought to pass the saying that is written, Death is swallowed up in victory" (1 Cor. 15:54).

Christ has conquered the last enemy, and even after death, as I have already shown you, when you stand before God in the judgment and God's law speaks against you, it is already answered, it is forever settled. "Who shall lay any thing to the charge of God's elect? It is God that justifieth. Who is he that condemneth? It is Christ that died, yea rather, that is risen again, who is even at the right hand of God, who also maketh intercession for us" (Rom. 8:33-34).

Or again, let me give it to you in the eloquent language of the author of the letter to the Hebrews. Here in chapter 7 is the resurrection message for you. The writer is comparing the Lord Jesus Christ and His way with the old way of the temple and the priests, and he says:

> *And they truly were many priests, because they were not suffered to continue by reason of death: But this man, because he continueth ever, hath an unchangeable priesthood. Wherefore he is able also to save them to the uttermost that come unto God by him, seeing he ever liveth to make intercession for them.*
>
> —*vv. 23-25*

We do not need earthly priests. We do not need popes and cardinals. We have one high priest, the only one, Jesus, the Son of God. He is changeless, and He always lives to make intercession for us. There is one God and one mediator, and only one, between God and men, the man Christ Jesus. I do not even need Mary, His mother. He is enough. He has proved it in his resurrection.

He helps, He aids, and, of course, this is the thing that thrilled the minds and hearts of these New Testament writers. Listen to Hebrews 2 again:

> *Wherefore in all things it behooved him to be made like unto his brethren, that he might be a merciful and faithful high priest in things pertaining to God, to make reconciliation for the sins of the people. For in that he himself hath suffered being tempted, he is able to succour them that are tempted.*
>
> —*vv. 17-18*

He is God, I know, and is at the right hand of God; but He became man and knows what it is to suffer and to be tempted.

> *Seeing then that we have a great high priest, that is passed into the heavens, Jesus the Son of God, let us hold fast our profession. For we have not an high priest which cannot be touched with the feeling of our infirmities; but was in all points tempted like as we are, yet without sin.*
>
> —*Heb. 4:14-15*

We have a faithful and a merciful high priest. He knows all about us.

In every pang that rends the heart,
The Man of Sorrows had a part.

M. Bruce

He is there in the glory, but He is still man as well as God, and He is able to sympathize with us, and He sends us His help. The writer of Hebrews continues:

Let us therefore come boldly unto the throne of grace, that we may obtain mercy, and find grace to help in time of need.

—*v. 16*

It is the resurrection that tells me all this. The one who was in this world and lived and endured the contradiction of sinners against Himself is there in heaven; He is the same one. I can go to Him and know He will never refuse me but will give me all I need. But more, our Lord has been made a Prince: The universe is in His hand. Just before returning to heaven, He said, "All power is given unto me in heaven and in earth" (Matt. 28:18). Paul puts it all together in that tremendous statement of his in Philippians 2:

Who, being in the form of God, thought it not robbery to be equal with God: but made himself of no reputation, and took upon him the form of a servant, and was made in the likeness of men: And being found in fashion as a man, he humbled himself, and became obedient unto death, even the death of the cross. Wherefore God also hath highly exalted him, and given him a name which is above every name: that at the name of Jesus every knee should bow, of things in heaven, and things in earth, and things under the earth; and that every tongue should confess that Jesus Christ is Lord [Prince, Governor], to the glory of God the Father.

—*vv. 6-11*

The resurrection proves that. The world has been handed to Him. It is His. He sits, He reigns, and He is waiting until His enemies shall be made His footstool.

And, finally, His resurrection and ascension, His going back to heaven, are excellent proof that He will come back again to judge the world in righteousness. He Himself said that the Father had committed judgment unto Him because He was the Son of man: "For as the Father hath life in himself; so hath he given to the Son to have life in himself; and hath given him authority to execute judgment also, because he is the Son of man" (John 5:26-27). But listen to it as it is expressed by the apostle Paul—in Athens, of all places. The citizens of Athens were very philosophical; they did not believe in judgment and hell. Such people still do not believe in them, and I gather that they are surprised that some of us do not share their skepticism.

The apostle Paul, preaching to such men, puts it like this: "Forasmuch then as we are the offspring of God, we ought not to think that the Godhead is like unto gold, or silver, or stone, graven by art and man's device." We ought not to believe in images, says Paul. Some people are very anxious to go back and worship them, are they not? But God cannot be represented by an image. The Second Commandment tells us not to worship God in that way.

Paul continues, "And the times of this ignorance God winked at; but now commandeth all men every where to repent"—why?—"because he hath appointed a day, in the which he will judge the world in righteousness by that man whom he hath ordained; whereof he hath given assurance unto all men, in that he hath raised him from the dead" (Acts 17:29-31).

The resurrection of Jesus Christ is a proclamation and announcement to the effect that God will judge the whole world by this person, which simply means that in this life and in eternity our fate is decided by our attitude to Him. If you say that Jesus is only a man and, like the Jews, are a bit annoyed with Him and dismiss Him and kill Him and think you have got rid of Him, then you will receive judgment, and that judgment is eternal punishment. But if you believe that God has raised up this Jesus and made Him a Prince and a Savior, and that it is in Him alone that you can have forgiveness of sins and become a child of God, with the hope of glory, why, the verdict is that you will have all you have believed! This is why these men said to the Sanhedrin, "We must obey God rather than men."

The apostles said in effect, "We are preaching the Gospel even to you. You have to die. You are the judges now, but you will soon be the judged. And how are you going to face God? How are you going to face the law of God? You cannot. The only one who can save you from the penalty of God's law is the one whom you have slain and hanged upon a tree. He is the Prince; He is the Savior; He is the Messiah. He is the only one who can satisfy the law and can conquer all our enemies and reconcile us to God and make us His children. Repentance is only possible in Him. There is no forgiveness of sins apart from Him. Members of the Council, we cannot keep silent—we must obey God rather than men. The souls of men and women are in jeopardy. There is no hope apart from this blessed Jesus. Kill us, if you like. His name will go on, and the power of His name will persist."

All this is why the apostles would not be silenced. This message is the truth of God. Easter reminds us of a fact of history. One has risen from the dead. He is Jesus, the Son of God, the only Savior. He is the only one who can save us in this life, and He is the only one who can take us safely through death. He is the only one who can justify us before God's holy law and introduce us to the blessings and the joys of the bliss of eternity in the presence of God.

How can one keep silent? The Gospel is so glorious, and men and women are dying in sin and in ignorance. Let them scoff at us, let them ridicule us, let them do what they will, we will go on preaching. We cannot but preach. We cannot but repeat that we bear witness to these things. Christ is the only hope; He is the only Savior. Have you believed in Him? Have you believed these facts? Have you seen their relevance and their significance for you? Have you gone to Him and cast yourself upon Him, asking Him to receive you? If you do, I have His authority for telling you that He will receive you. Blessed be his name. He says from the glory to any frightened soul, "Him that cometh to me I will in no wise cast out" (John 6:37).

10

THE WITNESS OF THE HOLY SPIRIT

Then Peter and the other apostles answered and said, We ought to obey God rather than men. The God of our fathers raised up Jesus, whom ye slew and hanged on a tree. Him hath God exalted with his right hand to be a Prince and a Saviour, for to give repentance to Israel, and forgiveness of sins. And we are his witnesses of these things; and so is also the Holy Ghost, whom God hath given to them that obey him.

—Acts 5:29-32

I want now to deal in particular with that very last statement in verse 32, Peter's final words in his great speech to the Sanhedrin: "And so is also the Holy Ghost, whom God hath given to them that obey him." We are looking at Peter's speech for one reason only. We are living in a time in which many people are saying in various ways the very thing that the Sanhedrin said to the apostles. We are told that Christianity is an anachronism in the modern world, that it is ridiculous, foolish. "The idea that anybody should believe this kind of thing!" The clever people of the Sunday papers are amazed that anybody should still believe in Christianity. They say, "It's out-of-date, finished. Christianity is an insult to modern men and women!" They are trying to put a stop to it in various ways here in the West, not by throwing us into prison, but by ridicule and contempt.

And our answer is the same as that of the apostles to the Sanhedrin. It is the only answer we can give, and it is the reason we ignore everything our opponents have to say and go on preaching "this old, old Gospel, which is ever new and ever true."

We have looked at the message itself and have seen that we are not saved by ideas but by the Lord Jesus Christ, God's only begotten Son, who brought about our full salvation by dying for us on the cross. Furthermore, we have seen that the apostles could say, "We are his witnesses of these things," but they did not stop at that. They continued, "but so is also the Holy Ghost, whom God hath given to them that obey him." Now it is "these things," and these alone, that explain to us the origin and continuation of the Christian church. I know that the church is in trouble today; she has been in trouble before, and she would have ended long ago had it not been for "these things" that were witnessed to by the apostles and by the Holy Spirit.

But what does Peter mean by his statement that the Holy Spirit is also a witness to these things? That question raises one of the most important matters that we can ever consider. What makes a church meeting unique? What differentiates a church from every merely human gathering, even human gatherings at their best and highest? It is the presence of the Holy Spirit. The unseen presence! God the Holy Spirit among us! Were it not for the Holy Spirit, the outlook for the church would indeed be completely hopeless. But with the Holy Spirit as a witness, the future is full of hope, as I shall try to show you.

How, then, is the Holy Spirit a witness? And the first answer must be that His very coming on the Day of Pentecost was a witness to "these things." Once more we are in the realm of historical fact. Something happened ten days after the ascension of our Lord. There were these disciples, these men who had been with our Lord for three years. They had been filled with joy and hope as a result of the resurrection, but something was still lacking in their lives. So in obedience to our Lord's command, they were in Jerusalem, waiting and praying. Suddenly, as they were all together in an upper room, there was a sound as of "a rushing mighty wind" (Acts 2:2). It was the mighty wind of God, the wind that blew the church into being, the Holy Spirit coming upon and into the Christian church. And that was, in a sense, the inauguration of the Christian church. There had been a church in the old Testament—let us not forget that—but the church as we know her was inaugurated on that Day of Pentecost.

Now I know, of course, that modern men and women do not accept the Holy Spirit's coming on the Day of Pentecost. There are so many things they do not accept as facts. Like the members of the Sanhedrin, they only believe what they wish to believe. If they do not like something, they try to explain it away. That is what the Jewish leaders were doing with our Lord's resurrection, and their successors have been behaving in the same way ever since.

But the solid fact is that if this had not happened, there would never have been a church, and none of the subsequent events would ever have taken place.

As the result of the descent of the Holy Spirit, something so extraordinary began to happen that people came crowding, rushing together from all over Jerusalem asking, "What is it?" People from countries throughout the Empire were utterly confounded and perplexed when they heard their own languages being spoken by these simple, ignorant men. Then the apostle Peter preached to them and explained what it all meant, and we are told that as a result of this one sermon, three thousand people were added to the church, to the company of disciples (Acts 2:41).

Now it was no small matter for a Jew to become a Christian. It is hard for us today to realize quite how difficult it was. It meant persecution and ostracism; it meant being disowned and having your name erased from the family records. From the beginning, it was desperately hard. Nevertheless, they became Christians, three thousand of them, and soon another two thousand were added.

The appearance of the Christian church is a matter of historical fact. It came about as a consequence of the descent of the Holy Spirit. Both events are part of "these things" to which the Holy Spirit bore witness. We must start with the facts. We must always realize that the coming of the Spirit on the Day of Pentecost was one of a series of mighty events. Notice how these people who heard and saw the apostles put it on that Day of Pentecost in Jerusalem. What surprised them was this: "Behold, are not all these which speak Galileans? And how hear we every man in our own tongue, wherein we were born? . . . Cretes and Arabians"—and many others—"we do hear them speak in our [own] tongues the wonderful works of God" (Acts 2:7-8, 11). The apostles had been giving a recital of the things God had done.

The Bible is not a record of men's thoughts or aspirations, nor of men's attempts to arrive at a knowledge of God. Quite the reverse—it is a record of God's actions. "In the beginning God created . . ." You start with the action of God, and you go on. The Old Testament recounts the way God dealt with the children of Israel, creating a nation, sending prophets and teachers. And then we are told: "When the fulness of the time was come, God sent forth his Son, made of a woman, made under the law" (Gal. 4:4). God acting! God delivering His Son unto death. That is what happened on Calvary. I know the nails were actually driven in by the hands of men, but it was God acting. "God was in Christ, reconciling the world unto himself" (2 Cor. 5:19). "Him, being delivered by the determinate counsel and foreknowledge of God, ye have taken, and by wicked hands have crucified and slain" (Acts 2:23). And then God raised His Son from the dead. The great facts of the resurrection and the ascension were all the actions of God!

Another of the wonderful things God did was to send the Holy Spirit on the Day of Pentecost. It is not merely that a certain spirit began to manifest itself among the disciples as the result of their talking together. Not at all! "Suddenly there came a sound from heaven as of a rushing mighty wind," and the Spirit fell upon the apostles in all the glory and wonder of His power. So that is the first way in which the Holy Spirit is a witness to "these things": by His coming, by this concrete event in history.

But, second, the Spirit's coming was a fulfillment of prophecies—it had all been anticipated. We, as Christians, do not start with the Gospel of Matthew but with the book of Genesis. That is what the apostle Peter did here in his statement to the Sanhedrin. We have already looked at the way he put it: "the God of our fathers." He was a Jew, addressing Jews. He did not say, "Now we suddenly have a new idea that nobody has ever thought of before." "No," he said in effect, "you know, this thing that you cannot understand is the fulfillment of all that you claim to believe. You cannot see that, but that is what it is. 'The God of our fathers'! The God of your fathers as well as ours. The God of our Old Testament, the God of our Scriptures. The God of whom we have always boasted and whom we claim as our God over against the idols of the nations. He is the one who has done this. There is a continuity."

Do you have doubts about your Christian faith? Do you get shaken by modern criticism? Here is the answer: The New Testament is the fulfillment of the Old. "These things" had all been foretold. And that is the astounding fact. There is nothing more staggering than verified, fulfilled prophecy. This same Peter, when he was an old man on the verge of the grave, wrote in his last letter: "We have not followed cunningly devised fables, when we made known unto you the power and coming of our Lord Jesus Christ, but were eyewitnesses of his majesty" (2 Pet. 1:16). We saw Him transfigured. "There came such a voice to him from the excellent glory, This is my beloved Son, in whom I am well pleased" (v. 17). Peter wrote that he was a living witness; he had been there.

But Peter does not expect his readers only to rely on his word and witness. In his letter he adds, "We have also a more sure word of prophecy"—which is better translated, "We have also a word of prophecy made more sure." How? Because the events that have happened are the verification and the fulfillment of the Old Testament prophecies. And then Peter goes on to say, "Knowing this first, that no prophecy of the scripture is of any private

interpretation. For the prophecy came not in old time by the will of man"—
how then? "Holy men of God spake as they were moved"—carried along,
led, possessed by—"the Holy Ghost" (vv. 19-21). These verses from 2 Peter
1 expound that one sentence spoken by Peter to the Sanhedrin.

If you go back and read the Old Testament prophets, what will you find?
You will find that they prophesied that God would raise up a Deliverer. It is
amazing to read the detailed knowledge that they were given. They knew that
He would be of the tribe of Judah, of the seed of David. They prophesied, eight
hundred years before the event, that He would be born in a little town called
Bethlehem. They wrote about His death, about His riding into Jerusalem on
the foal of a donkey. They forecast His burial and His resurrection.

But the prophets did not stop with the resurrection. They prophesied that
when our Lord had completed His work, He would send down His Spirit
upon His people, and on the Day of Pentecost Peter made use of this
prophecy. Here they were, these apostles, now baptized and filled with the
Spirit, talking in unknown tongues, and the crowd came together. Then we
are told:

> Others mocking said, These men are full of new wine. But Peter,
> standing up with the eleven, lifted up his voice, and said unto them,
> Ye men of Judaea, and all ye that dwell at Jerusalem, be this known
> unto you, and hearken to my words: for these are not drunken as ye
> suppose, seeing it is but the third hour of the day. But this is that
> which was spoken by the prophet Joel; and it shall come to pass in
> the last days, saith God, I will pour out of my Spirit upon all flesh:
> and your sons and your daughters shall prophesy, and your young
> men shall see visions, and your old men shall dream dreams: and on
> my servants and on my handmaidens I will pour out in those days of
> my Spirit; and they shall prophesy: and I will show wonders in
> heaven above, and signs in the earth beneath; blood, and fire, and
> vapour of smoke: the sun shall be turned into darkness, and the
> moon into blood, before that great and notable day of the Lord
> come: and it shall come to pass, that whosoever shall call on the name
> of the Lord shall be saved. Ye men of Israel, hear these words. . . .
> —Acts 2:13-22

Peter than began to tell everyone how all this had been fulfilled in Jesus
of Nazareth—this was the only explanation of what had been happening
among them. He said:

*Men and brethren, let me freely speak unto you of the patriarch
David, that he is both dead and buried, and his sepulchre is with us
unto this day. Therefore being a prophet, and knowing that God had
sworn with an oath to him, that of the fruit of his loins, according to
the flesh, he would raise up Christ to sit on his throne; he seeing this
before spake of the resurrection of Christ, that his soul was not left
in hell, neither his flesh did see corruption. This Jesus hath God raised
up, whereof we all are witnesses. Therefore being by the right hand
of God exalted, and having received of the Father the promise of the
Holy Ghost, he hath shed forth this, which ye now see and hear.*
                                                        —Acts 2:29-33

Now that is the point of this argument. The Old Testament prophets—
Joel, Ezekiel, and others—had received revelation from God, from the Holy
Spirit Himself. It was He who had given these men this knowledge and understanding. It is an utter travesty of the teaching of the Bible to think of the Old
Testament prophets as just wise philosophers, men surrounded by books,
comparing thought with thought, trying to understand the times in which
they lived and giving a contemporary message. They did have a contemporary message, but they had a future message also. They foretold as well as
forth-told. And never forget this element of foretelling. It is the great argument that was used not only by the apostles but by the Lord Jesus Christ
Himself. He was always referring people to the Scriptures. He said, "Cannot
you see that I am fulfilling them?"

So it was the Holy Spirit who gave the prophets their knowledge, and
when He came upon the church on the Day of Pentecost, the prophecies were
fulfilled. The Holy Spirit was a witness to the truth of "these things." His
coming was the last event in this great series, these "wonderful works of
God" (Acts 2:11).

Or we can put it like this: John the Baptist, this strange man, was the fore-
runner of our Lord. There was a silence of some four hundred years after the
writing of the prophet Malachi, and then people began to hear of an amazing man in the wilderness—John, preaching a baptism of repentance for the
remission of sins. And they crowded out to hear him.

The people had never heard or seen anybody like John, with his blazing
eyes, his ascetic life. He was clad in a camel-hair shirt, and he ate nothing but
locusts and wild honey. He was a man speaking with authority and calling
people to repent. Unafraid of Pharisees and doctors of the law, he spoke to
all alike, denouncing their sin and hypocrisy. He told them that they were

unworthy to be called the children of Abraham and that God could raise up children of Abraham even out of stones.

As the people listened, they began to muse in their hearts and ask, "Could this be the Christ?" But John heard them and turned upon them. He told them that he was not the Christ, and he said, "I indeed baptize you with water; but one mightier than I cometh, the latchet of whose shoes I am not worthy to unloose: he shall baptize you with the Holy Ghost and with fire: whose fan is in his hand, and he will thoroughly purge his floor, and will gather the wheat into his garner; but the chaff he will burn with fire unquenchable" (Luke 3:16-17). "That is it," said John. "I am not the Christ. The Christ is the one who will baptize with the Holy Spirit."

And when the Holy Spirit came, the baptism descended! What does that tell us? Oh, this is the Christ! Jesus is the Christ! The resurrection alone does not prove it. The descent, the baptism, of the Holy Spirit is the final, the ultimate proof.

Or consider the coming of the Spirit in terms of what we read in a most important statement in John 7: "In that last day, the great day of the feast, Jesus stood and cried, saying"—listen to this, beloved friend! Are you in trouble? Are you "weary and heavy laden"? Are you tired and exhausted? Are you thirsty in life and defeated? This is what he said, "If any man thirst, let him come unto me, and drink. He that believeth on me, as the scripture hath said, out of his belly shall flow rivers of living water." And then comes John's explanation: "But this spake he of the Spirit, which they that believe on him should receive: for the Holy Ghost was not yet given; because that Jesus was not yet glorified" (vv. 37-39).

Our Lord's words on the "great day of the feast" were words of prophecy: He Himself prophesied the coming of the Spirit. He claimed that He was going to send the Spirit, and He said that the result of the Spirit's coming would be that men and women would be so satisfied that out of their innermost selves would flow "rivers of living water." If the Holy Spirit had not come, our Lord would have been a false prophet. But the Spirit did come! Therefore the Holy Spirit is a witness. I repeat, the Holy Spirit is the final proof that our Lord was who and what He claimed to be. The apostles said, "We are not the only witnesses; 'so is also the Holy Ghost, whom God hath given to them that obey him.'"

Or take it as it is put in the fourteenth chapter of John's Gospel. Listen to our Lord, just before the end of His life: "I will pray the Father, and he shall give you another Comforter, that he may abide with you for ever; even the Spirit of truth; whom the world cannot receive, because it seeth him not, neither knoweth him" (vv. 16-17). It is not surprising that people do not believe in the Holy Spirit and in the baptism with the Holy Spirit that came on the Day of Pentecost. Our Lord told us that the world cannot believe in Him; it never has, and it never will.

There is nothing new about disbelief. Do not regard denial of the Gospel and this message about the Holy Spirit as the hallmark of modernity. It is the old sin of the Pharisees, the self-righteous people who think they can please God without being born again and without being filled with the Spirit. Our Lord said of the Spirit: ". . . whom the world cannot receive, because it seeth him not, neither knoweth him: but ye know him; for he dwelleth with you, and shall be in you. I will not leave you comfortless: I will come to you. Yet a little while, and the world seeth me no more" (John 14:17-19). Our Lord was giving His disciples a promise.

Our Lord went on to say, "It is expedient for you that I go away." Was it possible? How could it be good for the followers and the disciples that the Teacher should leave them? He had only been with them three years, and now He was going to leave them and was saying that was good! Then he continued, "for if I go not away, the Comforter will not come unto you; but if I depart, I will send him unto you. And when he is come, he will reprove the world of sin, and of righteousness, and of judgment" (John 16:7-8). "He" is the Holy Spirit.

Our Lord had said, "I will not leave you comfortless" (John 14:18). He would not leave His followers alone; He would send them another Comforter. Again, if the Spirit had not come on the Day of Pentecost, Christ would have been shown to be a false prophet and teacher. The Holy Spirit was the witness to these things, much more so than the apostles. This is the meaning of the words in Acts 5:32.

And then at the very end of His earthly life, after the resurrection even, immediately before His ascension, our Lord told the disciples to wait in Jerusalem "for the promise of the Father," about which He had told them. And He added, "For John truly baptized with water; but ye shall be baptized with the Holy Ghost not many days hence" (Acts 1:4-5). That is it! "But ye shall receive power, after that the Holy Ghost is come upon you: and ye shall be witnesses unto me both in Jerusalem, and in all Judaea, and in Samaria, and unto the uttermost part of the earth" (v. 8). Here is His promise; here is His claim, a claim and promise He fulfilled and proved true when He sent the Holy Spirit on the Day of Pentecost. So the second way in which the Holy Spirit bears witness is that by His coming He witnessed to the truth of the prophecies.

The third way is the change in the apostles. "We are his witnesses of these things; and so is also the Holy Ghost." What change was to be seen in the apostles themselves? Oh, read the Gospels and then read the Acts of the Apostles. Look at these men and see what they were. We are told that the members of the great Sanhedrin, in their patronizing manner, "perceived that they were unlearned and ignorant men" (Acts 4:13), and so they were. Perfectly right. They had no knowledge, no training; they were not Pharisees, scribes, or Sadducees. They were artisans, fishermen, ordinary workmen.

Not only that, the apostles were cowards. This was the greatest friend they had ever known, this Jesus, and yet they all forsook Him and fled when He was arrested and brought face-to-face with death. Craven-spirited men! Peter denied knowing Him and backed up his words with oaths and curses. After our Lord's death they met together in an upper room and locked the doors because they were afraid of the Jews. That is what they were.

But look at Peter and the apostles here; listen to them. Peter stands up on the Day of Pentecost and preaches without fear. And here in Acts 5, he is preaching again, though he has been in prison twice and though he is threatened with death. He looks into the face of this great authority, the Sanhedrin, and says, "We ought to obey God rather than you." What has happened? What is this?

This is Christianity! Christianity is not just about criticizing the policy of South Africa and apartheid. That is not Christianity. There are people who are not Christians at all who do that and do it very well. Christianity is not just a constant protest against atomic bombs and war. Again, people can do that who are not Christians at all. No; Christianity is that which transforms men and women completely, giving a new birth, a new mind and understanding, as we see with these apostles. Thank God that it is! It is not a wonderful idea or theory with philosophical jargon and terminology that I can only follow if I have a university degree. No, no! "The common people heard him [Jesus] gladly" (Mark 12:37). The descent of the Holy Spirit is the only explanation for the change in the apostles. You cannot explain it in any other terms. And that is why the Holy Spirit is a witness, even through them and their witness to the truth of the gospel message.

Now people today, in their cleverness and supposed wisdom, try to persuade us that they can explain away the whole of Christianity. And the favorite explanation in this present century has been the psychological one. People say, "Look at these Christians. What accounts for them?" And having analyzed a large number of people, they conclude that there are certain personality types, among them the emotional, religious type. So they say that some people are born religious, and some are not.

"All right," they add, "there's no need to quarrel. If you are helped by religion, by all means keep on with it. But don't say that everybody else should take it up; don't say that it is essential. You are just the religious type; you have a religious complex." And the events of the Day of Pentecost are dismissed as "mass hysteria."

But the difficulty is that, like the members of the Sanhedrin, those who put forward psychological explanations are flying in the face of facts. They are trying to weave a little theory to explain their little understanding. You cannot explain the apostles in terms of men who were suffering from mass hysteria. Could a man suffering from hysteria write the Epistle to the Romans and the Epistle to the Ephesians, do you think? If you want a little intellectual exercise, there it is for you. Begin to read the Epistle to the Ephesians, and come and tell me whether you have really understood it. I do not expect to see you for some time!

As for the theory that there is a "religious type," the fact is that among the apostles themselves, there were men of many different temperaments and psychological makeups. And that also applies to the wider group of Christians who comprised the early church. I cannot imagine two more different men than Paul and John, or John and Peter. There is every conceivable type here.

And as you come down the centuries, what do you find? Are the only people who are Christians the ignorant and unlettered? No; some of the giant intellects of all time have been humble Christians. I could give you a long list. I always rather like doing it, it is so wonderful! Athanasius, for example; there he was, one man, with his gigantic understanding, standing up against the whole church and the world, as it were. And Saint Augustine—what an intellect! What a colossus of a man! What a giant!

Why do you not face the facts, my friend? We find all types of people varying in temperament and ability—giant intellects, sinful people, the great sage and philosopher, and the little child—all brought to a common denominator, all believing the same message, all participating in the same new life, all rejoicing together in the great salvation. You cannot explain it away in terms of psychology. A man tried to do it a few years ago. I was privileged to write a little reply[10] to him, and I was told that he was going to answer me at once. But he still has not, and there is only one reason for that—he cannot.

There is only one explanation for the change in the disciples and for the origin of the Christian church. It is not mass hysteria; it is not psychological types; it is the filling of the Holy Spirit. Look at the apostles' joy and exultation. Look at their courage. See how their fear suddenly left them. Look at the way in which they spoke, not only with other languages but in their own language also. Look at their new understanding of the Scriptures and at Peter's ability to expound them. He could not have done that before.

What accounts for it all? It is the power of the Holy Spirit, and this is the very essence of the Gospel. The Gospel is not about what men and women can do, but about what God can enable them to do. It is God coming into them in the Holy Spirit and giving them life anew, a new ability, and all that they stand in need of.

Look at the miracles worked by the apostles; indeed, that is one reason why they were on trial. Peter and John could no more work a miracle than I can. When they healed the lame man, they said, "Why look ye so earnestly on us, as though by our own power or holiness we had made this man to walk?" (Acts 3:12). It is not us! "And his name [the Prince of life] through faith in his name hath made this man strong . . . hath given him this perfect soundness in the presence of you all" (v. 16). Peter said they had been enabled to cure the lame man because God had put His Spirit upon them and in them, and they had been filled with a divine energy. They were repeating the miracles that Christ had done when He had been here Himself in the flesh. That was the argument.

And that is how Christianity spread. Did it turn the world upside-down because a group of fishermen and women and illiterate people banded together to have a prayer meeting? The idea is quite monstrous; it is insane! There is only one explanation: The followers of Christ were transformed, transfigured, renewed, and given power above themselves. They became the vehicles and the channels of the power of the Holy Spirit who was working in them and through them.

That is argued everywhere in the New Testament. The author of the Epistle to the Hebrews, in telling us why we ought to listen to the Gospel, says:

> *Therefore we ought to give the more earnest heed to the things which we have heard, lest at any time we should let them slip. For if the word spoken by angels was steadfast, and every transgression and disobedience received a just recompence of reward; how shall we escape, if we neglect so great salvation; which at the first began to be spoken by the Lord, and was confirmed unto us by them that heard him; God also bearing them witness, both with signs and wonders,*

and with divers miracles, and gifts of the Holy Ghost, according to
his own will?

—2:1-4

That is how the Gospel spread. There would never have been a Christian church but for this. And yet people tell us that they do not believe in the Holy Spirit, nor in signs, wonders, and miracles because of the scientific knowledge of the mid-twentieth century! I am not surprised they are emptying their churches! What I am amazed at is that anybody troubles to go and listen to them. You can get that from your newspapers or on the street corner. That is a denial, not a preaching, of the Gospel. No, no! "God also bearing them witness" (Heb. 2:4). And if He had not, I repeat, the Christian church would never have come into being, and she certainly would never have continued. But the Holy Spirit has come, and He acts in the way that we read about in the second chapter of Acts.

The Holy Spirit can do the impossible. I cannot save a soul, nor can anybody else. I know some men who claim that they can, but all they get are decisions. The Holy Spirit alone can save a soul. No man and his speaking and his argumentation can ever convince anybody of sin and righteousness and judgment to come. The Holy Spirit alone can do it, and on the Day of Pentecost, even through the mouth of an ignorant fisherman like Peter, that is what He did. As Peter was preaching, we are told, the people were "pricked in their heart," and they cried out, "Men and brethren, what shall we do?" (Acts 2:37). That was not Peter—it was the Holy Spirit.

Three thousand believed on the Day of Pentecost; it was solely the result of the operation of the Holy Spirit of God. It was the Holy Spirit who filled those first converts with new life. We read that they "did eat their meat with gladness and singleness of heart, praising God, and having favour with all the people" (Acts 2:46-47). Not only that, "they continued steadfastly in the apostles" doctrine and fellowship, and in breaking of bread, and in prayers" (v. 42). They were afraid of nobody! They had new life. They were born from the dead, and death had lost its terror. They had had a vision and a glimpse of glory with God in eternity. And the Holy Spirit had given it all to them. He not only began to do that on the Day of Pentecost and in the early church in the first century, but thank God, He has gone on doing it!

The Holy Spirit convicts us of our sin, making us face ourselves in a way that nothing and no one else can ever do. He shows us our emptiness and woe. He puts us on our backs in utter helplessness. And then—blessed be His name—He enables us to discern Jesus as the Son of God. He gives us insight into the meaning of His death upon the cross. We see, as John the Baptist said, that He is "the Lamb of God, which taketh away the sin of the world" (John 1:29). The Holy Spirit reveals the Lord to us as God's paschal Lamb. We see God laying on Him the iniquity of us all and punishing Him so we might be forgiven. No man or woman can understand that. I am not surprised that people do not believe in the doctrine of the atonement. To human wisdom it is not only impossible, it is ridiculous. But not to those who are enlightened by the Holy Spirit. Then we see "Christ the power of God, and the wisdom of God" (1 Cor. 1:24).

And because the Holy Spirit is continuing His work today, I say that in spite of all appearances, I am not dejected and I am not discouraged. I have faith in—what? Modern scholarship? Most certainly not! Scholarship denies the power of the Spirit because it is bound by human understanding. Modern scholarship would take everything from us, everything that really is the Gospel, the power of God through the Holy Spirit. No, no; my faith is in the Holy Spirit as a witness of these things.

What do I mean? Look at the story of the Christian church throughout the centuries. What do you see? Well, here it is starting at Pentecost with this great outpouring of the Spirit. But troubles began even in the time of the New Testament. Then as you go on through the centuries, you find the church becoming institutionalized. It becomes important. Bishops appear, and other accretions. The church becomes rich and can no longer say, like Peter, "Silver and gold have I none," because it has so much wealth, so much that it is afraid to tell the public how much.

The amazing thing is that the church is still here at all! Men and women have tried to destroy it times without number. There is only one thing that explains the persistence of the church: the Holy Spirit. If you read the story of the church, you will find a story of reformations and revivals, of repetitions of the events on the Day of Pentecost. The church becomes weak and ignorant and worldly and moribund, but then suddenly, and in an utterly inexplicable manner, God again pours forth His Spirit, perhaps on a man, perhaps on a company. And they are renewed and filled with power. Their word becomes irresistible, and the church goes on to a new period of revival, renewal, and reawakening. And were it not for that, the church, I repeat, would long since have ceased.

You cannot explain revivals in terms of psychology and mass hysteria. The question you must answer is this: How did the first man get changed? What happened to Whitefield and to Wesley? The only explanation is that the Spirit who first came upon the apostles came upon these later followers

154   *Victorious Christianity*

as well. All the denominations started as a result of revival. And there we see the one hope for us today, because the Holy Spirit is still here, and He still witnesses to "these things."

That is why we go on preaching. That is why I, unworthy as I am to be mentioned in the same breath as the apostles, and living in this degenerate twentieth century of ours with all its pride of learning, learning that does not produce much good living and that leads to a world of chaos and shame and sin—that is why I, too, say: Let men say what they please, we ought to obey God rather than men. This message is God's truth, and thank God for it.

11

MOLDED BY THE GOSPEL

Then Peter and the other apostles answered and said, We ought to obey God rather than men. The God of our fathers raised up Jesus, whom ye slew and hanged on a tree. Him hath God exalted with his right hand to be a Prince and a Saviour, for to give repentance to Israel, and forgiveness of sins. And we are his witnesses of these things; and so is also the Holy Ghost, whom God hath given to them that obey him.

—Acts 5:29-32

I want now to deal again with that last part of the statement in verse 32: "We are his witnesses of these things; and so is also the Holy Ghost, whom God hath given to them that obey him." That is how Peter's sermon ends. And our treatment of this paragraph, this message, cannot end without the same vital emphasis. Peter was not merely making a statement to the authorities; he was out to convince them and to help them. He was out to win them, though they had put themselves in a position of enmity against him and all the other apostles. The members of the Sanhedrin were acting in a very unjust and unrighteous manner, and because the apostles were concerned about them, they pleaded with them. By saying, "the God of our fathers," Peter was calling upon their knowledge of the Scriptures, in this way making use of an argument that he trusted would appeal to them. The apostles were anxious that these men should have the gift of the Holy Spirit, even as they had.

The apostles were what they were and were able to do what they were doing because of the Holy Spirit. And Peter was telling the members of the

Sanhedrin that they might be the same if they had the same gift. But there was one condition: obedience. "So is also the Holy Ghost, whom God hath given to them that *obey* him." In other words, Peter was calling for a response. And this is a vital part of the Christian message.

Let me therefore put it in this way: The Gospel is to be obeyed. Let us be clear about this. Some people misunderstand these words spoken by Peter and think they mean that if you obey God, if you keep the commandments, if you live a good life, you will be rewarded with the gift of the Holy Spirit. But they cannot mean that because that is the exact opposite of the Gospel, as I will show you. None of us is rewarded by God for what we have done. It is all of grace. It is all the free gift of God. So Peter is really saying here that God gives the Holy Spirit to those who have believed the Gospel. The obedience is an obedience to the Gospel.

I start, then, with the first proposition: The Gospel of Jesus Christ, this message, is something that is to be obeyed. This is stated in many places in the Bible. In the apostle Paul's introduction to his letter to the Romans, he talks about himself as a preacher and an apostle and says, "By whom [the Lord Jesus Christ] we have received grace and apostleship"—what for?—"for obedience to the faith among all nations" (v. 5). That is Paul's way of describing how people become Christians: They give obedience to the faith.

In another place Paul says, "For they being ignorant of God's righteousness, and going about to establish their own righteousness, have not submitted themselves unto the righteousness of God" (Rom. 10:3). He is breaking his heart, he says, about his fellow countrymen, the Jews: "My heart's desire and prayer to God for Israel is, that they might be saved" (v. 1). Here he is, a Jew himself and preaching the Gospel to Gentiles who are believing it and crowding into the kingdom, but the bulk of his own nation are rejecting it. The Pharisees and scribes, the Sadducees and others are bitterly opposing it. He says, "I bear them record that they have a zeal of God, but not according to knowledge" (v. 2). They are, he says, busy doing this, that, and the other all over the world to establish their own righteousness, but they have not submitted themselves to the righteousness of God.

This teaching is put still more explicitly in Romans 10:13-16. Here Paul says, "Whosoever shall call upon the name of the Lord shall be saved." Then he takes up a series of questions. "How then shall they call on him in whom they have not believed? and how shall they believe in him of whom they have not heard? and how shall they hear without a preacher? and how shall they preach, except they be sent? as it is written, How beautiful are the feet of them that preach the gospel of peace, and bring glad tidings of good things!" And then he says, "But they have not all obeyed the gospel." Notice how Paul puts it. He does not say they have not all believed the Gospel, but that they have not all *obeyed* it.

It is not possible to avoid this word *obey*. And at the very end of the Epistle to the Romans, where Paul is talking about the Gospel, he says, "Now to him that is of power to stablish you according to my gospel, and the preaching of Jesus Christ, according to the revelation of the mystery, which was kept secret since the world began, but now is made manifest, and by the scriptures of the prophets, according to the commandment of the everlasting God, made known to all nations for the obedience of faith" (16:25-26).

We always return to the question of obedience, and lest somebody think this is a doctrine peculiar to the apostle Paul, listen to Peter writing his first epistle. He is addressing Christian people, and he tells them that they are "elect according to the foreknowledge of God the Father, through sanctification [the separating work] of the Spirit, unto obedience and sprinkling of the blood of Jesus Christ" (1:2). And I could give you other examples.

The need for obedience, this great point that is made here by Peter at the end of his address to the Sanhedrin, is a most important matter. The Gospel is not something that we listen to in a detached manner. People say, "Well, yes, I'm interested in your Gospel. I'm interested in all religions. I've read about other religions, and I like to read about Christianity too. I see that one has this, and others have that, and I like to evaluate them. There's a bit of good, of course, in all religions, and I grant you there is something about this Christian religion too." No; it is not merely a matter of opinion.

Nor is the Gospel something that you and I may simply enjoy listening to. There are things about this Gospel that make one admire it tremendously. But the Gospel is not even to be admired. It is to be acted upon.

But let me go further. The Gospel is not something that is to be accepted merely in an intellectual manner. This is a special word of warning for some of us. I know from personal experience what it is only to accept the Gospel intellectually. There is nothing in the whole universe comparable to the Christian philosophy as expounded by some of the great masters—Augustine, for example, or Thomas Aquinas, or a man with a magisterial mind like John Calvin. The Christian system is marvelous. It is the only complete and entire view of life. And there are people who regard themselves as Christians because they have accepted this intellectual system. But we are reminded by this one word *obey* that this position is of no value.

The Gospel calls for a response. It calls for action. It calls for a decision.

It calls for obedience. The Gospel of Jesus Christ is meant to affect the whole of one's life. It is meant to be the controlling, the central thing in life, that which governs the whole of one's outlook. That is what is meant by the word *obedience.*

Now there is a statement in Romans 6:17 that again puts it very well: "God be thanked," says the apostle, "that ye were the servants of sin [the slaves of sin], but ye have obeyed from the heart that form of doctrine which was delivered you." Some commentators say, and I think quite rightly, that here Paul is really using an illustration. They say that the words, "you have obeyed from the heart that form of doctrine which was delivered you" should really be translated, "you have obeyed from the heart that form of doctrine into which you have been delivered."

The illustration is this: Imagine a lot of molten metal—iron or steel perhaps—that a craftsman wants to form into a particular article. What does he do? Well, he pours the molten metal into a mold, and then as the metal cools, it hardens in the form of the mold. And that, according to the apostle, is what happens when men and women become Christians. Christians are people who have been poured into the mold of the Gospel, which means that they have taken on the appearance and the size and the shape of that mold. And this is vital.

Indeed, I go one step further. The teaching on obedience tells us that anything short of such a result is of no value. There is no point in saying that you think the Christian faith is wonderful and that you admire it unless it has made a difference to you. It is either the controlling factor in your life or else it is nothing. Now you may say, "I don't agree with that because oftentimes when I've listened to it, I've been affected and have really been determined to live a better life; and I have tried to do that."

That is all right, my friend, but it is not enough. The road to hell is paved with good intentions. Christians are people who have obeyed the Gospel. They have been poured into the mold. They are governed, controlled, and determined entirely by this teaching: ". . . the Holy Ghost, whom God hath given to them that *obey* him."

But now let me ask: Why is this so? Why the necessity for obedience? And here we come, of course, to another vital matter in connection with the Gospel of salvation. Obedience is essential because the very essence of sin is disobedience to God: "The carnal mind is enmity against God: for it is not subject to the law of God, neither indeed can be" (Rom. 8:7). The Bible describes sin as the transgression of the law, as breaking God's law. Sin occurs when men and women do not conform to the mold in which God made them.

God made them in His own image and likeness. That is the mold. But they have broken the mold and have rebelled against God. To put it another way, they have defaced the image.

Now it is absolutely essential, it is the necessary preliminary to the Gospel, that we should realize what sin is. We must not think of sin as merely doing something that is wrong. That is what we tend to do. We recognize certain acts as good and others as bad, and we tend to think that sin is just doing particular things that are bad. It is that, but that is not its essence. I repeat that the essence of sin is rebellion against God.

It is very important that we should be clear about the nature of sin, because if sin were merely a matter of committing particular types of actions, many people would feel that they were not sinners at all. Indeed, I have met many such people. They really do not think they are sinners. Some of them have even told me that. I remember a lady saying to me once, "You know, I've never really felt that I'm a sinner." And another lady, who used to attend my church—with a very critical attitude, I understand—once said about me, "This man preaches to us as if we were sinners!" She had never got drunk. She had never committed adultery. She had never committed murder. Therefore she was not a sinner.

Let me use an illustration. There is all the difference in the world between the symptoms of diseases and the diseases themselves. How do you decide whether or not a man is ill? Well, there are some people who say, "If you show me a man with a temperature of 105, I'll say he's ill. A man who is delirious is ill." And if you show them somebody who has no raised temperature at all—it may even be subnormal—and who is not delirious but is lying quietly and placidly on the bed, they will say, "There's nothing wrong with that man." Their idea of illness is something dramatic, something exciting, something flaring, as it were. But that is a very misleading standard. There are diseases that work their way quietly in the system, and you are hardly aware that anything is happening at all. But the disease is progressing. It is not the symptoms that matter, but the disease itself. And it is exactly the same with the whole question of sin.

We tend to think that respectable people cannot be sinners. Take the typical modern man who is not a Christian—the self-contained, decent, moral, good-living man. He does not come to church or read the Gospels. Why not? Because he does not need to. He does not do anything wrong, and so he is not a sinner. But why does he think that? It is because he has never understood that the essence of sin is rebellion against God.

Here is your respectable man, spending Sunday in his garden, perhaps with his children. Perhaps he has a tennis court or even a swimming pool. He is never drunk; he is loyal to his wife; he is perfectly honest in his business dealings. But has he thanked God for this day, for the sunshine? Has he lifted up his voice and his heart with others in acclaiming the great and glorious Creator? Is he living life to the glory of God, according to the mold in which men and women were originally made? No! He is self-contained and self-satisfied—and he has broken God's law just as much as the drunkard, the wife-beater, or the adulterer. He is as abominable in the sight of God as any flagrant sinner.

Nor, in spite of what people seem to think, is sin merely that which makes us sad. Because they are miserable after they have done certain wrong things, people look for help. They go to one another. They go to preachers. They try the cults and various other treatments, psychotherapy and so on. They long to be delivered from their misery, from whatever it is that is getting them down. They say, "I keep on falling into this thing; can't you help me?"

I often find that it is extremely difficult to get such people to stop talking about their misery and their failure and to see themselves in the sight of God. I generally bring it home to them by putting it like this: "If you could get rid of this, you would be all right, would you?"

And they always reply, "Yes, I would."

"Well, then," I say, "you probably won't get rid of this until you come to see that the real trouble is not this particular thing that gets you down and makes you miserable afterward. Your trouble is that you haven't even thought of God. He has never entered into your calculations, and you're not concerned at all about obeying Him and pleasing Him and living to His glory. That is sin."

This is the way to look at the problem of sin. God is the one who made us. He is the controller of all life. He made men and women for Himself. He made them according to His mold, His pattern, in His image and likeness, and He made them like that so that they might be His companions, that He might enjoy their company. Furthermore, in the Ten Commandments and the Sermon on the Mount, in the preaching of the Old Testament prophets and the teaching of the New Testament epistles, He has clearly revealed the kind of life He wants them to live.

As God controls the sun in the heavens and raises the moon and gives nature its laws, so He has made men and women for Himself. And He intended them to live according to His pattern and law. But they have refused. They have rebelled against Him. They have smashed the mold. They say they do not need God and they can make their own lives. So they do not obey Him. That, I repeat, is the essence of sin.

If you read or listen to the reports of political speeches, you will see that some politicians are themselves beginning to acknowledge people's self-centeredness. A man in a position of considerable responsibility said recently that if this country [England] is not to perish and go on the rocks financially, we have to stop thinking that at one and the same time we can shorten working hours and increase wages. What makes people think that such a foolish thing is possible? What is it that makes working men and women commit suicide, in the financial and industrial sense, and their employers do exactly the same? It is just selfishness. And when people are selfish, they have broken the mold and are living for themselves instead of for God. Some of the country's leaders are now saying that you cannot deal with these things by acts of Parliament. They are quite right—you cannot. You will never change human nature by making new laws. Here is the problem: Men and women are in trouble because of their disobedience to God. As a result, they are under the wrath of God.

And it is at this point that the Gospel comes in—it is exactly as the apostles stated here to the Sanhedrin. "Listen," they said, "you are telling us to stop preaching. You are telling us not to teach anymore in the name of this man or to do anything more in His name. But we must. We cannot keep silent. Why? Because God has commanded us, and 'we ought to obey God rather than men.' We have been sent by God."

And that was how the apostle Paul argued also. He wrote, "How shall they preach, except they be sent?" (Rom. 10:15). How can men and women believe in a Savior of whom they have never heard? How can they hear unless there is a preacher? But where does the preacher come from? What makes him a preacher?

There is only one answer: He is called of God; he is commanded of God. I do not decide to come into this pulpit. I did not decide to become a preacher. I say that honestly in the presence of God. I could have been doing something else; indeed, I was doing something else. But I was commanded by God. And what I preach is not my theory, not my clever idea. I am an exponent of God's Word. I am simply unfolding to you the message that is here before me, inscripturated, this teaching that God by His Holy Spirit has caused men to write and to write infallibly. I am a man under commission. I dare not preach anything else. I am commanded, and I am obeying. I say this to you now, and this is also how the apostles put it. No preacher of the Gospel can ever say anything else.

What is this message that has been given to us? It is a message about God and his Son. "The God of our fathers raised up Jesus, whom ye slew and hanged on a tree. Him hath God exalted with his right hand [of power] to be a Prince and a Saviour." This is the message, and here are the apostles preaching it to the Sanhedrin. "Listen," they said in effect, "you rejected Him, but you didn't know what you were doing. We are offering Him to you. We are appealing to you. Can't you see? He is Prince; He is Savior; He is God's way of salvation. You can be forgiven; you can have new life; you can have the gift of the Spirit, if only you believe this message and obey it."

The Gospel, therefore, is also a command. It is just as much a command from God as the Ten Commandments. Does that come to you as a surprise? It should not. God commands men to go out and preach it, and He commands men and women to believe it. So believe the Gospel. I say again—it is His commandment. And if you want my authority for saying this, let me quote our Lord Himself. Our Lord said to the people one day, "Labour not for the meat which perisheth, but for that meat which endureth unto everlasting life, which the Son of man shall give unto you: for him hath God the Father sealed. Then said they unto him, What shall we do, that we might work the works of God?" (John 6:27-28). In other words, they were asking Him to tell them what God commanded them to do in order to have the eternal life about which He was speaking.

And our Lord answered, "This is the work of God, that ye believe on him whom he hath sent" (v. 29). "What you must do," He said, "is believe on Me, because I have been sent by God. That is the work you have to do. That is the commandment you must keep."

Remember, too, Romans 1: "for obedience to the faith" (v. 5). Or again we read in John's first epistle: "This is his commandment"—God's commandment—"that we should believe on the name of his Son, Jesus Christ" (3:23).

Now what does obedience mean when it is translated into practice? It is no good listening to the Gospel if it does not change the whole of your life. Without obedience, there is nothing. What, then, are the commands that are to be obeyed? Well, the first command is to repent. When the apostle Paul was preaching in Athens, that, in essence, was his message. He began:

Ye men of Athens, I perceive that in all things ye are too superstitious.
For as I passed by, and beheld your devotions, I found an altar with
this inscription, TO THE UNKNOWN GOD. Whom therefore you
ignorantly worship, him declare I unto you.

And Paul concluded:

But now [God] commandeth all men every where to repent: because he hath appointed a day, in the which he will judge the world in righteousness by that man whom he hath ordained; whereof he hath given assurance unto all men, in that he hath raised him from the dead.
—Acts 17:22-23, 30-31

The first command is to repent. But what does repentance mean? First, just as Paul urged upon the Athenians, and Peter upon the Sanhedrin, repentance means that you stop for a moment and think about your life. It means that you stop living from day to day and hand to mouth and stop being governed by what happens to you. Instead of living as if you have an endless lease on life and will never have to die, you stop. You think. You meditate. You ask, What am I? How am I living? What is the purpose of it all? What is the end? And when you have started thinking, you see that you have a soul. It is then that you begin to realize the truth about God.

Furthermore, repentance means that you ask yourself certain questions about God: Where does God come in my life? Does He make any difference to me? Does my life in any way conform to His holy laws? And you soon realize that you have been forgetting God. You know what happens to a person who behaves in an unworthy manner in the presence of the Queen, but how do we all behave in the presence of the King of heaven? We are told that we must never turn our backs upon the Queen, but look at men and women turning their backs on the God of heaven, laughing at Him, walking away from Him in arrogance, deliberately breaking His laws.

Now when you repent, you realize that you have spurned God and that He calls you to account. He has a right to do that. As the psalmist says, "It is he that hath made us, and not we ourselves" (Ps. 100:3). Our times and our lives are in His hands; He is the Judge, and not we ourselves. And having realized this, you confess that you are wrong and that you have been a rebel against God. You see that you have spat upon His law and desecrated His sanctities; you see that you are vile, a reprobate, a sinner, and you acknowledge it without defending yourself. You realize that there is nothing to be said for you at all, and you acknowledge that you deserve nothing but punishment. You have flouted the law of God who has given you everything you have ever enjoyed—the gift of life, health and strength, food and clothing, your birth into a family that surrounded you with love and care and attention. God has given you all this, and you have turned away from Him.

But now you fall before God in utter acknowledgment of your rebellion and your sin. There's no defense, you say. And you cry out to Him for mercy. "For whosoever shall call upon the name of the Lord," says Paul, "shall be saved" (Rom. 10:13). And those who obey the command to repent begin to call on the name of the Lord. There is nothing to be done but to cry to God for mercy and compassion, for forgiveness, for love. We are commanded to do this: "God commandeth all men every where to repent."

And then, second, God commands us to believe this Gospel. He says, "I am setting this message before you. I first of all raised up My Son Jesus as the Savior. I sent Him from heaven and made Him, who was with Me in eternity, into flesh. I sent Him as a man 'in the likeness of sinful flesh' (Rom. 8:3). I caused Him to humble Himself in order to save you. Then I raised up preachers and told these men to hold My Son before you."

So when God commands us to believe the Gospel, He means us to believe this record, this witness of the apostles, that Jesus of Nazareth was none other than the only begotten, eternal Son of God. "We are his witnesses of these things," says Peter, "and so is also the Holy Ghost, whom God hath given to them that obey him." Obey what? Obey the message concerning our Lord Jesus Christ. Peter had preached Him on the Day of Pentecost, and three thousand people had obeyed the message. They had believed the truth concerning this Jesus, that He is the Son of God, that He is God's own way of salvation, that God sent Him to the cross, that God put all our sins on Him and punished them in Him. Do you believe that? That is obedience to the Gospel.

And then do you believe that though Jesus of Nazareth was buried, He rose again in the body on the third day? That is the proof that He is God and not only man. He ascended into heaven; He is seated at the right hand of God and will come again to judge all His enemies and to set up His kingdom of glory and of grace. Do you believe that? That is what God commands us to do.

But to be more particular, God commands you to believe that in His Son and in Him alone is salvation. He commands you to believe what is called the doctrine of justification by faith only, which means that those who obey the Gospel believe that here and now, without any delay whatsoever, they can become Christians.

"But surely," says someone, "I can't become a Christian in a moment. I must go out and live a better life. I must start reading my Bible. I must start to pray. I must do this, that, and the other."

No, no, my friend; if you say that, you have not obeyed the Gospel because it means that you regard Jesus as just a teacher who tells you how to save yourself. And that is a contradiction of the Gospel. The Gospel states that it is what He has done that saves: His death upon the cross, His rising again in the resurrection and presenting Himself on our behalf. You must really believe that "though your sins be as scarlet, they shall be as white as snow" (Isa. 1:18). You must say from the very heart:

> *Just as I am, without one plea*
> *But that thy blood was shed for me,*
> *And that thou bid'st me come to thee,*
> *O Lamb of God, I come, I come.*
>
> *Just as I am, poor, wretched, blind;*
> *Sight, healing, riches of the mind,*
> *Yea, all I need, in thee to find,*
> *O Lamb of God, I come, I come.*
>
> Charlotte Elliott

To believe the Gospel means that you stop all self-justification, every reliance upon your good deeds, your own efforts. You see that God justifies not the godly, but the ungodly. As Christ put it, "They that be whole need not a physician, but they that are sick. . . . I am not come to call the righteous, but sinners to repentance" (Matt. 9:12-13). If you do not come as you are, you do not obey the Gospel.

You do not impress God at all if you say, "I see now that I have been forgetting You and ignoring You. I have been breaking Your commandments; so I have decided, I am determined, to live a better life from now on. I am going to live in obedience to Your commandments." If you say that to God, He will tell you that you are now disobeying Him more than you have ever done in the whole of your life.

Why is that? It is because He has told you that He has raised up His Son Jesus "to be a Prince and a Saviour, for to give repentance to Israel, and forgiveness of sins." He has told you that He has done what you cannot possibly do for yourself, and if you do not accept what He has done, then you are disobeying Him. You must say, "I don't understand, but I believe, and I am coming to You in obedience to Your commands." You must cast yourself utterly and entirely upon the Word of God. That is obedience to the Gospel. That is what makes you a Christian.

But, of course, you must immediately give proof that you have really given obedience to the Gospel. You must give proof that this is not merely some trick you are playing, or trying to play, on God.

How? You show you have turned to God with all your heart by turning your back upon the idols that you have been worshiping and by turning with all your might away from the world and the flesh and the devil. Your desire now is to please God, to show your gratitude to the God who has so loved you that He has done this amazing thing and raised up His child Jesus and made Him to be a Prince and a Savior.

You are no longer ashamed of Christ. You are no longer afraid of being laughed at in the office or factory or at school or college. No, no; you glory in this Christ. You confess Him with your mouth and in your life. This is obedience. If God has done this for us, then surely we can do nothing else.

Obedience means that you act upon what you believe, and you are now molded by this teaching. So you become a member of the visible body of Christ, the Christian church. You take your stand with those who say, "The world is mad and going to hell, but I belong to the redeemed." Like those people who believed on the Day of Pentecost, you are "added to the church." And like them, if necessary, you submit to baptism, which is but a way of publicly acknowledging and confessing your sins and publicly taking to yourself God's statement that you are forgiven in Christ and are raised as a new person, to new life.

And your greatest desire now is to know more about these things: "They continued steadfastly in the apostles' doctrine and fellowship, and in breaking of bread, and in prayers. . . . And they, continuing daily with one accord in the temple, and breaking bread from house to house, did eat their meat with gladness and singleness of heart, praising God, and having favour with all the people" (Acts 2:42, 46-47). You now desire above all else to live to the glory of God and His dear Son, our blessed Lord and Savior.

The apostle John says, "He that believeth on the Son of God hath the witness in himself: he that believeth not God hath made him a liar; because he believeth not the record that God gave of his Son" (1 John 5:10). Do you realize what it means not to believe this Gospel? Do you realize what you are doing if you have not obeyed it? I would not dare to say a thing like this, but John, the inspired apostle, says it: You are saying that God is a liar. Not only that, you are turning your back upon God in His most glorious manifestation of love: "God so loved the world, that he gave his only begotten Son, that whosoever believeth in him should not perish, but have everlasting life" (John 3:16). Does that mean nothing to you? Have you not so seen this that you have to say, "Surely nothing else matters. That is everything to me. Henceforth this is the only thing about which I am concerned"?

So I end by asking once more: Have you obeyed this Gospel? You have heard it many times, but has it led to anything? Have you conformed to the mold of the Gospel? God is holding this Gospel before you, and He commands you to believe.

12

THE NATURE OF UNBELIEF

When they heard that, they were cut to the heart, and took counsel to slay them. Then stood there up one in the council, a Pharisee, named Gamaliel, a doctor of the law, had in reputation among all the people, and commanded to put the apostles forth a little space; and said unto them, Ye men of Israel, take heed to yourselves what ye intend to do as touching these men. For before these days rose up Theudas, boasting himself to be somebody; to whom a number of men, about four hundred, joined themselves: who was slain; and all, as many as obeyed him, were scattered, and brought to nought. After this man rose up Judas of Galilee in the days of the taxing, and drew away much people after him: he also perished; and all, even as many as obeyed him, were dispersed. And now I say unto you, Refrain from these men, and let them alone: for if this counsel or this work be of men, it will come to nought: but if it be of God, ye cannot overthrow it; lest haply ye be found even to fight against God. And to him they agreed: and when they had called the apostles, and beaten them, they commanded that they should not speak in the name of Jesus, and let them go. And they departed from the presence of the council, rejoicing that they were counted worthy to suffer shame for his name. And daily in the temple, and in every house, they ceased not to teach and preach Jesus Christ.

—Acts 5:33-42

Peter has just come to the end of his defense to the Sanhedrin, and as we have studied his words, we have seen that the Gospel always calls for obedience, surrender, and total allegiance. But now, as we continue with the story in Acts 5, we read, "When they [the Sanhedrin] heard that, they were cut to the heart, and took counsel to slay them." But then Gamaliel, one of their own company, a Pharisee, stood up and reasoned with them and persuaded them not to kill the apostles. So we are told, "And to him they agreed: and when they had called the apostles, and beaten them, they commanded that they should not speak in the name of Jesus, and let them go."

The story ends with a wonderful description of the apostles, threatened with death at one moment and only set free for the time being, going on their way "rejoicing that they were counted worthy to suffer shame for his name." And we read that they continued to preach and teach in the name of Jesus Christ.

So we are looking at the reaction of this great Council to the answer given by the apostles. They had put their case, they had put it reasonably and briefly, but the Council members were "cut to the heart, and took counsel to slay them." We have seen that it is impossible for anybody to listen to this Gospel without responding to it. And we have also seen that we respond either by submitting to it and obeying it or by opposing it; and it is always amazing to me that in the New Testament we are given an account of both of these responses.

We are shown here very plainly and clearly that the Gospel always produces a result. The New Testament gives us a very honest picture of the church and of the reactions to her preaching. We are not presented with a picture of universal success. Quite the reverse! This is proof to me that it is a divinely inspired account, not a worked-up version of events. Of course, we always try to produce a good balance sheet. We always make out that we have good results. But the New Testament tells us the bad results as well as the good. Nothing is concealed. It is the truth of God.

But Acts is more than an honest account of historical events. Why are we given a record such as this one in Acts 5—and it is only one of many? To me, there is only one answer. It is in order that we may see some of the great fallacies that afflict the human mind with respect to this Gospel. I believe that God, in His infinite mercy and kindness, has given us accounts of the reactions of various people to the Gospel in order that we might learn valuable lessons from them.

Now we are all aware, are we not, that it is always much easier to learn a lesson when we see it through the experience of somebody else. We are always on the defensive. We do not like to be addressed too directly. You remember the old story of how Nathan the prophet went to David? David had committed a terrible sin, but he was quite happy about it. He seemed to have gotten away with it. But then God sent His servant Nathan to David, and Nathan, very wisely, did not tackle David directly—he applied the strategy of the indirect approach. Nathan told David a story about a very grave injustice, and David, filled with a sense of righteous indignation, said, "The man that hath done this thing shall surely die." Then Nathan looked at him and said, "Thou art the man" (2 Sam. 12:1-7).

We are all remarkably like David. We are on very good terms with ourselves; we are experts at excusing ourselves. God grant, therefore, that we may see ourselves, some of us, as we look at the case of the Sanhedrin. Here we see a clear depiction of unbelief in one of its particular forms. It is not the only one, but it is one. Here is unbelief blatant and violent, determining to kill these apostles and to put an end to this teaching.

The verses we are now looking at are important for many reasons. One is that through an incident like this we are enabled to understand the world as it is today. Why all the trouble and the anguish and the pain, all the misery, all the failure, especially in view of the fact that there is a Gospel that can put it right? Why does the world reject this message? That is the great question, and by showing us the depths of human sin, this incident helps us come to an answer.

The tragedy of all tragedies in the modern world is that however much we may be aware of our problems, we are still not aware of their depth and of their real nature. While people still go on thinking that politics and education and culture can solve the problems of the human race, there is no hope whatsoever. That is the tragedy, especially, of this twentieth century. We have believed that we have the knowledge to put things right. But look at our world! It is deteriorating rapidly, openly, before our eyes. When will we realize the nature of the problem? When will we realize that the real problem is the depths of sin in the human heart?

So let us look at the members of the great Sanhedrin. Do not forget that they were most important people. They were certainly the most important people in Jerusalem. We have seen the description of them at the beginning of chapter 4. The Sanhedrin consisted of "rulers, and elders, and scribes, and Annas the high priest, and Caiaphas, and John, and Alexander, and as many as were of the kindred of the high priest" (vv. 5-6). They were the leading people, the religious and political leaders, the great thinkers of the age. And these were the people who rejected the Gospel.

As we look at the reaction of the Sanhedrin, as we listen to what they said and what they proposed to do, we shall be given an insight into the real nature of men and women, unregenerate and without God, and it is enforced for us by the advice that was given to the Sanhedrin by Gamaliel, who was one of their company.

I have sought to extract the principles out of this incident—they are here quite plainly—and the first is this: Unbelief is not new. Now I start with that because the popular assumption today is that rejection of the Gospel is something that is new to the twentieth century. You know the way in which it is commonly put. People say, "You don't believe that, surely? Everybody knows by now that the biblical stories are only myths." And they think that the average person today who does not believe would have been a believer if he had lived a hundred years ago. The popular idea is that in the past people were Christians because they did not know any better, because they lived in times when everybody believed in the supernatural and the miraculous, but things are different today.

Now I must not waste your time. Even if we had nothing else, this one story would be more than enough to show that such a view stems from nothing but ignorance and self-deceit. Here, at the very beginning of the church, the Gospel was rejected in exactly the same way as it is being rejected today. Go back nineteen hundred years and more, and here is the very attitude that people are boasting of as the hallmark of modernity. Of course men and women do not believe the Gospel. But there is nothing new about that. It is as old as Christianity itself.

Today's unbelief is often explained in this way: The Gospel must be rejected because of twentieth-century knowledge. Oh, what pride that shows! People say, "In the light of modern science, you cannot possibly go on believing all that." Now I must keep on opposing this view because it is put forward so frequently. Indeed, the value of one soul is such that I will go on repeating my condemnation as long as there is one person left who goes on believing such nonsense. People believe that they are rejecting the Gospel because of the splitting of the atom! They think somehow that has made belief in the Gospel impossible. But this one incident in Acts is enough to show you the complete fallacy of that idea. I say again, here were people who rejected the Gospel in exactly the same way as it is rejected today.

I can easily prove in almost endless ways that modern knowledge has nothing whatsoever to do with the refusal to believe. I am not here to say a word against modern knowledge. Anyone who does is a fool. It is wonderful, I agree with you. Split the atom! Conquer the force of gravity! It is amazing. I am with you 100 percent. But all I am asking you is this: What has that to do with human beings as human beings? What has that to do with morality? Look at the horrible cases reported in the newspapers. They have been committed after scientists split the atom. Is it not about time we began to think clearly? We are concerned with men and women and God and life and living and purity and cleanliness and chastity and honesty. These are not in any way affected by all your modern knowledge. Modern knowledge casts no light upon death, nor upon eternity. We are in exactly the same position as these people were in the first century. So let us get rid of false ideas about modern knowledge.

We must start thinking. We are all the creatures of prejudice. We repeat slogans and clichés. We say, "Nobody any longer believes all that." But stop and examine that statement. We should drop that "any longer," because time does not come into this at all. The problem of unbelief is the same today as it was in the first century, and as it was even before that. Unbelief has been a universal problem ever since the Fall.

Unbelief is not the consequence of modern knowledge, but neither is it based upon reason, intelligence, or understanding. That it is, is the second popular modern fallacy, is it not? People today think they are not religious because of their ability to reason, because of their intelligence. "All right," someone says, "I'll accept your point about scientific knowledge, but I maintain that any thinking person must see through the claims of religion."

It is said that religion is just sob stuff, emotionalism, the opium of the people. Those are the terms that have been used, and they have been swallowed and repeated *ad nauseam*. It is claimed that people who are Christians have committed intellectual suicide and allowed themselves to go soft in the head. Unbelievers, on the other hand, are controlled by their brains. There's no emotion, just understanding and thought! So let us examine the members of the Sanhedrin in the light of that contention.

Now I think I shall be able to prove to you without much difficulty that unbelief, far from being based on the intellect, is nothing but sheer irrationality, that it is utterly unreasonable, with nothing to be said in its defense. Now that is a strong statement, but I can substantiate it. Look at the position here. There are the members of the Sanhedrin; here are these apostles. And we are told that when the members of the Sanhedrin heard Peter's message, they were "cut to the heart, and took counsel to slay them." They wanted to kill the apostles.

But wait a minute! Let us ask a few questions. Why did the Sanhedrin want to kill the apostles? What had they done? What crime had they committed? What law had they broken? What evidence could be produced against them? Now the answer is that there was no evidence. They were innocent men. They had not broken any law, and nothing at all could be said against them. The apostles were getting the same treatment that our Lord had received before them. He had told them that it would happen. He understood human nature. He knew it all. His enemies had done their utmost to bring a charge against Him, and they had completely failed. And yet they had killed Him. Was all this reasonable? Was this a calm, dispassionate, logical response to the situation? You cannot say that it was, can you? Let us examine ourselves. Ask yourself as I make these points: Why am I rejecting the Gospel? Am I like the members of the Sanhedrin?

Then look at another aspect of this first-century trial. Not only was there no charge against the apostles and no justification for imprisoning and beating them or for plotting their death, but look at their message. They said, "The God of our fathers raised up Jesus, whom ye slew and hanged on a tree. Him hath God exalted with his right hand to be a Prince and a Saviour, for to give repentance to Israel, and forgiveness of sins." The apostles were telling men and women that they could be reconciled to God, have their past sins blotted out, have a new start in life, new power, new desires, new hope. They told them that God would be their Father and that they would receive all they stood in need of. And yet the effect of the message upon these people was to make them take counsel together to slay the apostles.

Have you ever thought of it like that? Why do people today reject this Gospel? What is wrong with it? It is treated with sarcasm, with scorn, with derision; people hate it and insult it. But why? What is there that can be said against the gospel message? Let me repeat what I have often said: If only everybody in the world today were living according to the Ten Commandments, our world would most certainly not be as it is. If only everybody on earth today were living according to the Sermon on the Mount, we would not have the industrial, the moral, and the social problems that we are now facing. There would be no wars anywhere. If only everybody lived like this! If only each person lived as a child of God, with a new nature and with the Holy Spirit as the gift of God, the world would be revolutionized. So what is the reason for rejecting the Gospel? That is the sort of question that modern men and women do not face.

Well, now I am asking you to apply your reason. Where does it lead you? Does it really help you live? Does it help you understand the problems of life? Does it help you live as a decent individual? What is the objection to this Gospel that offers you all this and that, demonstrably, is a true message because these very men were witnesses to it? This is not reason. This is unreason. It is irrationality.

But let us continue. The apostles had been arrested. But what had they done? What they had actually done was heal a man who had been born lame. Everybody knew this poor fellow. He was forty years old. For years and years he had been carried to the Beautiful Gate of the temple, and the members of the Sanhedrin had passed him when they went into the temple to offer their prayers. And now there he was, standing solidly on his feet before them, praising God, able to walk and leap. Concrete evidence! These apostles had done that. And yet the Sanhedrin wanted to kill them. Was this reasonable?

Similarly, what has been the influence and the effect of the Christian church and the Christian Gospel throughout the centuries? It is now agreed by everybody that when the Goths and the Vandals sacked Rome, it was the Christian church that preserved whatever was left, even of civilization itself. In the so-called "Dark Ages," the only light came from the church. And again, you cannot understand the history of modern Europe apart from the Protestant Reformation.

There has been no greater civilizing force in the history of the human race than this Gospel preached by the Christian church. When did the Poor Law commence? Poor relief was started by the Christian church centuries before the politicians ever thought of it, and the same is true of education and health care. The oldest hospital in London, St Bartholomew's Hospital, was founded by a monk over eight hundred years ago. All the greatest and most beneficent institutions have come through the medium of Christians. That is the Christian religion.

Yet these Christians are the people whom the world wants to destroy, and modern men and women think they are so clever in dismissing them with derision. Is this reason? We are being told that we no longer need God and the supernatural, that everything can be put right by acts of Parliament. My dear friends, the whole trouble is that people no longer think. They are repeating the clichés of the comedians and the clever newspaper columnists—the sneers, innuendoes, and insinuations. Think for yourself, acquaint yourself with the facts, and I think you will soon find that unbelief is not based on reason.

And then take the final manifestation of the unreason of the Sanhedrin. They wanted to kill the apostles at once, but Gamaliel advised them to be careful, and apparently he persuaded them. They decided they would not put the apostles to death. Yet even then they only half-listened to him. They did not kill them, but they beat them—and they had no more reason for beating them than they had for killing them. But this, again, is a manifestation of utter irrationality.

But let us go on to the next principle. If unbelief is not the consequence of modern knowledge and is not linked to intellectual ability, what is the cause? The answer, obviously and simply, is that it is always a matter of the heart, of feeling. People always reject the Gospel because of morality. The very words tell us that. We read, "When they heard that, they were cut to the heart." In the Greek, "cut to the heart" is a very powerful term. It means they were cut asunder; their hearts, as it were, were broken in two. There was such sharp vexation within them that it amounted to an inward rage. They were bursting, almost in a literal sense, in their desire to kill the apostles. Now this is not reason—it is rage. It is a raving mania and nothing else.

How different the members of the Sanhedrin were from the people described in the second chapter of Acts. There I see Peter preaching to a crowd, and I read, "Now when they heard this, they were pricked in their heart, and said unto Peter and to the rest of the apostles, Men and brethren, what shall we do?" (v. 37). There is a difference between being pricked in the heart and being torn asunder. It is good to be pricked in the heart. That means that you are disturbed and convicted; it means that you are made to see the truth, and it leads you to repentance. But the other is passionate, insensitive, vituperating rage that puts the mind to one side. Now this was a court, a court that tried people, but there was no reason there.

Now I am saying all this not because we are interested in this old Sanhedrin of so long ago, but because, as I have said, it is such a perfect representation of the case of modern men and women. Why were the members of the Sanhedrin so furious? Why were they filled with such a rage against these apostles that they wanted to kill them? First, it was partly a matter of conscience. The religious leaders were clearly troubled about the way in which they had crucified the Lord Jesus Christ. That is why they said, "Behold, ye have filled Jerusalem with your doctrine, and intend to bring this man's blood upon us" (Acts 5:28). They knew that they had crucified Him. They had rejected Him. They had said, "Yes, away with Him!" They had pleaded with Pilate to put an end to Him. Pilate had tried to set Him free, but they had insisted upon His being crucified (John 19:15), as they were reminded by the apostles: "The God of our fathers raised up Jesus, whom ye slew and hanged on a tree." And you cannot do a thing like that and live at ease. Their consciences were condemning them, and a troubled conscience always tends to infuriate us. They were annoyed. This thing was there, and they wanted to get rid of it.

Oh, men and women fight against the Gospel and pretend the reasons are intellectual. But the real reasons, I repeat, are generally in the realm of the conscience. We attempt to cover up our misdeeds. There is something in us that tells us that this message is absolutely right, but we do not want to listen to it. We prefer the darkness. As our Lord put it, "This is the condemnation, that light is come into the world, and men loved darkness rather than light, because their deeds were evil" (John 3:19). So we fight against our conscience. We kick against the pricks, as Saul of Tarsus did later on (Acts 9:5). Is that not the whole trouble at this present hour?

The difficulty about the Gospel is that it inculcates a life of obedience to God's laws, and by nature men and women do not like those laws. They prefer to be promiscuous rather than to be faithful. They want premarital sexual experiences when the Gospel says, "No" and the Ten Commandments say, "Thou shalt not."

"But," people say, "I want." That is why they hate the Gospel. It is not reason, as I have shown you. This Gospel disturbs them, and their consciences attest the disturbance. So they fight against it. This is a miserable state to be in. It drives them to a fury.

Then there is another factor. The Sanhedrin thought of the apostles as "unlearned and ignorant men." Yet they could see them addressing the crowds with great success. And this infuriated them. They thought, *Who are these men? What do they know? They've had no teaching; they've had no learning. We are the teachers—we are the members of the Sanhedrin.* And so the element of pride came in. And this is still part of the explanation of unbelief. There is something in men and women that makes them say that a Gospel that was true nearly two thousand years ago cannot possibly be adequate for the twentieth century. This, again, is another of those prejudices by which we are all governed by nature. We say that because we are in the twentieth century we are of necessity in an advantageous position, and it is an insult to be offered a Gospel that was acceptable to people in the first century.

Do we not all know something about that sort of pride? How can the same Gospel be as adequate for a great philosopher as it is for a man who has never read a book in his life? It seems wrong to us, does it not? Who are these men who are setting themselves up as teachers? How can ordinary Christians of past centuries teach us in the twentieth century? The thing is monstrous! But this response is not rational. What does it matter how old the teaching is? It is not the age of the teaching that matters, but its character and quality. But men and women governed by prejudice do not stop to think of that. In their pride they say, "Surely you are not asking me, with my brains and knowledge and understanding, to believe what you say can save the most ignorant person in any part of the world at this moment?"

The Gospel humbles us. It hurts our pride. And then, when we find that we cannot understand it, the whole situation becomes aggravated, and we find it quite impossible. What is this Gospel? we say. How could these ignorant men have spoken as they did? How could they have worked those miracles? We don't understand it! We think we understand something about the atom and about many other scientific marvels, but here is something we cannot understand. And so we insist that the supernatural is nonsense. We cannot follow it, and so we dismiss it. I say again that is not reason but sheer passion.

But then, I think, we come to the greatest source of trouble, and that is that this Gospel always tells us the truth about ourselves—and nothing else does that. The Gospel is a message that tells us that we are all sinners and that our brains and knowledge make not the slightest difference. The great geniuses have been as great in their moral failure as anybody else. Drunkenness is not confined to the ignorant. There are men of the greatest culture who are alcoholics. Every other message praises our knowledge, our brains, our understanding. Here is the only message that comes to us with honesty and says, "You are a sinner like everybody else." It tells us, "All have sinned, and come short of the glory of God" (Rom. 3:23). "There is none righteous, no, not one" (Rom. 3:10). Every man and woman is a failure. Everyone is blind and "dead in trespasses and sins" (Eph. 2:1).

But the Gospel goes further and tells us that it is impossible for us to deliver ourselves out of this condition. And this again, of course, is a terrible insult to self-confident, modern men and women. Is there anything that we cannot do? Look at what we are doing. Look at the knowledge we now have. Surely by the application of the principles of psychology, sociology, and philosophy we can put ourselves and our world right? But the Gospel starts by telling us that we cannot. We are as helpless in the twentieth century as people have always been. We cannot rehabilitate ourselves in a moral and spiritual sense.

So the Gospel finishes by telling us that we are all lost and helpless and hopeless, quite unable to save ourselves. Prophets could not save us. All the great thinkers and teachers have failed to save us. The world is so rotten that God had to send His only Son out of heaven in order to save us. The world hated Him, as He said it would. "If the world hate you," He told His disciples, "ye know that it hated me before it hated you" (John 15:18). Why was He hated? It was because the very presence of the Son of God in this world is a condemnation of the world. It is a proclamation that men and women cannot save themselves.

And then when the Gospel goes on to tell us that Christ even had to die before we could be saved and delivered, it becomes still more objectionable and offensive. The offense of the cross! "The preaching of the cross is to them that perish foolishness . . . unto the Jews a stumblingblock, and unto the Greeks foolishness" (1 Cor. 1:18, 23). Christ crucified—this was the cause of the hatred of the Sanhedrin, and it is still the same today.

If Jesus Christ had been only a man, nobody would hate Him. If He had been only a great teacher or a moral example, nobody would object to Him. But He is the Son of God. Why was it necessary for Him to come? Why did He die? Here is the cause of the problem. He says you cannot be improved—you must be made again: "Ye must be born again" (John 3:7). You must be regenerated from the very foundation. You need a new nature and a new start. So we say, "It's infuriating. We can't listen to it. Away with these people—whether Christ Himself or His followers. They must be stopped. Get rid of them! Put them to death!" Now that is the reason why the Sanhedrin rejected the Gospel, and that is why men and women are still rejecting it.

I ask you again: Why do you object to this Gospel? Consider it quietly and rationally. What is wrong with it? Is it not as I have been suggesting? Do you not feel that a Gospel that could save someone in the first century is an insult to you in the twentieth? Do you not feel it is insulting to be told that you are so rotten in your inner nature that nothing can save you but a new nature? Do you not maintain that it is insulting to be told that you are caught so helplessly in the grip of sin and evil that it takes the Son of God to come from heaven and to die on the cross and rise again in order to deliver you? Is that not it? The Gospel touches your pride.

Then let me come to the last principle that is so evident here. Unbelief is always against God. The members of the Sanhedrin were not really against the apostles—they were against God. Gamaliel began to feel this, and that is why he said, "Refrain from these men, and let them alone: for if this counsel or this work be of men, it will come to nought: but if it be of God, ye cannot overthrow it; lest haply ye be found even to fight against God."

The most appalling and terrible aspect of unbelief is that it is based upon a hatred of God. There are many statements to that effect in the New Testament. "The carnal [natural] mind is enmity against God: for it is not subject to the law of God, neither indeed can be" (Rom. 8:7). "But the natural man receiveth not the things of the Spirit of God: for they are foolishness unto him: neither can he know them, because they are spiritually discerned" (1 Cor. 2:14). What a terrible thing unbelief is!

As I pointed out at the very beginning, humanity is in a state of rebellion against God. "This is the condemnation, that light is come into the world"—in Christ—"and men loved darkness rather than light, because their deeds were evil" (John 3:19). Those are the depths of unbelief. The world rejected the Son of God because it hates God. It has not only rebelled against Him—it is filled with a spirit of malice and of antagonism toward Him, the holy God! Why do people hate the Ten Commandments? Why do they make fun of what they call the "narrowness of the Gospel"? This "narrowness" makes men and women keep their marriage vows, remain clean and pure, refrain from theft and robbery and violence and malice and hatred and spite—yet they hate it. What a terrible condition to be in!

But the terrible thing, as Gamaliel pointed out, is that unbelief leads men and women to fight God. Gamaliel said, "Be careful what you are doing, for you may find yourself fighting against God. If this is of God, you cannot stop it."

To reject the Gospel is not to fight me, it is not to fight the Christian church—it is ultimately to fight God. It is God who raised up His "holy child Jesus" (Acts 4:27). It is God who sent His Son into the world. And in that hatred we see the final folly of unbelief. Can you not see the blindness of this Sanhedrin and its members? Why did they not face the facts? They had great brains—why did they not apply them? Why did they not say to themselves, "We know that these men are ignorant and unlearned; so how, then, are they able to act like this?" But they were so filled with passion and rage that they did not ask such intelligent questions. If they had, they would have seen that there was only one answer: This Jesus, whom the Sanhedrin had slain, had risen and ascended into heaven and was directing the apostles. He had sent the Spirit, and His power was at work through the apostles. If only the Sanhedrin had reasoned like that, they would very soon have seen that they were not fighting men but were fighting against God.

If the Gospel had been only of men, it would have ceased long ago, as Gamaliel argued so rightly. But it is still going on. It is still "the power of God unto salvation" (Rom. 1:16). And that is the only explanation for the history of the church throughout the centuries. So I repeat that in rejecting the Gospel, you are fighting against the God who can give perfect soundness to a man who had been born lame, a God who can conquer death and the grave. You are up against the almighty power of God.

Oh, the madness and folly of the Sanhedrin. In trying to silence His witnesses, they were resisting God. They were fighting the Judge of the universe. This was sheer irrationality. This was the blindness of sin. This was man blinded to the glories of the God of heaven by the god of this world. Again I put this before us, not merely that we might entertain ourselves in looking back at an old story of the first century, but because we are still in the same world; we still have the same problems; we are still facing the same God. And there is still only one way of salvation. It is in "Jesus Christ and him crucified." So learn the lesson from the members of the Sanhedrin, see the real nature of unbelief, and turn from it. Cry out to God for mercy, and you will find that you will receive it.

13

GAMALIEL

Then stood there up one in the council, a Pharisee, named Gamaliel, a doctor of the law, had in reputation among all the people, and commanded to put the apostles forth a little space.

—Acts 5:34

I now want to consider with you the case of Gamaliel, who was a member of that great council at Jerusalem called the Sanhedrin. It is very important that, in considering Gamaliel, we should remember all that has gone before; otherwise we shall be in no position to assess him or what he said and proposed.

The apostles were on trial before the Sanhedrin because they had refused to stop preaching. Peter had begun and ended his defense with the need for obedience: "We ought to obey God rather than men. . . . We are his witness of these things; and so is also the Holy Ghost, whom God hath given to them that obey him." We have considered the reaction of the majority of the Sanhedrin to Peter's words: "When they heard that, they were cut to the heart, and took counsel to slay them." And in the violence of their unbelief, they would have done that, had it not been for the advice given to them by Gamaliel.

Again we must emphasize the importance of reading the whole of the Scriptures and of paying attention to everything that they say. The Bible is not only an exposition of the truth of God; it has a great deal to tell us about why people do not accept that truth. At times the Scriptures explicitly analyze unbelief, making it quite plain and clear. We read, for example, "The carnal mind is enmity against God" (Rom. 8:7). Now that is didactic teaching.

But at other times the Bible shows us unbelief by telling a story or by reporting an event in history. Now we are all helped by a picture. That is why we must always read the whole of the Bible. The history in the Bible is as important as the teaching, for there is teaching in the history, and sometimes, when we see the teaching being worked out in a person's life, it has greater impact on us than the more didactic passages.

The importance of an illustration is demonstrated very clearly in the passage we are now studying. We are sometimes tempted to think that unbelief only has one form and that all people who reject the Gospel do so in the same way. But that is not true. The devil is much too clever and subtle for that. No; he varies his methods, so much so that sometimes we do not even recognize what he is doing and fool ourselves. So it is important that we should look at all the biblical examples of unbelief. Then we shall see its real character and the various forms and guises in which it tends to appear.

So having seen an unmistakable picture of bitter hatred and malice and fury in the majority of the members of the Sanhedrin, we are now going to look at Gamaliel. He seems to be entirely different, does he not? Indeed, I have no doubt but that there are many people who think that Gamaliel was a very fine man. Many today would undoubtedly regard him as a Christian on the grounds that he showed a wonderful Christian spirit. But in this man, as I hope to show you, we see the same spirit of unbelief, though in a much more subtle form. So we should thank God for these records because unbelief in this guise is much more difficult to recognize.

We are living in an age that likes to think of itself, and to boast of itself, as "the age of tolerance," "the age of enlightenment." Indeed, this is the great problem of our age. It is an age in which we are almost ready to say that everybody is a Christian, and especially every reasonable person. To be fair-minded is, it is said, the very essence of Christianity, and the hallmark of Christianity is a tolerant spirit. That is why so many people say of those who know what they believe and have a very definite creed derived from the Scriptures that they are not Christians because they are intolerant. And so the case of Gamaliel is, I feel, particularly important at the present time.

Let us then look at this man; let us learn some lessons from him. The times are too desperate, the position is too terrible, for us to be indulging merely in some old historical inquiry, interesting though that may be. I know people like that sort of thing. That is what you go to see at the cinema, is it not, and watch on the television. People are moved and thrilled by a dramatic story or a character taken from history. But it is not real; it is only playing, and it comes to nothing. It begins, it ends, the next program comes, and you forget the previous one. God knows, I do not have the energy to indulge in something like that; the times are too serious.

I am calling your attention to Gamaliel because in him we see a picture of unbelief, and it is a terrible warning. We are dealing here with something that determines not only our condition in this world, but after death and for all eternity. Unbelief is the most urgent and the most vital subject in the world.

So what do we find here? Well, let us look first at the good things in Gamaliel, because there were good things, and we are told some of them by the record itself. "Then there stood up one in the council, a Pharisee, named Gamaliel, a doctor of the law, had in reputation among all the people." In other words, we are dealing here with a great man—there is no question about that. The world has its great men. In addition, he was a very learned man—he was "a doctor of the law." He had taught that outstanding genius who became the apostle Paul. Paul writes of himself, "[I was] brought up in this city at the feet of Gamaliel" (Acts 22:3).

Gamaliel was one of the great teachers among the Jews, a man who was highly respected and, as we are told, "had in reputation among all the people." He was also highly respected in the Sanhedrin itself, for it is clear that the council members were ready to listen to him.

Not only that, but we also notice, as we watch what he does, that Gamaliel was a man with a calm spirit; he was a cool and rational man. The other members of the Sanhedrin were "cut to the heart," which, as I explained, indicates violence. Their hearts burst, as it were, in their fury and passion. But Gamaliel was a controlled man who could keep his head in the midst of excitement, and that is a noble characteristic, a fine trait. The crowd is always ready to become passionate, and it does great harm in its violence. A man who is calm and self-possessed and collected is a valuable man in society.

But let us go further. It is quite clear that this man held some most excellent views. He was against violence. He disliked passion and hatred; he did not like people to be uncontrolled, gripped and governed by some violent emotion. Not only that, he had a legal, balanced mind, and he believed in justice and fair play. Gamaliel, at any rate, could see that the apostles had done nothing deserving of death. His fellow members of the Sanhedrin wanted to kill them, but Gamaliel knew perfectly well that there were no legal grounds for the death penalty.

Now these are all excellent virtues. If only there were more people with these qualities, the world would be a better place, would it not? Many troubles are caused by men and women who, controlled by their passions, act without stopping to think. That is the cause of wars. As James says, "From whence come wars and fightings among you? come they not hence, even of your lusts that war in your members?" (Jas. 4:1).

But here was a man who, believing in fair play and justice, could not allow this kind of violent action to be taken. So he counseled a better way. Why did he do this? Well, there is no doubt at all but that Gamaliel did see something right in these apostles. He made that perfectly clear when he said, "And now I say unto you, Refrain from these men, and let them alone: for if this counsel or this work be of men, it will come to nought: but if it be of God, ye cannot overthrow it; lest haply ye be found even to fight against God."

The other members of the Sanhedrin could not see anything good here at all. They thought that the whole thing must be stopped and the men killed. "No, no," said Gamaliel. "Be careful; there is something here that you have not quite seen." Gamaliel himself did not understand and could not explain the phenomenon confronting them, a phenomenon that consisted of the apostles themselves, their preaching, and particularly, as I have constantly pointed out, the glaring fact that before them all was the healed man. And Gamaliel, at any rate, had his eyes open to that. This made him cautious and careful: It may be of God.

The others, however, were so blinded by prejudice that they had even forgotten that lame man. They had dismissed him. They only saw what they wanted to see. "All seems yellow to the jaundiced eye" [Alexander Pope], and when you are filled with bitter hatred against something, you see no good in it at all and do not even see the facts that are staring you in the face.

Of course, Gamaliel was also aware of the facts concerning our Lord and Savior. He was a prominent man, living in Jerusalem, and he had heard all the reports about this Jesus of Nazareth, all that had happened during those three years. He did not believe in Him, but he knew about His death and had heard accounts of the resurrection. He had heard of the phenomenon on the Day of Pentecost and of the miracles worked by the apostles. Consequently, he felt that there was something here that could not be dismissed out of hand.

Now that is good. There are so many people today who would reject the whole of Christianity, even though they know nothing at all about it. Stop them sometimes and ask. The next time someone comes to you and says, "There's nothing in it, a lot of rubbish, all played out," ask, "Well now, would you tell me exactly what Christianity is?" And you will find your questioner has not the faintest idea and has never read the Bible and knows nothing of church history. Now that is unintelligent and irrational.

But Gamaliel was both intelligent and rational; so he advised caution.

And this, too, is a good characteristic. A man or woman who is ready to listen to the case for the Gospel and who is prepared to give it a chance is much better than someone who dismisses the whole thing and says, "I don't want to hear about such nonsense. Nobody today who knows anything about science can possibly believe it." All honor to Gamaliel! All honor to someone who is open-minded.

And more than that. Gamaliel was a man who obviously feared God. He believed in God and was afraid of fighting against Him. His caution was more than a desire for fair play and a readiness to listen and investigate. There was a kind of reverence here, and that is a wonderful thing. Would that there were more of this in our present world. The way people talk about God! If they but knew what they were saying, they would not use the name so casually. The Jews about this time, and before, never used the name Yahweh; they were afraid to do so. They were aware of the holiness, the sanctity, the greatness, the glory, the power, the majesty of God. And Gamaliel knew something about that fear.

Oh, the glib way that some of us have argued about religion in the past! God knows, I have done it myself, and nothing but His forgiveness could put me right with respect to it. Talking about God! Arguing! God ought to do this! Why does God do that? That is the way people behave, but not Gamaliel. He said, "Be careful. There's a possibility of fighting against God."

Now all this is good. People may be wrong or muddled, but as long as they have a spirit of reverence and an element of awe, as long as they are humble enough to say, "We're in a realm here where we do not quite know," that is always a sign of greatness. The more a man knows, the more humble he becomes. It is the first-year student who knows all about everything. He does not know so much in his final year when he is faced with his final examination. And those who have really studied the subject are much more cautious.

All these were excellent qualities. Because of them, Gamaliel pleaded that the apostles and what they stood for should be given a chance. May I ask a question before we go any further? Have you come as far as Gamaliel? Are you considering these things in order to dismiss and denounce them, or do you really want to listen and to learn? Is your mind open? Do you realize that we are dealing with something that not only involves you but involves the eternal God? Do you realize the seriousness of listening to this Gospel? Do you realize all that depends upon it? Do you realize these tremendous possibilities? Have you ever had a fear of fighting against God, or have you just been blasé and self-confident, talking about modern knowledge and "being up to date"? This is vital.

Oh, that I could stop at this point! In the light of the good and noble traits in Gamaliel, many say that he was a Christian. "Surely," they say, "that is just what we are longing to see—this tolerance, this open attitude, this readiness to find good in other people and in other points of view, this determination to stand up for them against the violent people who are always so ready to condemn. Surely that is the very spirit of Christianity." To people who think in this way, Gamaliel was the noblest kind of Christian.

Yet I want to try to show you from this very record that the truth about Gamaliel is that he was no more of a Christian than the other members of the Sanhedrin, that he was as much an unbeliever as any one of them, that he was as guilty of rejecting the Gospel as all the violent colleagues who sat with him on that bench. Is this possible? Let me put the evidence before you. I have no interest in condemning Gamaliel, God knows. I am here to learn from this man, and I see in him a terrible warning, especially, I repeat, for this lax, loose age that worships tolerance rather than truth.

What are the lessons we must learn? Well, we are shown here clearly— and this is very important—the difference between a good man and a spiritually minded man, the difference between being religious and being Christian. Gamaliel was a good man, he was a moral man, a just man, a religious man. But I want to show you that the real trouble with poor Gamaliel was that he was completely lacking in spiritual perception. He was nothing but a man who combined worldly wisdom at its best with a general belief in God.

Oh, how common this type is, especially in this present century! And these are the people who have done such harm in this generation. I remember reading a book once that put it very well. It was called *The Good Pagan's Failure*,[11] and this century has suffered more as the result of the teaching of "good pagans" than perhaps of anyone else. Because of their excellencies and their natural abilities, these people are the most convinced of all unbelievers, the most fervent of all the opponents of the Christian faith. Here is "the natural man," I suggest to you, at his very best; but I repeat that all he has is worldly wisdom coupled with an element of godliness.

Why do I come to such a conclusion about Gamaliel? First, in all he said he showed quite clearly that he had never seen the uniqueness of what these apostles were saying and doing. How do I know that? Well, his own argument gave him away. We are told that he said, "Ye men of Israel, take heed to yourselves what ye intend to do as touching these men." But why did he say that? Here are his reasons. He continued:

For [let me remind you] before these days rose up Theudas, boasting himself to be somebody; to whom a number of men, about four hundred, joined themselves: who was slain; and all, as many as obeyed him, were scattered, and brought to nought. After this man rose up Judas of Galilee in the days of the taxing, and drew away much people after him: he also perished; and all, even as many as obeyed him, were dispersed.

Do you see what Gamaliel was saying? "Don't get too excited," he said in effect. "Don't let your passions run away with you. These men have suddenly appeared on the scene. They are nobodies. We know nothing about them. They have no credentials. But, of course, they are attracting a crowd. So you are worrying about your jobs and your position and all the honor that you have, and you want to kill them. Don't be fools," he said. "We've seen this sort of thing before. Don't you remember the case of Theudas?"

Now there is some dispute as to who exactly Theudas was, but it seems quite clear that he had led a rebellion. He had some cause for complaint, and he was probably a good speaker; so he attracted a crowd and persuaded the people to join him in an insurrection against the authorities.

Then Gamaliel referred to a second man: "Judas of Galilee in the days of the taxing." The Jews, you remember, had been conquered by Rome, and Rome, as usual, had imposed taxes upon them. A party of patriots in Palestine had objected to paying these taxes, and Judas, who was obviously a natural-born leader, and probably an orator as well, had become their leader. "We have seen this kind of thing twice before," said Gamaliel in effect, "but don't you remember what happened? It all fizzled out."

But the significant thing to me is the comparison that Gamaliel used. He apparently saw no essential difference between this new phenomenon and those political insurrections that had happened some years previously. To him, the apostles were stirring up just another of these odd, sporadic disturbances, some form of rebellion, some popular movement. And thereby he betrayed his lack of spiritual perception.

Now here we see a most important principle. I suggest to you that the real failure of modern men and women is that they have never seen the uniqueness of Jesus Christ and the Gospel. Just like Gamaliel, they are betrayed by their words. You will hear them mouthing this failure from Christian pulpits; you will read it in their articles and books. They talk about "the great leaders of the centuries." They start with Moses perhaps and go on to Isaiah, Jeremiah, John the Baptist, Jesus, and Paul, taking in Plato, Socrates, and Aristotle on the way.

Some see Jesus as a political leader; others see Him as a social reformer or a religious teacher, someone with great insight. They put Him in the category of the world's great men, men who have led movements. They see Him only as a man among men, as someone who may or may not have been the greatest of the great leaders. And that was the very error of Gamaliel. He did not see the uniqueness of Christ.

And, of course, people today make exactly the same error about the Christian faith. They say, "You must not maintain that Christianity is the only religion that leads to God. If you condemn other faiths, you are proving that you are not a Christian, because that is to be intolerant, and the hallmark of the Christian faith is 'the spirit of tolerance.' We must have a congress of world faiths, world religions. Let us add together the insights of Islam and Confucianism and Buddhism and Christianity. They all have some truth and some error in them, and who are you to say that only Christianity is right?"

People like this do not reject the Christian faith violently; they display sweet reasonableness. "Very interesting," they say. "Of course, we want to hear what the Christian message is, what insight it has to offer. We must have Christians in our congress, but we must also have representatives of other faiths." And this is regarded as the very acme of the Christian spirit! That is the first error I detect in Gamaliel.

But let me put that still more strongly. The trouble with Gamaliel was that he never really faced the problem of the apostles, the problem of what they were and what they were doing. He looked at them in general only, as a movement that had suddenly appeared. Why did he not go beyond that and really look at them and try to examine them and explain them? If he had, he would not have spoken as he did.

Here Gamaliel was, confronted by men whom he and the others had agreed were nothing but "unlearned and ignorant men." They were fishermen, artisans, ordinary workmen; their clothing, everything about them, proved that. They were not cultured men; they had not been trained in the schools of the Pharisees. But Gamaliel never seemed to have examined this. He never said, "How do I explain these men? How can I possibly understand them? Listen to them speaking; look at the way they marshal their facts and put their arguments. What is it that enables ignorant men to do this?" He never faced that—their authority, their power, their ability, their miracles.

There was something amazing about the apostles, about their very appearance, about their faces. There was a brightness, a peace, and an assurance; there was a confidence. They had been told two or three times that if they went on behaving as they were doing, they would be put to death, but that did not frighten them. So what had happened to them? And why did Gamaliel not say, "How do we explain that event on the Day of Pentecost? What was it exactly? These men were speaking in other languages—so at least it has been reported to us. How did they do it? What caused it?"

Gamaliel merely said, "Ah well, another rising, another popular movement." In spite of his great wisdom and his judicial thinking, Gamaliel was as blind to spiritual reality as his more vociferous, violent colleagues.

Now I am elaborating this point for the good reason that modern men and women fail just as Gamaliel failed. There are many questions they should be asking. For example: How does one explain the origin of the Christian faith? How does one explain its influence in the world? How does one account for its persistence? The moment you face Christianity, you must answer these questions.

The apostles had said that they had not healed the lame man by their own power. They had said, "Who are we? Don't look at us, as if by our own power or godliness we had made this man walk." And, of course, they could not have done it. They were not magicians. And yet they had healed this man when nobody else had been able to do anything. So why did Gamaliel not face the facts? In his worldly wisdom he simply asked the others to leave the apostles alone for the time being. And in this way he demonstrated that he lacked spiritual perception.

I can demonstrate Gamaliel's spiritual blindness in a further way. With all his wisdom and all his knowledge, he had only one test to apply to such people, and it was not a spiritual test at all, but the test of worldly wisdom. It was the test of time and success. Listen to him: "And now I say unto you, refrain from these men, and let them alone: for if this counsel or this work be of men, it will come to nought"—you need not kill them; they will kill themselves; it will come to nothing—"But if it be of God, ye cannot overthrow it; lest haply ye be found to fight even against God."

Gamaliel had no test that he could apply immediately. It did not occur to him to think that all that had happened might, in and of itself, be evidence. He merely reasoned on the basis of past cases. That is typical of the legal mind, is it not? The lawyer quotes authorities, past events. So Gamaliel said, "Don't do anything to these men. Don't you remember the cases of Theudas and Judas? They came to nothing. People were excited then, as you are now, and some of the authorities wanted to do something immediately. No; leave it alone; time will soon prove it."

Time and success are tests that are commonly applied. In the past, many people were regarded as Christians simply because they went on these two principles. A hundred years ago Christianity was popular in Britain. This building we are in [Westminster Chapel, which Dr. Lloyd-Jones pastored] was built over a hundred years ago. They built it this size because the previous one, seating fifteen hundred, was too small! Spurgeon's Tabernacle was still bigger. London was crowded with great churches, and they were packed with people. Why? Because Christianity was successful; it was the thing to do, and people believed it, so they thought. It is my opinion that probably most were not believers at all. As we put it in our modern phrase, people were just climbing onto a bandwagon. And that was the mentality of Gamaliel. "If it is successful, then all right, we will be in with it; if it is not, it will come to nothing, and we have not committed ourselves."

Many are still like that. They will do "the thing to do." If there is a bit of excitement about religion, a campaign or something, they will be there, "making decisions for Christ." They do not understand, but they are always out for success. When, with time, something seems not to be successful, they are the first to leave. Like Gamaliel, they have no other tests, no spiritual tests, to apply.

But these are mere preliminaries. That is not really the explanation of Gamaliel. His real trouble was that, in all that was happening, he felt no personal challenge, and that is the most devastating thing you can ever say about a man like this. Cannot you see him looking at it all objectively? It was just another problem that had arisen for the Sanhedrin to deal with. Gamaliel had to pay attention to this new movement because, after all, he was a member of the Sanhedrin and an able man and a doctor of the law, and he had to have some sort of an opinion.

But notice, his opinion was entirely objective. He sat with what he regarded as his calm, judicial detachment, evaluating a movement, these transformed men, this healed man. The story was about Jesus of Nazareth, but to Gamaliel, it was only an episode in history, a kind of ripple on the surface of the water, something that had created a bit of a disturbance. He was simply giving an opinion on Christianity, just as people today give opinions on apartheid in South Africa or the race problem in America without becoming personally involved.

Now this failure to become involved is fatal; this is what is alarming about this kind of individual. Here was a man who could look into the face of the apostles, listen to them, and observe the healed man without his conscience being touched. Gamaliel's response was all in his head. He had not been convicted of anything; he had not started asking himself any questions; he had not seen the contrast between the apostles and himself. He had not said, "If they have the power to heal a man like that, why haven't I? I'm a learned man, one of the religious leaders. Why not me? What is all this?"

No, no; the personal element never comes in at all, and that is the final condemnation of this kind of man and this kind of attitude. He looks on at Christianity and its teaching in a detached and objective way. He picks up a book and listens to clever discussions on television and radio about the Christian faith and about all the religions and theories of life. He takes up a Christian teaching and puts it down; he may like it, he may not. It never occurs to this man that it is talking to him. He has never seen himself personally engaged; he never sees it in terms of his own need and the problem of his own life.

With a calm, judicial detachment, conscious of his culture and learning, such a man looks on with interest at movements as they come and go, as if he will go on living forever. Here he is, the judge on the throne of the universe. He has forgotten that he is a mortal man and that he is approaching death and must come face to face with it. And there is nothing more damnable than that. A man who can come into contact with these things without experiencing even an element of conviction or of disturbance, without being aware of his own need, is a man who is spiritually blind. Gamaliel was as blind as the raging colleagues on the Sanhedrin with him.

There, then, is our analysis of this great man Gamaliel. What conclusions do we draw from all this? This is the question, because if we do not draw conclusions, we have spent our time in vain. What does the case of Gamaliel teach every one of us? Consider this for your life; listen to what the Word of God is saying to you through this man Gamaliel. See him. I have been fair to him, have I not? Have I put anything into his mouth? Have I added anything? I have not. You must admit, it is a fair analysis.

What are the lessons to be learned? I have tabulated them for you in order that you may remember them more easily. Here is the first: Ability and culture and reasonableness and legal detachment and human wisdom are all utterly and completely irrelevant in the spiritual realm. When you go into a place of worship, the first thing you must realize is that all you have brought in with you is of no value to you. There is no difference at all between the doctor of the law and the wildest fanatic. None at all. This fact is here, on the very surface of this incident.

Only one thing matters in the spiritual realm, and that is spiritual understanding. And that is not natural. Nobody is born with it. Paul writes: "But

the natural man receiveth not the things of the Spirit of God: for they are foolishness unto him: neither can he know them, because they are spiritually dis-
cerned" (1 Cor. 2:14). "The carnal mind is enmity against God: for it is not
subject to the law of God, neither indeed can be" (Rom. 8:7). That is "the
natural man," the natural self.

You may have all the ability of a Gamaliel and all his judicial calm and
detachment, but not only is it useless, it may be your greatest hindrance.
Anything that you think you can rely upon is your greatest enemy. Our Lord
said that once and forever in these words: "Verily I say unto you, Except ye
be converted, and become as little children, ye shall not enter into the kingdom of heaven" (Matt. 18:3). "Little children"! Gamaliel, everybody—we
must all become little children. We must all realize that these things we are
so proud of—the learning of the twentieth century, for instance—are utterly
useless. They do not help us to the slightest degree. Gamaliel proves that.

Second, the way in which you reject the Gospel does not matter either.
All that matters is the fact of the rejection. You do not have to be violent in
your rejection of the Gospel as the other members of the Sanhedrin were. You
can reject it with the greatest politeness, praising it and saying in a detached
way, "Very interesting. I'm very intrigued by Christian teaching. Of course,
I study all these religions, and I find them all wonderful. They all have their
insights." You are not cursing; you are not blaspheming; you are not spitting
on the Gospel. I know you are not. But you are rejecting it quite as surely as
the person who does all those things. Politeness in rejection is of not of the
slightest value.

Third, a partial acceptance of this Gospel is, again, of no value. This man
Gamaliel, as I have been showing you, said, "Yes, there is something there."
He was not quite clear about it, but he saw that there was something that
ought to persuade them to give it a chance. And yet his whole case is here in
the Bible to tell us that to see something in Christianity is of no value—it is
either everything or nothing. Partial acceptance is rejection.

Many people do accept certain things in the Gospel. They say, "We like
the person of Jesus. He was the greatest man the world has ever seen." And
they praise Him. They say, "His teaching is incomparable. There has never
been anything like the Sermon on the Mount." Ah, yes, they accept that.

And then you say, "But you must be born again."

"Oh, no," they say. "We don't believe that, of course. That's just a little
bit of first-century thinking."

Then you ask, "What about the doctrine of the atonement? Do you
believe that Christ died for your sins?"

"Of course, we can't believe that," they reply, "that's immoral."

So they take out bits of the gospel message and then praise it and say that it is marvelous. But that is rejection of the Gospel. Gamaliel saw good things in it, but he rejected it. The fact that you may see certain good things in the teaching of Christianity does not mean that you are a Christian. If you do not see it all, you are rejecting it. It is all or nothing. You take it as it is, or you do not take it at all. Gamaliel proves that too.

But let us come to the ultimate test, which is this: Have you seen the uniqueness of the Gospel? Have you seen that it is in a class of its own? Have you seen that you must stop saying, "This is one of the great . . .?" Have you seen that it stands alone in utter, absolute uniqueness?

Further, to bring this test to the point where everything focuses, have you ever seen the uniqueness of Christ? "The God of our fathers raised up Jesus, whom ye slew and hanged on a tree. Him hath God exalted with his right hand to be a Prince and a Saviour." It all comes to this: What do you think of Christ? Do you recognize Him? Do you know who He is? Was He only a man? Was He one of the many great religious teachers of the centuries? Or is He uniquely the Son of God and Son of man? God in the flesh! "The Word . . . made flesh." He said, "I am the light of the world" (John 9:5); "I am the way, the truth, and the life: no man cometh unto the Father, but by me" (John 14:6). Paul wrote, "When the fulness of the time was come, God sent forth his Son" (Gal. 4:4). So the question is: Is He that to you, or is He not? It is one or the other.

Then are you clear about the facts concerning Christ? The Incarnation! His coming out of eternity into time! Born of a virgin—a miraculous birth! The miracles He wrought! His incomparable teaching! Do you say, "This was just another movement" or "It happened once and for all; it's unique"? Then His death upon the cross! His resurrection! Do you believe in the resurrection? Do you believe that He literally rose in the body from the tomb and manifested Himself, as these apostles were saying? Do you see the uniqueness?

What matters is not the opinion you may take upon various modern problems in the world; here is the only question: Do you believe the biblical record concerning Jesus of Nazareth? Do you believe that He was, indeed that He *is*, the Son of God?

But if this is the Son of God, why did He ever come into the world, and especially why did He ever die on that cross? This is the question that Gamaliel never asked himself. Have you asked it? And there is only one answer. It is this: "Him hath God exalted with his right hand to be a Prince and a Saviour." He died on that cross because it was the only way whereby anyone could be forgiven. What was happening there was that God was laying upon Him the iniquity of us all. God "hath made him to be sin for us, who knew no sin; that we might be made the righteousness of God in him" (2 Cor. 5:21).

Have you ever seen that? Have you ever seen your need of Him? Is Christianity something that you judge and evaluate with judicial calm? Or have you seen it as the only place of safety for you? Have you said:

> *Wash me, Saviour, or I die.*
> Augustus Toplady

Poor Gamaliel! He never looked at the gospel message personally. If he had, he would not have just given his great advice. Do you know what he would have done? He would have said to the Sanhedrin, "We are all sinners. We are relying on the law. We think we can put ourselves right with God. I've been wrong; you are all wrong; these men are right." He would have risked death in order to say that.

The Gospel does not want our opinions; it does not want our judgments. It calls for our obedience to God who sent His only Son to be our Savior. It calls us to repent and believe this message.

14

THE NAME

And they departed from the presence of the council, rejoicing that they were counted worthy to suffer shame for his name. And daily in the temple, and in every house, they ceased not to teach and preach Jesus Christ.

—Acts 5:41-42

What a contrast these last two verses provide, coming at the end of the chapter! In the previous verses we have had an account of the reaction of the majority of the members of the Sanhedrin to the testimony of the apostles, and then the response of the worldly-wise Gamaliel. But here the picture changes completely, and thank God for it. We are now going to look at those who believed and accepted the Gospel. What a difference!

We are looking at these verses, let me emphasize again, not because we have some mere historical or antiquarian interest in the story, though it is, incidentally, very important from that standpoint. As I have said, if you want to know what Christianity really is, the more you know of the book of the Acts of the Apostles the better. Here is the story of the origin of Christianity. The tragedy of the modern age is that people ignore this and put up their own ideas as to what the church and her message ought to be. But here is the only authentic account.

We, however, are studying this passage primarily because it is always helpful to see the reactions of other people. The Bible stoops to our level. It has its didactic teaching, but in other places, as here, it shows us the same truths through the lives of men and women. In the earlier studies we looked at unbelief so we may know whether we are guilty of it, and now, on the positive side, we turn to a picture of belief.

It is very wonderful to look at these early believers to see why they were believers and to examine how they behaved and lived. And, of course, as we do this, we shall be testing ourselves. The question for every one of us is this: Do we correspond to this picture that we are given? It is possible for us to think we are Christians when we are not. This has been one of the great curses in the church, as church history has demonstrated abundantly time after time throughout the centuries. History shows us people who have thought they were Christians when they were not, and it shows us their mistaken ideas as to what constitutes a Christian. And that, surely, is still the main trouble with the church. I believe that the high road to revival is for those of us who claim to be Christians to examine ourselves to make sure that we are and that we are putting our faith into practice.

The Book of Acts constantly underlines the fact that the spread and the triumph of Christianity in the early world was not only because of the preaching of the apostles. That was the first and vital factor, of course, but it was not the only one. The other great factor was the way Christian people lived their lives. That shook the ancient world. The apostles are described as men who "turned the world upside down" (Acts 17:6), but we are also told that when the ordinary Christians were "scattered abroad," they "went every where preaching [gossiping, talking] the word" (Acts 8:4).

Christianity spread by a process of "cellular infiltration," as it is called. That is how communism grew in this present [twentieth] century—not as the result of mass meetings, but by individual men working at their benches and speaking to their colleagues on the right hand and the left. That is an excellent way of spreading any teaching. Christianity in the first century advanced very largely through this process of personal testimony and living, and that method is as effective today as it has ever been.

So as we look at this picture, those who claim to be Christians will be under examination to see whether or not they really are genuine believers, and those who are not will, God granting it by His Spirit, be shown a picture of what it is that makes people true Christians. God grant that as they see it, they may be charmed and attracted, as so many were in the first century, and as so many have been ever since, in every time of reformation and revival.

What, then, are the principles that are taught here? Some are self-evident. The first is that the Christian is essentially different from the unbeliever. Now I put my emphasis on the word *essentially*. That is why I said at the beginning that one cannot but be amazed at the contrast between the apostles and the members of the Sanhedrin. We read, "When they"—the Sanhedrin—"heard that, they were cut to the heart, and took counsel to slay them." Gamaliel with his worldly wisdom was not as bad as that, but he was in the same boat.

Then look at the response of the other people to the same message—there could not be a more complete contrast. The difference between a Christian and a non-Christian is not slight. We are in another realm altogether. Here were people who thanked God and rejoiced in the fact that they were counted worthy to suffer shame for the name of Christ.

I am emphasizing this principle—this complete contrast—because it is so frequently forgotten at the present time. There are people who think that in their thinking Christians are remarkably like everybody else, except that they decide to add on certain special beliefs; there is no essential difference. Similarly, some people think that Christians live essentially the same lives as unbelievers and that the difference is only a difference in degree, the lives of Christians being a little bit better than the lives of non-Christians.

But that view is utterly impossible in the light of this one episode here, and indeed this is emphasized in the whole New Testament. The Christian is absolutely different from the non-Christian, as different as these apostles were from the members of the Sanhedrin, including Gamaliel. And the terms that the New Testament uses establish that difference beyond any doubt whatsoever.

There are two major differences between Christians and non-Christians. The first is that, according to the New Testament, Christians are men and women who are "born again," "born of water and of the Spirit" (John 3:3, 5). And there is no greater contrast than between being born of the flesh and being born of the Spirit. Indeed, the apostle Paul uses a term that is even stronger. "Therefore if any man be in Christ," he says, "he is a new creature" (2 Cor. 5:17)—which means, "a new creation"; something has come into being that had previously not been there at all. It is not that the original was taken and patched up, improved and painted and varnished. No; "a new creation."

Now this is vital, is it not? This is surely fundamental. Elsewhere the apostle puts it like this: "For God, who commanded the light to shine out of darkness, hath shined in our hearts, to give the light of the knowledge of the glory of God in the face of Jesus Christ" (2 Cor. 4:6). Paul says, "What has happened to me is comparable to what happened when God created the universe." There was nothing; then God said, "Let there be light," and there was light. That is creation—bringing something into being out of nothing. That is what has happened to all Christians. "Old things are passed away; behold, all things are become new" (2 Cor. 5:17).

Now that is Christianity. This difference between Christians and non-Christians is clearly evident on the surface of the account in Acts 5. People do not react in such opposite ways unless they have different natures within. And this leads to an entirely different outlook on life and death. That is why I emphasize the point that to be a Christian is to become absolutely new. God is dealing with the soul of the Christian, making it afresh, producing a new being.

Now it is important to emphasize the fact of the new birth because if we do not grasp this point we will probably try to make ourselves Christians. Many people try—we all have in the past. By trying to stop doing certain things, and by starting to do others, by taking an interest in reading the Bible and in praying, people hope that they will make themselves Christians. But it is a vain endeavor. I repeat, to be a Christian means to have the whole of our outlook determined and controlled by a new principle of life that has been put into us by God the Holy Spirit.

Then the second difference between Christians and non-Christians is in their attitude toward, and their relationship to, the Lord Jesus Christ. Here again is something that is absolutely basic. I shall not stay with this because I have already referred to it in passing, but I must repeat it because the point can never be stressed too frequently.

We are living in a world that does not like definitions, a world that is opposed to doctrine and theology and dogma, a world that likes indefiniteness, vagueness, comprehensiveness, all-inclusiveness, and that is why this point is so important. We are living in a time when people say, "All religions are of equal value; they all have a contribution to make, and they all lead to the same God. And what matters in the end is that we all believe in the same God." That is the climate of opinion in which we are living.

But here is one episode that, if we did not have any other, would be enough in and of itself to give the lie once and forever to the all-inclusive view. Let me put it as bluntly and as plainly as I can: People are not made Christians by believing in God. Christians do believe in God, but that is not what makes them Christians. Look at the division we find here at the end of chapter 5: the Sanhedrin and the apostles. What is the difference? The members of the Sanhedrin were Pharisees; they were Sadducees; they were the religious leaders and teachers of the people. They all believed in God.

Again, this is urgently important. How often people have said to me, "Of course I believe in God. I always have. And I have always said my prayers." They think that makes them Christians. But the orthodox Jew is a believer in God, and so is the Muslim, along with many others. No; the determining factor is not belief in God but a person's relationship to the Lord Jesus Christ. He is the center and the crux of it all.

Or to put it another way, you are not a Christian just because you are religious. The members of the Sanhedrin were quite as religious as the apostles, perhaps even more so. Again, this is a common misapprehension. People have the idea that in an age like this, when there is so much atheism and materialism, as long as you are religious, then you are of necessity a Christian. Not so! Indeed, the greatest opponents that our blessed Lord ever met in this world were religious people.

And in the same way, in spite of what is often said at the present time, the fact that you are a good, decent citizen does not mean that you are a Christian. You will frequently find people described as "outstanding and notable Christians" or "the greatest Christians of this century," who deny the person of our Lord. Because of their good lives and their good deeds and the sacrifices they have made to help others, they are regarded as Christians. The members of the Sanhedrin were upright men who did a lot of good. That is not the point. Only one thing differentiates the Christian from the non-Christian, and that is, as we are shown here, their attitude to this one person, our Lord and Savior Jesus Christ.

Let us be clear about this. Christianity is an exclusive teaching; it is an intolerant teaching. I do not say this because I am intolerant, but because I am concerned about your soul. If you say that Christianity is not exclusive and intolerant, then you must say that one religion is as good as another, and I am here to deny that.

Peter had already told the Sanhedrin that salvation came through Christ alone (Acts 4:12). And the next time he was brought before this council, he asserted that "The God of our fathers raised up Jesus. . . . Him hath God exalted with his right hand to be a Prince and a Saviour, for to give repentance to Israel, and forgiveness of sins." That is another way of saying, "Salvation is in this man, and in this man alone. There is no other; there is no second. He and He alone is the Savior."

Our Lord said the same thing when he told the people, "I am the light of the world" (John 8:12). There is no light apart from Him. Do not talk to me about Buddhism, Confucianism, Islam, or Judaism! No, no! *He* is sufficient; He does not need a glimmer of light from anybody else. The light is all exclusively in Him. This is Christianity. Like the members of the Sanhedrin, you may dislike it, but at any rate, I have shown you what you are disliking.

Our Lord also said, "I am the way, the truth, and the life: no man cometh unto the Father, but by me" (John 14:6). Nothing can ever be more exclusive than that. This was the issue that divided the Sanhedrin and the apostles. They were agreed about believing in God and about morality, but they were divided over our Lord and Savior Jesus Christ.

So the question I have to ask at this point is not about what sort of life you are living or how much good you do or how much you give to worthy causes or how concerned you are to help starving people. I do not want to know your views on war or atom bombs or the race question. No; here is the question of questions: "What think ye of Christ?" (Matt. 22:42). He Himself is the sword: "For I am come to set a man at variance against his father . . ." (Matt. 10:35); "I came not to send peace, but a sword" (Matt. 10:34). And He does. So what is He to you?

My third principle puts this difference in a yet more challenging manner. What stands out in these two verses at the end of Acts 5 is the fact that Christians not only believe in the Lord Jesus Christ—they rejoice in Him and glory in Him. Christ is everything to Christians. We see here two different ways of behaving: the Sanhedrin wanting to kill the apostles, wanting to get rid of them as they had the Lord Himself; and the Christians rejoicing! And it is obvious, is it not, that the Christians were different because they were controlled absolutely, in the whole of their life and living, by their relationship to Christ. Let us be clear about this. Christianity is not about deciding to live a better life or deciding to join a church. No, no; I repeat, it is about being controlled by the Lord Jesus Christ and rejoicing in Him.

In verse 41 we are told that the apostles "departed from the presence of the council, rejoicing that they were counted worthy to suffer shame for his name"—a better translation has, "counted it worthy to suffer shame for the name." Here is a true description of the Christian. The "name" that God has set before humanity stands not for Jesus appearing in the world as man, but for the totality of this blessed person in all His offices.

In other words, Christians are not ashamed of their faith. They do not hope that people in the office or school or factory or home will not find out that they are followers of Christ. No, no; they are proud to believe in Him and to belong to Him. They are proud of the name *Christian*. The word *Christian* means a person who belongs to Christ—the very name tells us that—and they are not afraid to claim it. The name of Christ is everything to them; they rejoice and exult in it; they boast of it.

Indeed, we are told here that the apostles were even proud to suffer shame for the sake of this name. They had been beaten and scourged—a very painful process—but the effect was that they "rejoiced that they were counted worthy to suffer shame for his name." It has been said that these words should be translated, "They were honored to be dishonored for his name." They gloried in being insulted and maltreated for this name.

We can go further: The apostles had been strictly ordered to stop speaking in the name of Jesus; three times over they had been threatened. At their last trial, the Sanhedrin had wanted to kill them, and would have succeeded had it not been for the intervention of Gamaliel. The apostles knew they had had a reprieve; they knew the great danger they were in. Yet this was their response: "And daily in the temple, and in every house, they ceased not to teach and preach Jesus Christ." They were ready to die for this name. They would sooner die than deny it. Death was nothing when this name was involved. That is what makes you a Christian. Not that you just decide to go into Christianity because you think that perhaps it will help you somehow or another. No, no; it is everything to you. You glory in "his name" in every respect. There is nothing you would not do for it, even to the extent of laying down your life.

That is Christianity. Have you realized that? Have you realized that it is great and glorious, not only dramatic but thrilling also? Here were men and women, noble souls, whom we call heroes. And they were only the first of very many throughout the centuries. Have you realized that this is Christianity? Or, like the members of the Sanhedrin, do you despise it? Or are you the sort of Christian who is half ashamed of your faith, half afraid of being challenged in this name? Here is Christianity, and once you really see it, you must react like these first believers.

Then, finally: Why did the apostles rejoice in the name of Christ? Why did they consider it the greatest honor that had ever come to them to be counted worthy to suffer or to die for it? Here are some of the reasons.

First, Christians have rejoiced in the name because their Lord is who He is. They rejoice to be associated with such a person. But who is He? Who is this Jesus to whom we belong, this Christ of whom we preach and whose name we use? Here is one description:

> *God, who at sundry times and in divers manners spake in time past unto the fathers by the prophets, hath in these last days spoken unto us by his Son, whom he hath appointed heir of all things, by whom also he made the worlds; who being the brightness of his glory, and the express image of his person, and upholding all things by the word of his power . . .*
>
> —Heb. 1:1-3

That is who He is! That is the Jesus the apostles refused to stop speaking about; that is the one they were ready to die for. He is the Lord of glory! He is the King of kings and the Lord of lords! He is the Creator of the universe and Jesus the man. That is why Christians like to use this name; that is why they like to be associated with it. He is the one who is now seated at the right hand of God in the glory everlasting.

The apostle Paul tells the members of the church at Ephesus that he prays that they may know certain things:

> *. . . that ye may know what is the hope of his calling, and what the riches of the glory of his inheritance in the saints, and what is the exceeding greatness of his power to us-ward who believe, according to the working of his mighty power, which he wrought in Christ, when he raised him from the dead, and set him at his own right hand in the heavenly places, far above all principality, and power, and might, and dominion, and every name that is named, not only in this world, but also in that which is to come.*
>
> *—Eph. 1:18-21*

You are proud to be associated with great people, titled people, kings, princes, emperors, presidents; you say, "I know them. I've had the pleasure of being in their company." If you can establish that you belong, however remotely, to the same family as some great man, you will stake your claim, will you not? People spend hours and much money proving that they belong to certain family lines, certain names. I am not criticizing that—it is all right; it is what men and women do. They feel the same about a country. Men and women are ready to die for their country. It is the name that they are dying for—they honor it; they are proud of it and exult in it. All right, if you think like this, then I say, follow your logic. Do you want dignity? Do you want glory? Then get associated with Christ! "The brightness of his [God's] glory, and the express image of his person."

Are you ashamed of the name of Jesus? Are you ashamed to acknowledge that you belong to Him? Is this something that you do not make known in your ordinary daily life and only bring out quietly on a Sunday? May God have mercy on you, and open your eyes, and let you know that you are ashamed of the Lord of the universe, the one through whom and by whom all things have been created, the one for whom it is God's desire "that in all things he might have the preeminence" (Col. 1:18).

The Christians in Colosse had thought it was clever to dabble in philosophy, but there is no greater folly than that! They had been listening to clever philosophical teaching and had thought they could add to Paul's Gospel. Paul asks, what are you doing? "Beware lest any man spoil you

through philosophy and vain deceit, after the tradition of men, after the rudi-
ments of the world, and not after Christ." Why? "For in him dwelleth all
the fulness of the Godhead bodily" (Col. 2:8-9). Deny this Jesus? Stop
preaching about Him? No, no, says the apostle. The man Jesus is the Son of
God! He is God incarnate! The absolute, utter fullness of the Godhead is in
Him in bodily form. And that was the apostles' first reason for rejoicing in
the name of Christ.

But then there was a second reason. Christians rejoice in the name and
are ready to suffer everything for it because of what the Lord has done for
them. God appointed His Son as a Savior. That is why He ever came into the
world, this Lord of glory. He came to save us. There was no other reason. He
did not come as a matter of interest or experimentation. He said, "For the
Son of man is come to seek and to save that which was lost" (Luke 19:10).
And Paul wrote, "When the fulness of the time was come, God sent forth his
Son, made of a woman, made under the law, to redeem them that were under
the law" (Gal. 4:4-5).

Oh, there is nothing more impossible than trying to preach the message
of the Gospel! What can a little man do with a theme like this.

From the highest realms of glory
To the cross of deepest woe.
Robert Robinson

Jesus Christ! The name high over all! The name of the Son of God. All
that He did, He did in order to reconcile us to God. "Who gave himself for
us, that he might redeem us from all iniquity, and purify unto himself a peculiar people, zealous of good works" (Titus 2:14). "Who his own self bare our
sins in his own body on the tree, that we, being dead to sins, should live unto
righteousness" (1 Pet. 2:24). He died for me! Can I be ashamed of Him? The
idea is ridiculous! The apostles knew that this was true, and they therefore
had no choice but to rejoice.

Then think of what our Lord has made of us. He has made us "kings and
priests unto God" (Rev. 1:6). He not only purchased pardon and forgiveness
and reconciled us to God, but He has made us children of God, "partakers
of the divine nature" (2 Pet. 1:4), "heirs of God, and joint-heirs with Christ"
(Rom. 8:17). Unbelief is madness, is it not?

Look at the world's social climbers. They try to be associated with a
name, to prove they belong to great families, and yet they do not want this
Gospel. The Sanhedrin rejected it and wanted to kill those who preached it.

People today think it is so clever to scoff and jeer. Is not unbelief blindness? Is it not the blindness of the devil and of hell? This is what you are offered. Listen to John: "Behold, what manner of love the Father hath bestowed upon us, that we should be called the sons of God: therefore the world knoweth us not, because it knew him not. Beloved, now are we the sons of God, and it doth not yet appear what we shall be: but we know that, when he shall appear, we shall be like him; for we shall see him as he is" (1 John 3:1-2). This is what He has done for us.

Your Lord has not only bought pardon for you and blotted out your sins—He has made you a new person, He has made you a child of God, He has put you into the royal family of heaven, and He has made you a joint-heir with Himself of the glory that is to come. He has sent His Spirit into you so that the Spirit that was in Him is now in you. This is what He has done for you; this is what He has made of you. That is why the apostles rejoiced in Him and would not be silent.

Then think of the difference our Lord makes to life in this world. He gives us an entirely new view of our life. There is nothing that I rejoice in more than in the understanding He has given me of the truth about this life—life in this world—and the older I get, the more I rejoice. I read my newspapers, and I see accounts of the deaths of men whom I knew years ago who went a different way. I, by the grace of God, am a preacher and a Christian. I thank God that He opened my eyes to the world and its glittering prizes, the emptiness of it all, the futility of it all.

There is nothing more wonderful than to be delivered from the power of the world, the flesh, and the devil; to see through all the vain show and all the sham and all the pretense; to be delivered, as Peter puts it, from "the corruption that is in the world" (2 Pet. 1:4). Corruption! Pollution! Foulness! Is it not wonderful to be delivered from that? That is what He does—He takes us out of it. My happiness does not depend upon what happens to me; my happiness does not depend upon the next program on the television or upon the amount of drink I can have or even the amount of food. No, no; I am made independent of the world.

Not only that, Christ helps you to live in the world; He helps you resist temptations. For while you are left in this world, Christians, you will be tempted, you will be tried—but you are no longer alone. "Wherefore in all things it behooved him to be made like unto his brethren, that he might be a merciful and faithful high priest in things pertaining to God, to make reconciliation for the sins of the people. For in that he himself hath suffered being tempted, he is able to succour them that are tempted" (Heb. 2:17-18).

Ashamed of Him? About to deny Him? Stop preaching about Him? No, no! You would be lost without Him.

> *He breaks the power of cancelled sin,*
> *He sets the prisoner free.*
> Charles Wesley

In your moral fight and struggle and endeavor, in your failure, He will be with you, if you will but believe it and know it and apply to Him. He is your great high priest. How can you pray to God? You cannot except with this person—you pray in His name. "Let us therefore," says the author of Hebrews, "come boldly unto the throne of grace"—through this great high priest—"that we may obtain mercy, and find grace to help in time of need" (Heb. 4:16).

And then Christ puts power within you. These apostles had already turned to the people and said, "Why look ye so earnestly on us, as though by our own power or holiness we had made this man to walk?" No, no! "His name, through faith in his name . . . hath given him this perfect soundness in the presence of you all" (Acts 3:12, 16). That is why they gloried in Him.

And the apostles gloried even in suffering because the effect of suffering is to put Christians into the same category as their Lord. If the world laughs at you and persecutes you and derides you and says you are insane because you are a Christian, they are paying you a great compliment—they are saying the very things they said about Him. You are following in His steps (1 Pet. 2:21).

What a difference our Lord makes to life in this world—and oh, what a difference He makes to death! That is why the apostles counted it an honor to be allowed to suffer shame for His name. That is why they went on preaching "daily in the temple, and in every house." They were no longer afraid of death. He transforms death; He transfigures it. Death has no terrors now. The non-Christian fears death, but the Christian can turn to it and, in the language of the apostle Paul, say, "O death, where is thy sting? O grave, where is thy victory? The sting of death is sin; and the strength of sin is the law. But thanks be to God, which giveth us the victory through our Lord Jesus Christ" (1 Cor. 15:55-57).

You can laugh in the face of death; you can defy the grave. Christ is the victor. He is the resurrected one, the ascended one. Paul writes to the Philippians, "I am in prison. I am an old man, and they are threatening to put me to death. But don't worry about me. 'For to me to live is Christ, and to die is gain'" (Phil. 1:21). Gain! Why? Because death means "to be with Christ; which is far better" (Phil. 1:23).

So we sing:

> *Till then I would thy love proclaim*
> *With every fleeting breath . . .*

Listen!

> *And may the music of thy name*
> *Refresh my soul in death.*
>
> John Newton

No other name will refresh your soul when you are dying. Your favorite film star, your pop singers, your actors—they will not refresh your soul; nor will your football team. They will be a mockery; they will offend you. But here is a name that can refresh your soul as you are dying and going out into the unknown eternity. What a name! Deny this? If you deny this name, you will have nothing left in life, and still less will you have anything left in death.

And then, to close on a theme that will occupy me and every other Christian throughout eternity, think of the difference this name makes not only in life, not only in death, but to all eternity. There He is, seated at the right hand of God, waiting "till his enemies be made his footstool" (Heb. 10:13). I do not know about you, but I like to be on the winning side. I want to be present on the day of victory, the day of final acclamation, the day of crowning. And that is why I am associated with this name; that is why I will not deny this name; that is why I rejoice in it.

He is "the King eternal, immortal, invisible" (1 Tim. 1:17). He is coming to destroy His every enemy; He is coming to reign; He is coming to set up His glorious kingdom. And I believe this word that tells me that when He comes I shall see Him, and that every Christian who sees Him will be "like him" (1 John 3:2). He is glorified; we shall be glorified. Paul puts it to the Philippians in some well-known words. Writing about this Savior who shall come from heaven, he says, "For our conversation is in heaven; from whence also we look for the Saviour, the Lord Jesus Christ: who shall change our vile body"—the body of my humiliation—"that it may be fashioned like unto his glorious body, according to the [mighty] working whereby he is able even to subdue all things unto himself" (Phil. 3:20-21).

He is coming! He will reign from pole to pole, and all who believe in

Him, and all who have stuck to Him, and all who have refused to stop speaking about Him, all who have gloried in Him, will be with Him sharing the reign, judging the world, judging angels. Paul writes, "At the name of Jesus every knee should bow, of things in heaven, and things on earth, and things under the earth; and that every tongue should confess that Jesus Christ is Lord, to the glory of God the Father" (Phil. 2:10-11). Those who know this, glory in Him whatever happens to them, whether praise or criticism, whether pleasure or pain. Nothing matters in life or in death except to be related to Him. Christians rejoice because of the glory that is coming to all who believe in Him and rejoice in Him.

My friend, do you regard Christ like that? Is that your relationship to Him? Is He everything to you? Does He control your view of life in the world, of everything that happens? Is he the center and circumference of your life? Are you His willing slave? If not, you are as blind as the members of the Sanhedrin.

Oh, I beseech you, look at Him again, and if you do, praying that the Holy Spirit may open your eyes and give you understanding, you will then be ready to join with me in repeating the words of Charles Wesley:

> *Jesus! the name high over all*
> *In hell, or earth, or sky;*
> *Angels and men before it fall,*
> *And devils fear and fly.*

> *Jesus! the name to sinners dear,*
> *The name to sinners given;*
> *It scatters all their guilty fear,*
> *It turns their hell to heaven.*

And here is my final confession, with Charles Wesley:

> *His only righteousness I show,*
> *His saving grace proclaim;*
> *'Tis all my business here below*
> *To cry: Behold the Lamb!*

> *Happy, if with my latest breath*
> *I might but gasp his name;*
> *Preach him to all, and cry in death:*
> *Behold, behold the Lamb!*

15

THE WORK OF THE HOLY SPIRIT

And now I say unto you, Refrain from these men, and let them alone: for if this counsel or this work be of men, it will come to nought: but if it be of God, ye cannot overthrow it; lest haply ye be found even to fight against God.

—Acts 5:38-39

Today is Whit Sunday, but what does that mean?

"Oh," says someone, "it's a festival in the church."

But why should the church regard Whit Sunday as a day of festival, a memorial day? I want to consider that with you, and to do so particularly in terms of Gamaliel's statement to the Sanhedrin. We have considered Gamaliel himself, and we have seen his serious lapses and deficiencies. This man, who looked so all right on the surface, was as blind to the truth as the most irate and vociferous members of the Sanhedrin.

But however deficient Gamaliel may have been in himself, in his understanding and insight, he certainly raised a very good question: How can you tell whether a work is the work of God or the work of men? And that is the question I would like to consider with you. But what is the relationship of this question to Whit Sunday? It is this: On the first Whit Sunday in Jerusalem, a very remarkable event took place. The trial of the apostles before the Sanhedrin would never have happened had it not been for that event on the Day of Pentecost, as it was called, the day we [in England] now call Whit Sunday.

Read the Gospels and these early chapters of the book of Acts, and you will find that it comes to this: There had appeared in Palestine a young teacher called Jesus of Nazareth. He had been known to some people as a carpenter who worked in a little place called Nazareth up in Galilee. But suddenly, at the age of thirty, He had embarked on a public ministry and had astounded everybody. He had never been trained, He had no learning, and yet He spoke with authority and obviously understood spiritual truth in a way that the Pharisees and scribes had never done. Moreover, He had worked miracles. And so He had become a phenomenon. At the end of three years, as the result of the machinations of the Pharisees, the scribes, the Sadducees, the Herodians, and other men of authority, He had been arrested. Early one Friday morning He had been condemned most unjustly and flogged. He had then been crucified, and He had died. Two of His friends had taken down His body from the cross and put it in a tomb. But this is the point: He had risen from that tomb!

During His ministry, this young teacher had collected a number of people around Him and, in particular, twelve men, His disciples, later called apostles. When they had seen Him arrested in apparent weakness and then dead on that cross, they had been completely shattered. They were honest enough to admit it. All their hopes had been dashed, and they had not known what to do. But on the third day some of their own company had reported that the stone had been rolled away and that the tomb was empty. And then He had suddenly appeared among them, and over the next forty days He had come to them a number of times. He had instructed them, explaining everything to them. And then, in the presence of some of them, on top of a mountain called Olivet, He had suddenly ascended into the heavens.

But just before that, He had told them to go back to Jerusalem and to wait because something mighty would happen: They would be baptized with the Holy Spirit. He had said, "Ye shall receive power, after that the Holy Ghost is come upon you: and ye shall be witnesses unto me both in Jerusalem, and in all Judaea, and in Samaria, and unto the uttermost part of the earth" (Acts 1:8). So the apostles had gone back to Jerusalem, and there they had waited and prayed for ten days.

In his dramatic account in Acts 2, Luke tells us what happened next:

> *When the day of Pentecost was fully come, they were all with one accord in one place. And suddenly there came a sound from heaven as of a rushing mighty wind, and it filled all the house where they were sitting. And there appeared unto them cloven tongues like as of fire, and it sat upon each of them. And they were all filled with the*

Holy Ghost, and began to speak with other tongues, as the Spirit gave them utterance.

—vv. 1-4

This had created a great sensation. People had come crowding together to see this extraordinary phenomenon, ignorant men speaking to them in their own dialects and languages about the wonderful works of God. The crowd had been utterly confounded and confused. So Peter had stood up to explain what had happened. He told the crowd that Jesus whom they had crucified was the Son of God, and the proof was that He had risen from the dead. Peter then said, "Therefore being by the right hand of God exalted, and having received of the Father the promise of the Holy Ghost, he hath shed forth this, which ye now see and hear" (v. 33). And he went on to show them the enormity of their crime in crucifying "that same Jesus" who is "both Lord and Christ." As a result of that sermon, three thousand had believed the message and had been added to the company of believers.

We have been considering together the events described in Acts chapters 3 through 5—the healing of the lame man and all that took place as a result. And now we come to the question upon which Gamaliel focuses our attention. What was all this? Was it as the apostles had said? Had this Jesus sent the Holy Spirit upon the apostles? They had testified to the Sanhedrin, "We are his witnesses of these things; and so is also the Holy Ghost, whom God hath given to them that obey him" (5:32). They were saying that what had happened was a work of the Holy Spirit. But the members of the Sanhedrin obviously disagreed, and that was why they wanted to kill the apostles. Gamaliel held the balance, as it were, and he put forward the question, Is it or is it not a work of God? And that is the question I would like to discuss with you: How can you tell whether or not something is the work of God?

"Dear me," says somebody, "why do you ask us to consider such a question? Is it relevant to our situation in the world today? Aren't you just propounding some old question that is perhaps of interest to you preachers who have nothing else to do except sit and read books and discuss questions like this? What has this to do with me?"

I will tell you. This question is urgently important because it determines your life in this world and in the next. Is this the work of God? Our whole eternal destiny depends upon our answer. So were the apostles right, or were the members of the Sanhedrin right? How can you tell? What are the authentic marks of a work of the Spirit of God? That is what we must discover.

Let me start by saying that it is not always easy to tell the difference between the work of the Holy Spirit and the work of a spirit that is opposed to God. There would have been no perplexity on the part of a man like Gamaliel if the issue had been plain and obvious. Our Lord Himself gives me authority for saying this. Consider His words in Matthew 24:24: "For there shall arise false Christs, and false prophets, and shall show great signs and wonders; insomuch that, if it were possible, they shall deceive the very elect." The New Testament is full of this kind of warning. Clearly this is a problem that caused great trouble in the life of the early church.

Not only have there always been false Christs and false prophets, but over the centuries there have arisen what are called the great world religions. Are they of God? Are they on an equality with Christianity? There are many movements that use the name of God. Take the cults that are around and about us at the present time—Jehovah's Witnesses, Christian Science, and many others. Here they are, all asking for allegiance and offering help and support to people in need. How can we tell whether that which claims to be a work of God is in reality such? This is the problem that confronts us, and we must face it.

This problem is at its most difficult when there is an element of truth in a wrong teaching and when Christianity in its very essence is being undermined. How can you tell the difference between the true and the false? The Christian church herself has found it difficult to answer this question. If you know anything about the history of revivals, you will know that the question has frequently arisen.

A powerful influence is at work in this world—the devil, the head of the evil spirits. This is not my idea—it is the teaching of the New Testament. The apostle Paul puts it like this: "For we wrestle not against flesh and blood, but against principalities, against powers, against the rulers of the darkness of this world, against spiritual wickedness in high [heavenly] places" (Eph. 6:12). It is the message of the whole Bible that an antagonist—a mighty power, a fallen angel called the devil—has arisen against God.

The devil has great forces, and his supreme ambition is always to spoil the work of God. He did it in the first creation. He does his utmost to do it in connection with the life of the church, which is the second or new creation. And he does it, of course, by trying to confuse the work of God. He tries to bring in a human element. And thereby he has often driven people to excesses, bringing genuine revivals into disrepute. I must not dwell on this, but it is important that we should be aware of it because it is sometimes difficult to discern.

In the eighteenth century, in the United States, there was a great man whose name was Jonathan Edwards. In many ways he was the most brilliant thinker the United States has ever produced. Certainly he was one of her greatest saints. Jonathan Edwards was involved in a tremendous religious awakening, a revival; but being a man with a spiritual mind who knew the Scriptures, he saw that another element tended to come in. The devil would take hold of certain men and use them, with their natural abilities and ambitions. As a result, the work of the Spirit of God was being confused. So Jonathan Edwards wrote a great book, *A Treatise on the Nature of the Religious Affections*, in which he shows us the difference between the true and the false. It is not easy, but we must persevere until we are certain because so much depends on our realizing the difference.

So how can we tell? To begin with some negative principles, there are certain tests that are quite inadequate. It is important to begin here because people often get confused by these tests, and we need to be clear about them. First, then, the fact that Christian terminology is being used is not a guarantee that a movement is the work of the Spirit of God. I can easily demonstrate that from the story of revivals. Obviously, in the eighteenth-century revival in the United States, the people who brought in the false element were using Christian terms. Indeed, has that not been the whole tragedy of the church in this present century? The theologians who have given rise to the so-called higher criticism, which has so undermined the authority of the Scriptures, have not stopped using traditional language. But though they talk, for example, about "Christ as Savior," they do not mean by that what you and I mean, what the church has meant throughout the centuries, and what the apostles meant. They use the term but empty it of its meaning. They hold on to the phraseology, but the truth is gone.

So the test of truth is not whether Christian phraseology is used. Rather, it is whether, when talking about the Lord Jesus Christ and His death on the cross, that is understood to be the work of God and not merely of man.

Second, success and popularity are not criteria. The fact that a teaching wins support does not prove that it is of God. False movements can gain adherents. There ought to be no difficulty with this point. Buddhism is very popular. Did you know that in Ceylon there has been a massive movement in the direction of Buddhism during the last ten years? This is also the case with many other religions and movements—think of the success of Islam.

Nor, third, can we say that God's Spirit is present just because people are being helped. Why do people become adherents of the cults? Obviously they seem to find help in them. I have known many such people. The testimonies of believers in Christian Science and other cults tell of the marvelous difference the teaching or method has made to them. But the fact that people begin to feel better and happier, that they can sleep whereas formerly they suffered from insomnia, or that they have physical healing does not prove that the work is of the Spirit of God. The counterfeit can produce these results, even as our Lord reminds us in Matthew 24:24.

Similarly, the presence of unusual phenomena does not prove that a work is a genuine work of the Spirit of God. False movements have their phenomena. Again in Matthew 24:24, we read our Lord's teaching that the false Christs will be able to work signs and wonders of such a startling character as almost to deceive the elect themselves. There is a well-known spiritist in this country—Mr. Harry Edwards, who says he is the medium of Louis Pasteur—who undoubtedly achieves healings. We must not dispute facts. Then there are tongues. Mormons and spiritists speak in tongues. Psychological influences can make people speak in tongues.

Fifth, what of zeal and enthusiasm—surely this is proof? Is it? Are not the followers of the cults zealous in their propaganda? Why, I have had them at my own door, young men and women giving up their Saturday afternoons to come around trying to sell their literature. They will give their time, their money, and their energy, and some of them are ready to give their very lives. So zeal and enthusiasm, and a concern to proselytize, are not proof of a genuine work of the Spirit of God.

Last, I would say that the test that is propounded by Gamaliel is not a good one. He puts it like this: "If this counsel or this work be of men, it will come to nought: but if it be of God, ye cannot overthrow it." If a thing lasts, he says, it must be of God. But he is wrong. Confucianism, Buddhism, Hinduism, and Islam have lasted for centuries. The teaching of Roman Catholicism did not immediately collapse when it departed from the Scriptures. No, no; there is an element of truth in this test, but it can lead you astray. If you base your position upon it, you will be in difficulties when you come to answer the various critics who appear before you and who want to test your Christian faith.

All those appear to be good tests, but they are not reliable, they are inadequate.

"What, then," asks somebody, "are you suggesting are the true tests?"

In answer to that question, let us first have a look at the characteristics of a work of man and then let us contrast them with a work of God. It always comes back to those words in Acts 5:28-29: "If this work be of men . . . but if it be of God." Let us try to consider this as dispassionately as we can, aware of its very great importance, knowing that we can be deluded, we can be deceived. The devil deceived Adam and Eve at the beginning, and he has continued to deceive people through the centuries. If he can get us to espouse the false, he is delighted—it is one of the best ways of keeping us from the true. As Paul reminds us, Satan even transforms himself into an angel of light (2 Cor. 11:14), and he quotes Scripture and appears to be a fine Christian in order to mislead us.

What, then, are the characteristics of a work of man? First of all, one very important test you can make is to ask the question, Can I understand and explain what is happening? If you can, then you may be certain that it is of human origin. Many works claiming to be the works of God can be understood and exposed by the application of this test alone. If you see a work and feel that you can explain it quite simply and adequately in psychological terms, then you are right to do so.

This is the test you apply, for example, to miracles. Some people seem to think that miracles are happening by the thousand every day! By definition, that is wrong. A miracle is exceptional. How do you tell whether or not a miracle has taken place? One of the best tests is to see if it can be explained scientifically. If it can, you can be sure it is not a miracle. A miracle is supernatural, beyond the natural. It is beyond understanding, therefore. If you can explain a thing, then do so. I plead with Christians especially to do this. Do not claim that something is miraculous if it can be explained in purely natural terms.

It is the same with any general religious or supposedly Christian movement. Do not say that something is a work of God if you can see there is a human explanation for what is happening—if you can see, for example, that there is a psychological influence either upon an individual or upon a crowd. There is such a thing as the psychology of the mass or mob. We are all aware of this, unfortunately. Hitler has taught us all about it. You may remember seeing the crowds as they listened to Hitler, and you may remember their shouting. You may have seen films of them. Oh, the power that man could exercise upon the mob! They were worked up with singing and with bands beforehand, and then, with his particular type of oratory, Hitler could do what he liked with them, and they were ready to die for him. They were enthusiastic; they were convinced. It was all the result of a brilliant psychological technique. Similarly, when we read of many freak religions or watch some of them on television, we can easily see the way people are manipulated.

Now I am saying all this because people are writing books in an attempt to discredit Christianity. They appear on television and give you pictures of freak religions in South America or somewhere and show you people with snakes and so on. But you can see those poor people being gradually worked up until they do not know where they are. The explanation is perfectly simple: It is entirely psychological.

So if you are confronted by something and you are not quite clear as to what it is, ask, Can I understand this? Can I explain it? We all need to apply this test, every one of us. And every preacher of the Gospel has to examine himself constantly along this very line.

The second test looks at the methods used in connection with any movement. If it is man's work, then man's activity and organization are always the most prominent elements. Take that word from the prophet Zechariah: "Not by might, nor by power, but by my Spirit, saith the LORD of Hosts" (Zech. 4:6). What is might? What is power? Well, there is nothing more powerful than money, is there? Money. Influence. Organization. That is power. Might and power are always prominent in the work of man. He relies on it. Obviously he has to. He cannot succeed without it; so he manipulates power.

In the same way, man relies upon his methods, his techniques. We see these methods being used, and we read about them in books. Some men even claim to preach the Gospel when in reality they are teaching nothing but psychology. They have their results. They have their adherents. People almost worship them. How have they done it? Sometimes results have even been achieved by manipulating electric lights. Different colored lights. A cross, perhaps, is illuminated on the central light, and as the service goes on, the lights slowly go out at given points until at the end you are in almost total darkness looking at this one thing and the preacher under it. These are the methods of psychology, methods with which we are surely familiar.

Then there is the use of repetition: You do the same thing and keep doing it on and on and on. To anybody who knows anything about psychology and hypnotism, the use of repetition and suggestion is elementary. They are necessary if results are to be achieved, and so they are evident in any movement that is the work of man.

The other characteristic with regard to methods is that a great deal of pressure is always brought to bear upon people in order to break them down and to convince them and to gain their support. Mohammed, of course, was a striking example of someone who used this method. He actually made people accept his message at the point of the sword. He said, "This is the truth, and I believe it is right," and he took armies and forced people to follow his religion. That may be an extreme, but to a lesser extent, it is always the method of man. He will bring pressure to bear in every way possible to get people to make a decision immediately.

But the outstanding characteristic of a work of man is always that it is man-centered, as is illustrated by Gamaliel's two examples, Theudas and Judas. A man or woman is always prominent, always at the center. But not only that. Watch the message, and you will find that in all instances it starts and ends with man. It is always about human needs, human problems, human difficulties.

Take the cults again. They would never succeed and flourish if they did not focus on human need. They know there is a lot of suffering in the world and that people are in trouble; so they come and say, "Are you in trouble? Are you worried? Do you find it difficult to sleep? Are you conscious of some aches and pains or some kind of paralysis? Now come along," they say, "we can put you right. We can deal with you. That's what we're here for—this is our message." They offer people the benefits they seem to stand in need of. They are human-centered the whole time.

A further characteristic, of course, is the superficiality of man's work. Man is incapable of profundity. Though appearing at times to be the work of God, man's work is superficial in its intellectual content—that is a part of its success. But not only that, it is even superficial in its emotional content. This emotional aspect is very interesting because it sometimes veers from one extreme to the other, from emotionalism to sentimentalism, and neither of these two extremes is true emotion. Sentimentalism is quiet and respectable and never in any way obtrusive or offensive, while emotionalism is riotous, violent, and irrational. I shall go on in a moment to show you the contrast with the truth.

Now these human movements generally make an onslaught upon the will, a direct appeal to the will. Consequently, because they are dependent upon human activity and manipulation, their results are generally not lasting. Let me tell you a story—forgive me for telling you this out of my own experience—to illustrate what I am saying. Before I came here [to Westminster Chapel, London] I was in a church in South Wales. The church building was much smaller than this, and at the end of the service I used to stand at the exit to shake hands with people as they went out.

Every Sunday night I would notice a man in the gallery. We all knew him well. He was a butcher. Poor fellow, he used to be drunk every Saturday night, but he always came to our service each Sunday night. One particular Sunday I happened to look at the man while I was preaching, and I could see tears streaming down his face. *Well, now,* I thought, *is it happening to him tonight?*

At the end I went to the door, and this man came along. I said to myself,

Shall I challenge this man? But I decided not to; so I shook him by the hand as usual and prayed that God would bless him. Out he went.

The next night I was walking up to my prayer meeting, and who should be coming toward me but this very man. He came up to me and said, "You know, Doctor, if you had asked me to stay behind last night, I would have done so."

I said, "Well, I'm asking you now."

"No, no," he replied, "if you had asked me last night, I would have, and I would have joined the church."

"Well," I said, "come with me now to the prayer meeting."

"No," he said again. "I would have done it last night."

"But, my dear friend," I said, "if what happened to you last night doesn't last twenty-four hours, it's not the work of the Spirit of God."

That had been emotionalism. Perhaps I had been partly responsible. Perhaps I had been doing something that I should not have in the presentation of the Gospel. There had been a temporary emotion, a superficial influence upon the mind or the conscience or heart or will.

Now in the great revivals of history there have always been what are called "temporary believers," people washed up, as it were, on the shore by the impetus of the movement. They do not last. They seem to be all right, but when the influence goes, when the stimulus has ceased, they have nothing. It has only been a superficial work; they kept going only as long as they were in a certain atmosphere.

Superficial and temporary responses have been very frequent in this present century. I have known university students who, while still at university and attending daily prayer meetings or regular meetings of their evangelical Christian Unions, appeared to be wonderful Christians. But when they finished their university courses and were back out in the world, away from the atmosphere that had carried them along, they had nothing. Their religious fervor had been the temporary work of man. The religions of the world continue only because they are religions of fear, because of the tyranny of fear.

Those, then, are the characteristics of man's work. Now what are the characteristics of God's work? What a relief to turn to this! It is here before us in the early chapters of Acts, and you can see it in every revival that has ever taken place in the history of the world. So let me apply my same tests. What, then, about the general criteria?

Here is the first: A work of the Spirit of God is always inexplicable. Notice that word at the beginning of Acts 2: "Suddenly" (v. 2)! No preparation, no conditioning, no working up. No, no! It happens, and it cannot be understood. Revivals, movements of the Spirit of God, take place in spite of human weakness. They are never worked up by man. I have known many men who have tried to bring about revivals. It can never be done. They say, "If you do this, that, and the other, you will get a revival." You will not. Revival is always from God, and it is amazing. "What is this?" said the people on the Day of Pentecost.

Psychologists will try to explain revivals, but they cannot. A few years back I had the privilege of writing an answer to Dr. William Sargent's book *Battle for the Mind*.[12] And he was unable to answer me because he could not explain revivals. I was able to show that Dr. Sargent's explanations did not apply here. He could not explain the Day of Pentecost. He could not explain the origin of a single revival; still less could he explain why revivals suddenly stop. He could not explain why, in spite of using all their human techniques, men have never produced a revival. They cannot, because revivals are the work of God. They are always surprising; they always elude human ingenuity and human understanding. That is the great test.

But consider the second—the methods. "Not by might, nor by power, but by my Spirit, saith the LORD of hosts" (Zech. 4:6). A work of God does not depend upon man's organizational skills, nor upon special techniques. And it does not depend upon applying human pressure to the will. Now let me give you my authority for saying all this. We are fortunate in having the great apostle Paul as the basis for what we are saying. Here he is, writing to the Corinthians:

> *And I, brethren, when I came to you, came not with excellency of speech or of wisdom, declaring unto you the testimony of God. For I determined not to know any thing among you, save Jesus Christ, and him crucified. And I was with you in weakness, and in fear, and in much trembling. [Self-confident? The exact opposite!] And my speech and my preaching was not with enticing words of man's wisdom, but in demonstration of the Spirit and of power: that your faith should not stand in the wisdom of men, but in the power of God.*
> —*1 Cor. 2:1-5*

And to the Thessalonians Paul writes:

> *Our exhortation was not of deceit, nor of uncleanness, nor in guile: but as we were allowed of God to be put in trust with the gospel, even*

so we speak; not as pleasing men, but God, which trieth our hearts. For neither at any time used we flattering words, as ye know, nor a cloke of covetousness; God is witness: nor of men sought we glory, neither of you, nor yet of others, when we might have been burdensome, as the apostles of Christ.

—1 Thess. 2:3-6

The principle is plain and never varies. The apostle Paul deliberately decided not to use his human abilities and powers: "I determined not to know anything among you . . ." This was a brilliant man who could have used philosophical arguments. Here was a man who could have brought his mighty logic to bear. He could, if he had wished, have spoken eloquently, using all the skills of rhetoric—Paul proves that in his epistles—but he deliberately eschewed such methods. He says, "I put them aside. I wanted it to be clear that my message was of God and not of man."

Paul did not try to please and flatter his listeners or seek to put them into a good mood and joke and laugh with them and entertain them. No, no; it was inconceivable. He wanted it to be seen that what was happening was nothing but the power of the Spirit of the living God. He wanted the marks of the work of God to be perfectly plain and clear. When the Spirit of God is acting, there is no need for man to use his power.

Look at Peter preaching on the Day of Pentecost. He was expounding the Scriptures, and to us it seems to be rather a dull sermon. But this is what I read: "Now when they heard this, they were pricked in their heart, and said unto Peter and to the rest of the apostles, Men and brethren, what shall we do?" (Acts 2:37). That is the work of the Spirit of God. He does not rely upon human methods and techniques but searches minds and hearts and consciences, and as He deals with people, they cry out.

Some twelve years ago there was a revival in the Congo. A man called Ivor Davies later wrote a book in which he included a description of what happened. I will never forget hearing him speak when he came back to this country. He told us that for twenty years he had been a missionary in the Congo. He used to preach his heart out and would plead with people to come forward in decision at the conclusion of the services. But not a soul would respond. As a result his heart was almost breaking. But then he had to go away somewhere, and in his absence a revival broke out. He said, "This is what I found when I went back and began to preach: Halfway through my sermon, people began to move forward, in agony of soul, wanting help."

This man had been trying to bring about conversions, but nothing had happened. He had not been able to do it. But now it had. He was not an expert in psychological methods. The Spirit had done it.

Then, third, I said that the characteristic of man's work is its superficiality. So what are the characteristics of the work of God? Read your Bible, read your New Testament, and you will be impressed by the greatness, the glory, the majesty of the message. Truth is in control.

What else? Read these early chapters of Acts, and keep your eye on the words "fear" and "awe." "For our God is a consuming fire" (Heb. 12:29). Man is out of sight. God is filling the place, and when God is present, and His glory and His truth and His majesty are evident, there is a sense of awe and profound seriousness.

And what of the message? Well, it never starts with man. You notice how Peter put it to the Sanhedrin: "We ought to obey God rather than men." Did he get up and say, "Let's go on preaching because we're helping people and making them much happier than they were"? Not at all! Listen: "The God of our fathers raised up Jesus." The true message is always a message that starts with God, not with man and his aches and pains and his little unhappinesses and problems, his psychological state. No, no; rather, man face to face with the everlasting and eternal God, with His honor, His glory, His majesty, and His great plan and purpose of redemption.

The Bible is interested in sin, not because it makes us unhappy, but because it is an affront to God. Because it is rebellion. Because it is arrogance before a holy God. We are subjective, self-centered, and selfish, always wanting something for ourselves, and the first thing we need to know is that we are accountable to God, that He is there, and that His glory is what matters. Whatever may be true about you and about me, the Gospel always starts like that.

The result is, of course, that what the fathers used to call "a law-work" is always very prominent in a true work of the Spirit of God. By this they meant that a true work of God always humbles and abases us. It always convicts us of sin. We forget our little troubles, our little problems, and see ourselves as sinners—"Men and brethren, what shall we do?"—conscious of God, conscious of His Son, conscious of the vileness in us that made us reject Him. We are driven to repentance, and we become concerned about our souls, even though this means, perhaps, that we may have to go on being ill physically and go on suffering from insomnia.

And then, of course, a true work of God always glorifies the Lord Jesus Christ, as we see from these early chapters in Acts. He is the one who matters. Not the teaching, not the experience, but this blessed Lord: "The God of our fathers raised up Jesus, whom ye slew and hanged on a tree. Him hath God exalted with his right hand to be a Prince and a Saviour." The message is about Him, not about the petty problems of today—these are but little symptoms. What matters is not the particular sins, but the whole person in total relationship to God, man's lost estate. The one central trouble is that men and women are enemies and aliens before God, rebels under the wrath of God, and the only one who can reconcile them is the blessed Son of God, our Lord and Savior, Jesus Christ.

Oh, this is a great and glorious message. Look at this truth in the New Testament. How big it is! I have been trying to preach it for nearly forty years, and I feel I am but a beginner. It expands before me in ever-widening vistas— the glory, the profundity, the largeness of this truth as expounded by these apostles. My mind is filled; my mind is enlarged. The content of the message—how wonderful!

And, likewise, the Gospel deals with the heart in depth. It does not drive me to a wild, irrational ecstasy, nor does it leave me with a kind of maudlin sentiment. It moves me in such a manner that it gives me thoughts that are often "too deep for tears" [William Wordsworth, "Ode on the Intimations of Immortality"]. It moves me to the very depths of my heart and emotions. And the Gospel persuades the will by its mighty truth, so that when the meeting has ended or the days have passed, I still believe. The truth has taken hold of me, and I am convinced and convicted and enlightened. I see it; I am governed by it. I am a slave of Jesus Christ and a slave to His blessed truth. That is the work of the Spirit of God.

And the Spirit of God goes on to produce His fruit in us. If our lives are not entirely changed, we have not been moved by the Spirit of God. People can do many things. They can get adherents; they can get decisions; they can get people to join their church. We have all done this. We can all do it if we are worth our salt. It is not difficult to get people to make decisions or to become members of churches or to decide to be religious. I can do all that. But what I cannot do is give men and women new natures. I cannot renovate them in the totality of the personality. But the Spirit of God can, and He does. And when people are born again, they show it in their lives.

The new life given by the Spirit is progressive. It becomes deeper and deeper. People acquire a love for the Word of God—and this is a very good test. I hear of people who seem to have been influenced, and everybody thinks they have become Christians, but then I find they do not like the profound teaching of the Bible. They do not want that and say, "Oh, no, that's too deep."

Too deep? But look at these people who were saved under the preaching of Peter on the Day of Pentecost. We read, "And they continued steadfastly in the apostles" doctrine [teaching], and fellowship, and in breaking of bread, and in prayers" (Acts 2:42). The people to whom Paul wrote his mighty epistles were but slaves and soldiers, but they wanted his teaching, they gloried in it. They did not just demand a twenty-minute sermon and then say, "That's too deep—we can't understand it. We want something to make us feel happy." No, no! When people have been born again and have the Spirit of God in them, they want to understand, they want teaching, they love the Word, they want to pray, they enjoy the fellowship of God's people. So I do not care what has happened to you—if you do not have a thirst for this teaching, it has not been the work of the Spirit of God.

There, then, are these great and essential distinctions between the work of man and the work of the Spirit of God. Which of them has taken place in you? Do you know that you have experienced a work of the Spirit of God? Nothing else will be of value in the sight of God. Beware, says the whole of the New Testament, of the counterfeit, the false.

Make certain that the work that is done in you is a work of the Spirit of God. I have told you how to test it. Are you full of your experience and of what has happened to you, or are you taken up with God and His glory and His great plan of redemption and the Lord Jesus Christ and the fact that you, a miserable sinner, have been saved by Him, that He even came on earth and went to the cross and was laid in a tomb and rose again for you?

Are you always talking about yourself, or are you lost before Him with a sense of wonder, love, and praise? Are you humbled? Do you magnify God and His grace in the Lord Jesus Christ?

Have you become a problem and an enigma to yourself? Are you amazed at yourself and at this new life that is in you? If you can understand yourself, I tell you, you are not a Christian. Christians cannot understand themselves. They say with Paul, "I live; yet not I, but Christ liveth in me" (Gal. 2:20). That is the only explanation.

May God give us grace to make certain that the work that has happened in us is the work of the Spirit of God.

16

PRIORITIES

And in those days, when the number of the disciples was multiplied, there arose a murmuring of the Grecians against the Hebrews, because their widows were neglected in the daily ministration. Then the twelve called the multitude of the disciples unto them, and said, It is not reason that we should leave the word of God, and serve tables.

—Acts 6:1-2

I should like now to deal with the statement that was made by the twelve apostles: "It is not reason that we should leave the word of God, and serve tables." In this sixth chapter of Acts we come to a new incident in the life of the early church, a most important incident from many standpoints, telling us, as it does, about the growth and development of the Christian church.

God had granted His blessing upon the work of the apostles—their preaching and their miracles. We are told, "when the number of the disciples was multiplied." That was the situation, and it is interesting to notice, therefore, how, in spite of the difficulties that are described in chapter 5, the church still went on from strength to strength.

This statement describing the growth of the church is also particularly interesting as it gives us our first insight into a developing organization. Much of the present confusion about the church hinges upon the point that people cannot differentiate between the church itself and the organization of the church. The tragedy is that the church that we read of in the New Testament has, over the centuries, become a great institution with many offices and dignitaries, with cathedrals and all that we are so familiar with.

Organization is essential—you have to organize the life of the church. But the question is, to what extent? This is important because when the organization becomes more important than the message, the New Testament position is reversed, and tragedy follows. Though we shall not be going into that now, it is interesting to notice that the issue is raised here because of a difficulty that had entered into the life of the early church.

We are told, "There arose a murmuring of the Grecians against the Hebrews, because their widows"—that is to say, the widows belonging to the Grecians—"were neglected in the daily ministration." Now the Grecians were probably not Greeks, but Jews who were Greek-speaking. The Jews at that time were living in many countries, and some had become Greek-speaking. Probably some had come from other countries to live in Jerusalem, while others were on a visit, perhaps making a prolonged stay. The "Hebrews," of course, were Jews from Palestine.

So a dispute arose. Now we have already been told at the end of chapter 2 that from the beginning, the Christians were in the habit of meeting together in one another's houses to share their meals, those who were in need being helped by those who had plenty. But now, apparently, the Grecians were saying that their widows were not being treated as fairly as the widows belonging to the Hebrew Christians, and, moved by nationalistic prejudices, they said that this was unfair. There was a "murmuring," and this dispute was now threatening the life of the church.

That is the background, but what we are really concerned about is the apostles' response—what they said and did. What they did, of course, was tell the church to pick out seven men who had certain qualities and characteristics, men "of honest report, full of the Holy Ghost and wisdom." These seven men were to be brought to the apostles, who would set them apart to "serve tables." And that is the beginning of the whole idea of the diaconate—having deacons in the church to look after the finances and the business of the church and to be responsible for the care of the poor, the suffering, and the needy. That, then, was what the apostles did.

But we are concerned here with what the apostles said. This is the reason they gave for appointing these seven deacons: "It is not reason that we should leave the word of God, and serve tables." Church numbers were increasing, people were being converted—among them these widows—and this had become a problem. It had been simple at first, but the larger the numbers, of course, the more difficult it became to minister to the needs of these widows and others who were suffering. Furthermore, there seems to have been a suggestion that the apostles should have been spending the whole of their time in this work. But they said that suggestion was not acceptable to God or to them.

I should like to consider the apostles' reply because it raises a very contemporary, indeed a most urgent question. Let me therefore put the whole subject in the form of three propositions. Here is the first. We are told here what is the *primary* task of the Christian church.

Now one of the phrases used today—this is an age of phrases—is the phrase, getting your priorities right. We are very fond of saying this, are we not? Yet it is almost ludicrous because the real trouble with the present age, as I shall show you, is that it has got its priorities wrong! But it is always talking about them, and here we are reminded of the church's primary task.

What is the church here for? This is a subject of considerable debate and dispute at the present time, and there is great misunderstanding about it. The popular teaching today—and it is increasingly popular, not only on the continent of Europe and in this country, but in most other countries also—is the idea of what is sometimes called "religionless Christianity."

What does "religionless Christianity" mean? Well, its advocates say that we must cease to carry on the tradition of meeting Sunday by Sunday in church buildings for services of worship at 11 A.M. and 6:30 P.M. with a preacher and so on. They say all that is finished, that belongs to the past, and in any case it was based on an entirely wrong idea of what Christianity is. The old idea was, they say, that you should preach a personal message, indulge in what is called "evangelism," and be interested in the personal soul. But that type of Christianity is entirely wrong. We should get rid of it.

"Oh, it is quite all right," they say, "to have discussions about religion. Let people ask questions and give answers. But what you really need to do— and surely this is the primary task of the church and the Christian faith—is to go out into the world and do good. There's so much suffering in the world, so much poverty in so many countries, not to mention the war in Vietnam, so why preach this Gospel? Why don't you do something about South Vietnam and the tragedy that's being enacted there and in these other troubled areas of the world?"

So the modern idea is that the business of Christianity is to indulge in philanthropic work. I remember a man once putting this very forcibly when he said, "If you want to make Christians of the people in pagan countries, don't send men there to preach your Gospel to them. Send men there who will enter into their politics, join in their life, get onto their local councils, and be part and parcel of the people; and if you do that, there is some hope that after a generation or two you will Christianize them and their whole outlook." In other words, you win converts not by preaching, not by holding the Word of God before people, but by doing good among them. The task of the Christian church, it is said, is to put an end to war and injustices and wrongdoing and to relieve every form of suffering.

People today are giving up the whole notion of public worship and listening to the preaching of the Gospel. Practical Christianity, they say, that's the thing. Get out into life, mix with people—that's the modern way to show the Christian spirit and the Christian teaching. You are familiar with this modern argument. This is undoubtedly a very serious issue.

First, of course, we must say that this view is not quite as modern as its proponents would imagine; indeed, it is very old. We see from the first two verses of chapter 6 that this problem confronted the Christian church right at the very beginning. It was a kind of crisis in the life of the early church. If she had gone wrong at this point, probably the church would not be here now. And here we see the wisdom given to these apostles by the Spirit. It was a turning-point, and they might have gone wrong once and forever. But they did not—and they did the exact opposite of what is being advocated today.

It is most interesting to notice that even before the dispute that we are now considering, the problem had already arisen. Our blessed Lord and Savior had to fight this battle. The miracle of the feeding of the five thousand had astonishing effects upon the people, one of which is described in John 6:15: "When Jesus therefore perceived that they would come and take him by force, to make him a king, he departed again into a mountain himself alone."

When the people saw the miracle, they said, "This is he. This is the Messiah. This is the Deliverer we've been expecting." But their idea of a Deliverer was someone who would set himself up as king, gather a great army, and lead that army of the Jews against the Romans and everybody else. He would be a world conqueror and would establish a political kingdom. They tried to "take him by force, to make him a king," but "he departed again into [to the top of] a mountain himself alone." He was facing again the terrible temptation to become an earthly king or a political deliverer.

Or take another instance, which is a tremendous illustration of the problem we are discussing. Our Lord was teaching the disciples, whom He was about to send out to preach and to work miracles, and He told them some wonderful things. He prepared them for opposition—and it soon came. Then He told them not to be worried, not to be troubled. He told them that they were God's people and that the world, finally, even though it might kill them, could not really touch them (Luke 12). It was an amazing sermon! Our Lord gave the disciples some great promises. He said, "The very hairs of your head are all numbered" (v. 7). Never had He led them further into the realm of the Father and of the Spirit; never had He given a more uplifting discourse.

But do you remember what happened? There was a man there, listening to all this, and he seemed to have been waiting for our Lord to take a breath because he suddenly burst in upon it all: "One of the company said unto him, Master, speak to my brother, that he divide the inheritance with me." There had been some dispute between these two brothers about an inheritance. Somebody had died, and this man felt that he was not receiving his fair share of the inheritance. The one thing that mattered to him was that his brother was not playing fair with him. And here he saw a great teacher, and he thought, *Ah, here's someone who will help me sort out this problem.* So he blurted it out into the midst of this amazing discourse.

But our Lord looked at that man and said, "Man, who made me a judge or a divider over you?" In effect He said, "Do you think I have come from heaven to earth to settle family disputes? Do you think I have left the courts of glory simply to sort out how much money you should inherit?" Then he looked at the assembled company and said, "Take heed, and beware of covetousness: for a man's life consisteth not in the abundance of the things which he possesseth" (vv. 13-15). And our Lord went on to tell the parable of the rich fool.

So our Lord was constantly confronted by the question of His purpose in coming to this earth. People said, "Haven't you come to do this, that, and the other?" And all the time He was preaching. Even John the Baptist got into trouble over this question, did he not? "Art thou he that should come? or look we for another?" he asked (Luke 7:19).

"Go back," said our Lord to the two messengers whom John had sent with that question: "Go your way, and tell John what things ye have seen and heard; how that the blind see, the lame walk, the lepers are cleansed, the deaf hear, the dead are raised, to the poor the gospel is preached. And blessed is he, whosoever shall not be offended in me" (vv. 22-23).

Poor old John! Sick and languishing in prison, having in his mind the old Jewish idea of the Messiah, he could not understand what was happening. He was unhappy. "Art thou he?" The answer was, "Reconcile your views to what I am."

And then there is one other striking instance. People came to our Lord one day and said, "We have a very difficult problem here." These were the Herodians, and they were politicians. They said, "You're a teacher, a master. We've heard you, and we greatly admire your teaching. Now tell us, should we Jews pray taxes to Caesar or not?" They regarded him as a kind of encyclopedia.

Our Lord replied, "Render therefore unto Caesar the things which are Caesar's; and unto God the things that are God's" (Matt. 22:21). That was his emphasis; and there, through the Holy Spirit, He gave these people this understanding and enlightenment. It is not surprising that later on the apostle Paul describes the church as "the pillar and ground of the truth" (1 Tim. 3:15). The primary task of the church is to hold up and to hold forth the truth before men and women, to hold it up on a pillar, to put it on a placard.

Now let us be clear about this matter of philanthropy, lest I be misunderstood. I am not saying that it is no part of the Christian message to teach people to be kind and helpful and philanthropic; quite the reverse. All I am concerned about is the question of our priorities. I am dealing with the modern contention that says that the primary, indeed virtually the only, task of the church is to do good, to right wrongs, and to mitigate injustices. But here is my answer, given by the Lord Himself and repeated here by the apostles. Philanthropic work does come in, but it is secondary.

Look at our Lord's own ministry. The primary feature was the teaching; the miracles, the healings, were always secondary. John, indeed, in his Gospel always refers to them as "signs." Why did our Lord work miracles? It was partly to do good and partly to show His love and compassion and kindness. His miracles were manifestations of love.

But still more important, our Lord worked miracles to attest His person, to prove that He was and is the Son of God. It was the miracles that helped to convince people. They supported His teaching and manifested its truth. I repeat, they were signs and were not the primary purpose of the Incarnation. Our Lord did not come to work miracles. He said, "I am the light of the world" (John 8:12). He is a teacher; He came to tell us something that nobody else could tell us.

If you are really interested in this, it would be very simple indeed for me to prove to you that all the benevolence and the philanthropy, of which the world talks so much, was started by the Christian church. The moment Christianity comes in, people become concerned about widows. We talk about widows' pensions, do we not? We pride ourselves on this—it is something this country [England] has done. But it was done in the first century by the Christian church! Again, provision for the poor first began in the church, long before the politicians and sociologists ever even thought of it, let alone put it into practice. Take the modern welfare state: You will find that most of its provisions have been anticipated by the church over the course of the centuries. Where did hospitals come from? From Christians. Where did public education come from? From Christians. The church has always led the world in matters of philanthropy and kindness to widows, to the poor, to children, to the suffering, to the wounded, and to those who are treated harshly by life.

It is about time we knew our facts; it is about time we gave answers to people who are so ignorant of history. While preaching the Gospel, the church has, at exactly the same time, been caring for people in need. Read the story! We have already seen, in the third chapter of Acts, the account of the man who was put to sit every day outside the Beautiful Gate of the temple. Why was he left there? Because beggars have always known that a church is a good place to be near. That is why you have always found people in need crowding outside the doors of churches. And they do it because people who believe in prayer are more likely to respond with pity and compassion to pleas for help, because Christianity makes men and women compassionate, as their Lord was.

Oh yes, practical care for the needy is here—but it is not the first priority. Right though it is to serve tables, we must not allow it to usurp the position of the Word of God. It must be done; so appoint capable men to do it. "It is not reason," the apostles said, "that *we* should leave the word of God, and serve tables."

But we cannot leave it at that. We must go on, in the second place, to point out why it is that the preaching of the Word is and should be the primary task of the church. How do you justify this statement of the apostles? Why is it right that they should put preaching before philanthropic activities? Why do I say today—yes, in this twentieth century!—that "religionless Christianity" is a contradiction in terms, that the primary business of the church is still to preach the Gospel "in season, out of season" (2 Tim. 4:2)? Indeed, I go further and assert that the greatest need of the world today is to hear this message, and what is needed is not less but more preaching. Continue with your philanthropy, but let us have more preaching.

There are many reasons for putting preaching first. I cannot give them all now, but I will try to give the more important ones. Undoubtedly, one reason why the apostles acted as they did was the Lord's commission to them. He had called them and had sent them to preach. Just before His ascension He had said, "Ye shall receive power, after that the Holy Ghost is come upon you: and ye shall be witnesses unto me both in Jerusalem, and in all Judaea, and in Samaria, and unto the uttermost part of the earth" (Acts 1:8). "Witnesses unto me."

During His ministry on earth, our Lord had already sent the apostles out to preach and to cast out devils, and in the upper room, after His resurrection, He had breathed the Holy Spirit upon them and commissioned them to go out. At that time He had said, "Whose soever sins ye remit, they are remitted unto them; and whose soever sins ye retain, they are retained" (John 20:23). Then there was the great, the grand, commission, recorded at the end of Matthew's Gospel: "Go ye therefore, and teach all nations, baptizing them in the name of the Father, and of the Son, and of the Holy Ghost: teaching them to observe all things whatsoever I have commanded you: and, lo, I am with you alway, even unto the end of the world" (28:19-20)—and we have not come to the end of the world yet. It is a commission to go out, to teach and preach. Our Lord gave His apostles the power, and oh, the wonderful things they were told to talk about!

Peter had already told these authorities in Jerusalem, and told them very clearly, that the apostles had been commanded to preach. Several times, as we have been seeing, the Sanhedrin had tried to stop them from preaching. We read in the fourth chapter of Acts that they had said:

> But that it spread no further among the people, let us straitly threaten them, that they speak henceforth to no man in this name. And they called them, and commanded them not to speak at all nor teach in the name of Jesus. But Peter and John answered and said unto them, Whether it be right in the sight of God to hearken unto you more than unto God, judge ye. For we cannot but speak the things which we have seen and heard.
>
> —Acts 4:17-20

And as we have seen, Peter reaffirmed his intention to continue preaching when he was later brought before that same council (Acts 5:30-32). And so now Peter and the apostles said to the Grecians and to their widows and to the whole company that they could not stop preaching. They said, "Are you suggesting that we stop telling people about Him, this blessed person who has come on earth from heaven, this Son of God, this only Savior and Redeemer? Are you telling us not to speak about Him, telling us to serve tables? The idea is monstrous. We cannot but speak. We must. We are heralds; we are proclaimers; we are announcers of the wonderful works of God."

The apostles' response is sufficient in and of itself to show the primary task of the church. If Christianity were merely some human theory and philosophy, then there would be some reason for telling people to spend less time preaching and more time doing good with their hands, feeding the hungry, and caring for the sick and the wounded and the lame and the blind and the halt. But listen to the theme! Oh, the wonder, the marvel! The Son of God becomes Son of man, the redeemer of the world. That was the apostles' message.

But there is another reason why the apostles were so right to speak as they did, and why we must still maintain the same priorities. This message alone deals with our fundamental need. The Grecians seemed to think that the fundamental need was for food and clothing, the need for money and attention—and this is still the idea, is it not? We are living in a materialistic age. People are interested in food, drink, clothing, pleasure, and possessions. That is what our Lord dealt with when He said to that poor fellow who had a problem about inheritance, "Man, who made me a judge or a divider over you? . . . Take heed, and beware of covetousness: for a man's life consisteth not in the abundance of the things which he possesseth" (Luke 12:14-15). The Old Testament had proclaimed this principle, and our Lord repeated it: "Man shall not live by bread alone" (Luke 4:4). It is false to say that the body and the needs and conditions of the body come before everything else, that food, health, saving life, and banishing war should be the primary concerns of Christianity. I repeat, they are not!

The apostles were right when they put preaching first, because it is only by the preaching of this Gospel that we are shown the source of our troubles. Humanity is so superficial in its thinking—that is why it goes so wrong. Before you begin to deal with physical needs and with war, greed, and selfishness, all these things, you ought to stop for a moment and ask why these problems have ever arisen in the world. Why is there suffering? Widows? Why is there death? Where has it come from? What is death? We do not think about that, do we? We have become so clever. We insure against death—we even take out insurance policies to cover our own funeral expenses; but we never stop to think about the meaning of death. That is where our superficiality reveals itself. We are always interested in the surface trappings, but as for the essential problem, we do not even know what it is.

The Gospel, this "word" that the apostles were talking about, and this alone, gets down to the real source of the troubles, the fundamental needs of the human race. It is here to tell us that our whole view of life is wrong and that our world is as it is because of that wrong view. Why are there wars? James answers that question. He says they are due to the "lusts that war" within us (James 4:1). Where have wars come from? Ultimately they come because of people's interest in money and in food and in clothing. One country sees that another has more minerals or oil or more and better land or something; so its leaders look with covetous eyes and hatch their plots. This is how empires have been built up; powerful leaders have seen riches and have grabbed them. That is the whole story of the human race, the history that we glory in. We even exult in the wars in which men have allowed this predatory instinct to get the upper hand. The shame of it all! But that is modern thinking. It starts at the wrong end. But the apostles say, "It is not reason that we should leave the word of God, and serve tables."

So let me put it to you like this: It is wrong to put "serving tables" before the preaching of the Word of God because it is always wrong to put man before God. That, in a nutshell, is the real trouble with the world. Man is at the center; man is everything. And God? He does not come in. The clever people do not even believe in Him; they have banished Him. They are talking and writing about "the death of God." "God is dead!" You can read it in the religious journals; you will see it in the books; you may sometimes hear it on the radio.

To put man at the center was a very subtle temptation for the apostolic church. Here was need. After all, the widows were suffering; they were not having enough food; their clothing was inadequate; they did not have sufficient money. Surely the first thing the apostles were called to do was to attend to them? But in doing that, in giving all their time to that, they would never have preached the Gospel. And the result would have been that humanity would not have known about God. All the troubles in the world today are due to the fact that people do not know about God. My problems, my suffering, my aches and pains, my little unhappiness, my insomnia—my everything—that is the emphasis. Man! God is not mentioned. But this "word" is the Word of God, the Word of the living God.

You must not put man before God because God is over all. Where has the world come from? Where has the human race come from? What is life? What does it mean? What is its purpose? You cannot answer those questions unless you know about God. God is the author of life, the giver of all being. He reigns; He rules over all. And if you do not start with Him, you are bound to go wrong. That is why the world has gone wrong.

Man sets himself up as God. Every man is a god; we are all gods. So we fight one another. Nations are gods. Each nation deifies itself and worships its own records and history. So nations are bound to fight; they cannot help it. That is why you get all these rivalries—rivalries between Grecians and Hebrews, and all the rivalries we see today.

God made the world perfect, and He put man into it perfect; there were no problems in the Garden of Eden. There would never have been the problems of poverty, death, or widowhood had it not been that man in his folly failed to realize as he should have the full truth about God, had he not rebelled against Him. This is what brought the chaos. Rich nations have too much corn; they dump it into the sea or burn it. What makes people do a thing like that when other nations are starving? There is only one answer—they do not live under God.

We think we are clever. We say we must start with the needs of people—we must start with one another, and we say there is only one commandment—"love thy neighbour as thyself." I remember once reading in the paper a statement by the then Lord Provost of the city of Glasgow. A religious conference was being held in Glasgow, and, as they will do these days, the organizers had invited this secular person to the opening meeting. As a way of honoring him, they had asked him to speak—as if a man like that had anything to say in a religious conference! That is the madness of which the church has become guilty. Those men are not to speak—they are to listen, and they need to be preached to. But this foolish man stood up and said that he was an ordinary plain man—they always are!—and he was a man who had no time for theology and dogma, doctrine and all that. He said, "I just want the church to tell me how I can love my neighbor as myself." He put the modern view perfectly, did he not? He put the second commandment first, and he did not mention the first commandment.

There was once a clever man who came to our Lord and asked a question. "Master," he said, "which is the great commandment in the law?" And our Lord said, "Thou shalt love the Lord thy God with all thy heart, and with all thy soul, and with all thy mind. This is the first and great commandment. And the second is like unto it, Thou shalt love thy neighbour as thyself" (Matt. 22:36-39). Did you notice the order? You will never love your neighbor as yourself unless you first love God. Men and women cannot love themselves rightly if they do not start with God. Without God, they have a false notion of themselves, and that leads to a false notion of their neighbors, so that they cannot love them. I repeat that you cannot start with the second commandment: It has to follow the first. Only as humanity realizes the truth about God does it get the right view of everything else.

That is why we must go on giving priority to the preaching of the Word of God. We must tell people about God and their relationship to Him.

So it is wrong to put man before God, and, second, in exactly the same way, it is wrong to put the body before the soul. In other words, we are not only wrong about God, we are wrong about man. What is man? According to the modern theory, man is only body, and so you must attend to everything to do with the body; give it plenty of food, plenty of drink, clothing, shelter, medical care, plenty of sex. Oh, the tragedy that humanity should think it is complimenting itself and exalting itself by turning its back upon God to concentrate on physical needs. And this is what this Word of God encounters, what it denounces. What is man? This message of the Gospel, and this alone, can enlighten us.

When our Lord sent His disciples out preaching, He said to them, "And I say unto you my friends, Be not afraid of them that kill the body, and after that have no more that they can do. But I will forewarn you whom ye shall fear: Fear him, which after he hath killed hath power to cast into hell; yea, I say unto you, Fear him" (Luke 12:4-5). Do not put the body first; put your soul first.

Now I say again that the tragedy of modern men and women is that they are not interested in the soul; that they think only of the pleasures of this life. Indeed, they do not know they have souls, and it is only the Word of God that can tell them this.

"We cannot serve tables," say the apostles. It is insulting to suggest to people that they only have bodies; it is insulting to propose that they are only animals. No, no! They are living souls. God has set eternity in the hearts of men (Eccl. 3:11). He has made men and women to be His companions.

Our Lord once put it like this: "For what shall it profit a man, if he shall gain the whole world, and lose his own soul? Or what shall a man give in exchange for his soul?" (Mark 8:36-37). "Your priorities are wrong," says our Lord—and He made this point on many occasions. I am not disparaging the body; it is no part of Christian preaching to do that. The body is important; we ought to keep it healthy. The needs of the body must be attended to. We need food, clothing, all these things; they are perfectly right and legitimate. But I repeat that if you live for them, your priorities are wrong.

Man! Woman! There is in you something bigger than the world. Do you not feel sometimes that there is that within you crying out for "an ampler ether, a diviner air" [William Wordsworth], something searching into the infinities? That is your soul! You are a spiritual being. That is why all that the world can give is not enough to satisfy you. But the modern world is not interested.

Death! Oh, to people of the world that is a terrible thing. Why? Because they know of no life apart from this world. Because they know nothing about the soul. They are saving the body, they are gaining the world, but losing their own souls.

How terrible it is to put the body before the soul. Many of us know this, do we not, on a lower level? You are intelligent people, and I know that you are often sorry for the kind of person who never reads at all, who has no appreciation of Shakespeare or the great prose writers. Have you not known what it is to be sorry for people who cannot appreciate a great painting or feel nothing when they listen to Beethoven? "Poor things," you say, "they are more animals than people."

And you are perfectly right. They are living like animals. All they are interested in is the flesh; they know nothing about these higher aspects of being human.

But there is something infinitely higher than all the arts and all culture—and that is communion with God, entering into the unseen and the eternal, dwelling in the realm of the spirit. The soul that is in you has been given to you by God, and it is bigger than the whole world and all cultures; it belongs to eternity itself. So the Word of God must be preached to remind this modern age of what it is ignoring.

But, finally, is it not the height of folly and indeed the greatest tragedy to put time before eternity? The feeding of the body only belongs to time. A day is coming in the life of all of us when we will not be interested in food, and when food will not be able to help us at all; we will be beyond that.

But the world lives for the body, does it not? "Do good," people say. "What we want to see is a little practical Christianity. We want you to get out of your pulpit and go into the pubs. People are basically very good-hearted—they are very kind; they just need a little help and assistance. What about all the suffering in the world? Stop preaching every Sunday in your pulpit in Westminster Chapel, and go out and stop the war in Vietnam or do something about South Africa. Religionless Christianity. Burn down your chapels; stop preaching; get rid of your Bibles; do good. What matters is the spirit of love."

No, no; that is to put time before eternity. Listen to what I am saying. A final day is coming. Even with a welfare state, a National Health Service, with miracle drugs and millions spent on medical concerns, with the phenomenal advances of this century, men and women still have to die—the body comes to an end. Widows, wives, husbands, widowers, children—all must die and go on to eternity. And the modern world is as it is because it has forgotten that. This twentieth century? Scientific achievements? Think of those two Americans up in space at this moment[13]—this is marvelous, wonderful, this is what we want! Improve the world; apply science; lift it up!

But the whole world is coming to an end. There is to be an end to time;

there is to be an end to history: "For the things which are seen are temporal; but the things which are not seen are eternal" (2 Cor. 4:18). And there is only one thing that tells men and women about that, and that is the message of the Gospel. That is why nothing must come before it. If only every man and woman in the world today realized that he or she will have to die and stand before God in judgment, it would be a very different world. If every human being realized that we have to give an account of the deeds done in the body, whether good or bad, would they still go on living in the same way, living without thinking about the soul and about death and about the real meaning of life, living only to gratify the baser instincts and that which is merely bodily, forgetting the soul and spirit?

And remember this: The judgment is a judgment for eternity. There is no second chance. You decide in this life what your eternal existence is going to be.

"Ah, but," you say, "the modern man doesn't believe that."

I know. Modern people do not believe many things that are true; that is why they are the fools they are. Can you prove to me that there is not a judgment? How easy just to say, "No cultured person, no sane, reasonable, educated person, believes that any longer." But what does education have to do with this? Does education tell us about what is beyond the veil? Of course not. It knows nothing about it at all. These two men up in space at this moment know no more about heaven and God and eternity than we do—not a fraction more; nor do the clever men who put them up there. It is in the Bible that we find the teaching that eternity lies ahead of us and that it will be one of bliss beyond description or one of tragedy and shame and remorse, again beyond description.

Now that is why I say that this message, "the word of God," must always have priority, even before acts of benevolence and kindness. If you put any one of them first, you are reversing things that must never be reversed. God must be before man! The soul before the body! Eternity before time!

And, indeed, the modern world is proving the truth of what was decided here by the apostles. The apostles' argument was that other agencies could look after the needs of the body, the outward needs; and, of course, people today know all about this. That is why so many do not go to chapels now—the welfare state does it all. It is giving the food; it is giving the widows' pensions; it is giving the clothing; it is giving the housing; it is giving the health, the free National Health Service. So if the church had gone wrong at this point, had simply attended to physical needs and stopped preaching the

Gospel, you see what would have happened? The church would then have become what the world is now.

And what is the world now? We are in an age of materialism, an age of utter confusion. Long ago the Old Testament told us, "Where there is no vision, the people perish" (Prov. 29:18). Oliver Goldsmith saw it:

> *Ill fares the land, to hastening ills a prey,*
> *Where wealth accumulates, and men decay.*

All of us who are alive today, ordinary people as we are, are so much better off than we would have been a hundred years ago. "Never had it so good!" "The affluent society!"

But what of man? What is he doing with the world? How is he spending his weekends? There was a time when men and women spent their weekends listening to the preaching of the Word, and they would be discussing it the next day, and reading books and commentaries about it and discussing them. "Wealth accumulates, and men decay." With all our benefits, with all our concentration on secondary things and our forgetting of the priorities, this is what we have produced—a nation that has lost its vigor and is perishing. All the nobilities are vanishing, disappearing one after another. Moral confusion, moral decline! Theft, robbery, vice! Sneering instead of glorying in the great and the sacred—a decline that is so characteristic of our country.

Similar declines have happened so many times before. Look at the decline and fall of the great Roman Empire. As we have seen, the citizens of Rome went in for what? Bread and circuses! Putting the body before the soul; putting man before God; putting time before eternity.

There is a statement in the Old Testament that I find one of the most alarming in the whole Bible. God warns the nation through a prophet, and He says this: "Behold, the days come, saith the Lord GOD, that I will send a famine in the land, not a famine of bread, nor a thirst for water, but of hearing the words of the LORD" (Amos 8:11). And that is the final calamity because if you do not hear this word, you have nothing left. The things that are seen, on which you have been living, are taken from you, and you are left bereft and hopeless, without anything to comfort you, without anything to give you a glimmer of hope. "A famine of hearing the words of the LORD" is much worse than starving for lack of food or dying for lack of clothing or shelter or attention to your health.

So the great need, the supreme need, is to hear the Word of God, and the church alone can give it. Politicians and statesmen do not know it, and they do not believe in it. Philosophers scoff at it, and scientists ridicule it. Where can I find this "word" that can put me right in regard to God and myself and eternity? It is here and here alone! It is not the word of man—it is the Word of God. It is the living Word that came in the person of the Lord Jesus Christ, the Son of God. He stood up and said, "I am the light of the world: he that followeth me shall not walk in darkness, but shall have the light of life" (John 8:12). "Come unto me," He says, "all ye that labour and are heavy laden, and I will give you rest. Take my yoke upon you, and learn of me . . ." (Matt. 11:28-29). He alone can tell us about God. He alone can show us what men and women are meant to be. He alone can open the gate of heaven. And He alone can deliver us from our perilous, lost condition as the result of our ignorance of these things, for he came into the world "to seek and to save that which was lost" (Luke 19:10).

And that is why the apostles went on saying, "It is not reason that we should leave the word of God"—not even for the sake of serving tables and looking after widows, which is a right and a noble and an excellent thing to do.

So do you start with God or with human beings or with yourself or with scientific achievement? Which is it? Do you put your soul before your body?

> *Dost thou art, to dust returnest,*
> *Was not spoken of the soul.*
>   H. W. Longfellow

Do you know that there is within you that imperishable thing called the soul and that you are going on beyond death to meet God in judgment and on to eternity—do you know that?

And have you put eternity before time? Paul says, "For our light affliction, which is but for a moment, worketh for us a far more exceeding and eternal weight of glory; while we look not at the things which are seen, but at the things which are not seen: for the things which are seen are temporal"—and they will vanish away—"but the things which are not seen are eternal" (2 Cor. 4:17-18).

Are you basing your life on the Word of God? Are your priorities right?

17

THE WORD OF GOD

Then the twelve called the multitude of the disciples unto them, and said, It is not reason that we should leave the word of God, and serve tables. Wherefore, brethren, look ye out among you seven men of honest report, full of the Holy Ghost and wisdom, whom we may appoint over this business. But we will give ourselves continually to prayer, and to the ministry of the word. And the saying pleased the whole multitude. . . . And the word of God increased; and the number of the disciples multiplied in Jerusalem greatly; and a great company of the priests were obedient to the faith.

—Acts 6:2-4, 7

Now I want to call your attention particularly to statements made in the second, fourth, and seventh verses:

Verse 2: "Then the twelve called the multitude of the disciples unto them, and said, It is not reason that we should leave the word of God, and serve tables."

Verse 4: "But we will give ourselves continually to prayer, and to the ministry of the word."

Verse 7: "And the word of God increased; and the number of the disciples multiplied in Jerusalem greatly; and a great company of the priests were obedient to the faith."

I select these three statements because they have an inner connection that I am anxious to put before you. We have already begun a consideration of these verses, and, as I have indicated, this passage is important because it gives us an account of the first moves toward organization in the life of the church. We see here the formation of a kind of diaconate, the calling and the appointing of deacons, and that in and of itself is of great interest. That is not our reason for calling attention to this passage, but I would emphasize the importance of this subject. I think that we of this generation have neglected the doctrine of the church. As evangelicals, particularly, we have been too interested in movements at the expense of the church, and it is the church that is so central in New Testament teaching. However, let me remind you, because here we are given here an account of the character and the nature of the church of God, of her business and the way she is to put all this into practice.

As we have seen, the apostles were confronted by an acute crisis. What should they do? Should they or should they not give themselves to the charitable work of relieving the poverty of the widows? And their decision was one of the most important decisions the Christian church has ever made. In the last study we saw how the apostles, led by the Holy Spirit, declared that the primary task of the church was to minister the Word of God, to preach the Gospel. Everything else, even works of charity and of kindness, were to be secondary to that. And we saw the reasons for this decision.

Now, having done that, we come to what obviously follows from it. If it is the primary task of the church not to serve tables but to preach the Gospel, then how does she do this? And thank God, we are told here quite plainly.

Here, once more, is a most vital matter. Of all the confusion in the world today—and there is confusion politically, philosophically, and in every other respect—the most tragic is the confusion about the message that the church has to preach to people. The church, and the church alone, has been given the task of preaching the message; so what is this message? Now this is a subject of much dispute and debate at the present time. We are face to face with the primary and fundamental problem of authority—the authority of our message—and until we are clear about this, there is no point in proceeding. How can we know what our message is and be sure of it?

Now in a most amazing way, during this very last week, quite unplanned by me, I found myself reading an article that states the essence of the problem in a very succinct way. This article, which was written by a well-known man, appeared in one of the religious weekly papers. This is what it says:

Christianity as a way of life appeals perhaps to more people than ever before when it is presented as a translation into modern terms on the teaching and spirit of Jesus. At the same time, Christianity as a series of propositions about God, about heaven and hell, and in particular about metaphysics, is looked upon with increasing suspicion. In this field it is regarded as one of man's interpretations of his experiences, but not necessarily either a true one or a final one. Now it is this actual situation which determines the method of approach that evangelism must use. What I want to say in this article is that the authoritarian method of approach becomes increasingly ineffective; in fact, it is by its very nature precluded.

And the writer goes on in the article to say that any man who preaches on the authority of the Bible is of necessity doing something that is ineffective. According to him, the message is to be "the teaching of the spirit of Jesus." He denounces propositions of truth and faith—doctrine, dogma, and theology—which he regards as at the best useless and in any case altogether wrong. Modern man, he says, will not have it.

Now one could say a great deal in reply, but I do not want to waste your time. If our friend is interested in results, as he seems to be because he says that theology and preaching are ineffective, then it is very interesting to notice that, in spite of all the publicity he gets, he does not seem to be very effective with what he calls "his gospel." But that is not what chiefly interests us. The question is, Is he right? Is this man's diagnosis of the situation accurate?

Now it seems to me that the answer is given plainly and clearly here in Acts 6. All we must do is consider what the apostles and the first Christians did, because this is what brought the church into being. We read, "In those days, when the number of the disciples was multiplied . . . the word of God increased"—and we are told again—"and the number of the disciples multiplied in Jerusalem greatly; and a great company of the priests were obedient to the faith" (vv. 1, 7). Preaching was the first activity of the church, and that is what she has come back to in every period of reformation and revival. That is our answer to this writer who says that the preaching of the Word is ineffective. This and this alone has ever been effective. So since the church began with preaching, the essence of wisdom is to return to it.

The church, then, must not spend her time in serving tables but is to minister this "word." This emphasis runs right through the Book of Acts. And Paul exhorts Timothy to "preach the word; be instant in season, out of season" (2 Tim. 4:2). Notice the terms that are used in this passage in Acts: "the word of God," "the ministry of the word," "the faith."

Let me emphasize again that I am not interested in this because I enjoy polemics. I do not. God forbid that any of us should. The apostle reminded me tonight, as I entered this pulpit, that "the servant of the Lord must not strive" (2 Tim. 2:24). I do not want to strive, I do not want to argue and debate, but as I have concern about your souls and the souls of men and women, and as I know I shall have to answer for my ministry before the throne and the judgment-seat of Christ, I must warn you against the modern error, this dangerous denial of the truth and the message preached by the Christian church. That is my only motive. May God enable me to present this message in spirit and in truth, and may God grant unto you, my friends, the same spirit as you receive what I am trying to say.

What is the business of the church? It is to minister—it is the ministry of "the word of God," the faith. What, then, does this tell us about our message? What is our authority? I have tried to analyze it for you.

First, we must be clear that our message is the Word of God. It is a word from God. The apostles say, "It is not reason that we should leave the word of God, and serve tables." And here is the starting-point, the point at which so many modern ideas go hopelessly astray. When people talk about "the modern man" and "modern thinking," they have already departed from the practice of the early church. Christianity is not human thinking; it is not human theorizing or philosophizing. These apostles were incapable of that! We have been reminded so many times that they were nothing but "unlearned and ignorant men," incapable of producing a philosophy or a political or sociological theory. The great Greek philosophers could do that, but not fishermen, not ordinary workmen and artisans. If human philosophy, human ideas, had been the message of the church, these men would never have been preachers at all.

That, then, is our first proposition: The Christian message is not the product of human thinking or devising. Later on Peter wrote in his second epistle, "We have not followed cunningly devised fables, when we made known unto you the power and coming of our Lord Jesus Christ" (1:16). Learned men are good at producing such things; they are experts at it. But not apostles. No, no; the Gospel is not human in any shape or form. So what is it? And here is the most important fact we can ever discover: The Gospel is unique; it is absolutely apart. It does not belong to any class or any category whatsoever. It stands alone because it is the word of the living God. And this is the claim for this message that is made by the whole Bible. We preach the Bible because it is "the word of God" and not the words of men.

Let me put it to you like this: From beginning to end, the Bible claims to be a revelation from God. It is one of the great watersheds in the life of the world, and it is astounding to me that anyone can be confused about this. Revelation is the opposite of research; it is the opposite of human seeking and endeavor, and the opposite too of imagination and poetical inspiration or "the muse." Revelation is the veil drawn back by God; it is the truth given and made plain and clear to men and women.

I could quote many passages from the Bible to substantiate the fact that the biblical message comes by revelation from God. One well-known verse refers to the whole question of creation: "Through faith we understand that the worlds were framed by the word of God, so that things which are seen were not made of things which do appear" (Heb. 11:3). "Through faith"! By faith we are given this understanding. It is not that Moses or anybody else had an idea and worked it out into a theory of creation. It was a revelation.

By revelation we mean that God has been pleased, in His infinite mercy and kindness and compassion, to tell us about Himself. We read in Job, "Canst thou by searching find out God?" (11:7). The philosophers have tried throughout the centuries, but they cannot do it. "The world by wisdom knew not God"—and that was why "it pleased God by the foolishness of preaching [the thing preached] to save them that believe" (1 Cor. 1:21). God, by definition, eludes the grasp of human understanding.

The writer who wrote the article I quoted earlier keeps on talking about "the modern man" and what he will and will not accept. How ridiculous this is! No man or woman, whether modern or ancient, can ever arrive at a knowledge of God because He is in eternity, entirely beyond human reach in every respect.

So God has been pleased to reveal and to manifest something of the truth concerning Himself, the world, and humanity, concerning the cause of our ills and the only solution to our problems. Our blessed Lord Himself put this more plainly and clearly than anyone else when He turned to His Father and prayed, "I thank thee, O Father, Lord of heaven and earth, because thou hast hid these things from the wise and prudent, and hast revealed them unto babes. Even so, Father: for so it seemed good in thy sight" (Matt. 11:25-26). It is not the power of the babe that matters here; it is the revelation—it is the making plain and clear. God has "*revealed* them unto babes"—He has shown them, made them known, made them clear, exposed them, opened them out. Revelation!

Now revelation deals essentially with the knowledge that we stand in need of, the content of the message. Take the way that the apostle Paul puts it in writing to the Corinthians: "But as it is written, Eye hath not seen, nor ear heard, neither have entered into the heart of man, the things which God hath prepared for them that love him. But God hath revealed them unto us by his Spirit: for the Spirit searcheth all things, yea, the deep things of God"

(1 Cor. 2:9-10). God makes clear these "deep things of God"—the mystery of His being and all His great and glorious and gracious purposes. That is revelation. From beginning to end it is knowledge that is given to us.

But not only is there revelation, there is, accompanying this, a further element. The revelation has been given to men; the facts have been laid before them; the knowledge has been imparted to them. Now these men must pass it on to others. That is a great responsibility because it is knowledge that is beyond human grasp. How can human beings convey this knowledge that has been given to them freely by God? How can they convey it accurately and without being misleading? So we come to the further element, and this is the inspiration of the Bible. Christians claim that in the Bible there is an inspired record of the revelation that has been given.

Let me just give you one or two pieces of evidence to show what I am talking about. In 2 Timothy 3:16 Paul writes, "All scripture is given by inspiration of God"; that is, all Scripture is "God-breathed," God breathing into men. Inspiration does not mean mechanical dictation; it does not mean that the individual styles of the biblical writers are not brought into operation. But it does mean that God is controlling, God is safeguarding the writing against error or anything that will mislead us. God is breathing through His Spirit in order that the writers may perfectly record His revelation.

Take the way in which the apostle Peter puts it with reference to the great prophets of the Old Testament. In his second epistle he says, "We have also a more sure word of prophecy"—a word of prophecy made more sure—"whereunto ye do well that ye take heed, as unto a light that shineth in a dark place, until the day dawn, and the day star arise in your hearts: knowing this first, that no prophecy of the scripture is of any private interpretation" (1:19-20). That means that the Scriptures do not give a private understanding of life, a man saying something that he has thought out.

What is the Bible, then? Peter continues, "For the prophecy came not in old time by the will of man: but holy men of God spake as they were moved"—or carried along, borne along—"by the Holy Ghost" (v. 21). Now that is the essence of what is meant by inspiration, and Peter is telling us that all the Old Testament prophets were inspired.

Many of the prophets were great men, I grant you, but none of them say, "I've been thinking about this. I've been looking deeply at the problem, and having read about it, I have come to these conclusions." Not at all! "The Spirit of the Lord was upon me"; "the burden of the Lord"; "The Spirit of the Lord possessed me"—that is what they say. The knowledge is given, and they are filled with a kind of divine afflatus, and to their own amazement they utter God's Word. Indeed, Peter tells us that they did not always understand what they were writing. But they wrote it all the same because they knew that it was God who was dealing with them. That is the story of prophecy. It is the story, indeed, of the whole of the Old Testament.

And our Lord claimed the same inspiration for Himself and His teaching. The Holy Spirit came upon Him at his baptism by John in the Jordan; then He returned to Nazareth, entered the synagogue, and said, "The Spirit of the Lord is upon me, because he hath anointed me to preach the gospel to the poor. . . ." When he had finished reading, He said, "This day is this scripture fulfilled in your ears" (Luke 4:18, 21). It is the same principle. "For God giveth not the Spirit by measure unto him" (John 3:34). And the same is true of all the New Testament writers.

These apostles, as Peter had already reminded the Sanhedrin—we saw it in the previous chapter—were eyewitnesses of certain events. But that did not make them authoritative. We need something more. They were not only eyewitnesses; they were men who had been given to understand the meaning of the things they had seen and heard. That is what made them apostles; that is where they derived their authority.

The Lord Himself had expounded the meaning of His life, death, and resurrection. You remember how, with that extraordinary frankness and honesty that characterizes the four Gospels, we are told that after the crucifixion these very men were quite downcast and crestfallen and disappointed. They felt the whole thing had come to nothing. But our Lord appeared to two of His followers and said, "O fools, and slow of heart to believe all that the prophets have spoken: ought not Christ to have suffered these things, and to enter into his glory?" (Luke 24:25-26). And He took them through the Scriptures.

Later that Sunday evening, back in Jerusalem, in the upper room, we are told that our Lord said to the disciples, "All things must be fulfilled, which were written in the law of Moses, and in the prophets, and in the psalms, concerning me" (Luke 24:44). And He explained the teaching of the Bible, showing why He had to suffer and endure these things and rise on the third day. Indeed, in the first chapter of Acts, we find that immediately before His ascension, He had to continue with His teaching because the apostles were still muddled and confused.

"Lord, wilt thou at this time restore again the kingdom to Israel?" they asked (Acts 1:6), still thinking in that old Jewish political manner.

"No, no," he said, "you must not bother about these things: 'Ye shall receive power . . . and ye shall be witnesses unto me'" (Acts 1:7-8). He sent the apostles out to declare the Gospel with authority, with knowledge, and with understanding.

Then our Lord took the final action to make all this absolute, and that was the sending of the Holy Spirit on the Day of Pentecost—the baptism with the Holy Spirit. You remember how He had said to them, "I have yet many things to say unto you, but ye cannot bear them now. Howbeit when he, the Spirit of truth, is come, he will guide you into all truth" (John 16:12-13). There is the promise. God the Father, God the Son, and God the Holy Spirit gave the knowledge, gave the information, and gave the inspiration so that the apostles spoke and wrote it with accuracy.

"He will guide you into all truth," said our Lord. So the apostles were not declaring their words, but the words of God, as they themselves said. "It is not reason that we should leave the word . . ."—the word from God, the word of God, the word of which God is the author, the word that God has given to us—"and serve tables."

And what was true of the apostles, whom we are considering here, was equally true of the apostle Paul. He was not an apostle at this time, but "a blasphemer, and a persecutor [of the church], and injurious," as he later said of himself (1 Tim. 1:13). He was one of the greatest of all the opponents of the Gospel and the Christian church, but later we find him its greatest preacher, its greatest apostle, its greatest exponent of the truth.

How did he come to this? In Acts 26 we read a most lyrical account of what happened. Paul himself tells how the Lord appeared to him and said:

> *Rise, and stand upon thy feet: for I have appeared unto thee for this purpose, to make thee a minister and a witness both of these things which thou hast seen, and of those things in the which I will appear unto thee. [I want to send you to the people and to the Gentiles, that you may give light to them] . . . to open their eyes, and to turn them from darkness to light, and from the power of Satan unto God, that they may receive forgiveness of sins, and inheritance among them which are sanctified by faith that is in me.*
>
> —Acts 26:16, 18

So Paul was commissioned on the road to Damascus. He did not go out to preach as a brilliant Pharisee. No, no; he became a fool. "If any man among you seemeth to be wise in this world," he says, "let him become a fool, that he may be wise" (1 Cor. 3:18). Paul discovered that he knew nothing; he needed a revelation. "I have received of the Lord that which also I delivered unto you," he says of the totality of his message (1 Cor. 11:23). It was not his in any shape or form; it was all given. And so he says to the Galatians, "I certify you, brethren"—I will give you a certificate, if you like—"that the gospel which was preached of me"—by me—"is not after man. For I neither received it of man, neither was I taught it, but by the revelation of Jesus Christ" (Gal. 1:11-12). Surely this is enough once and forever to show that the Gospel originated with God.

Modern man, modern science, twentieth-century knowledge are all irrelevant, and to bring them in is to show that you do not believe that the Gospel is the Word of God. You must not even be nervous about it. This is the Word of God "once [and forever] delivered unto the saints" (Jude 3), and the passing of the centuries does not affect it to the slightest degree. It is a Word from the eternity where there is no time and there can be no change. It is the Word of the living God.

So there is our first point, and it is here before us in Acts, plainly and simply. But we are also told something else here that is equally important. The Word can be defined—it can be stated in propositions. I put it like that because of the modern objection to a propositional gospel. You see the denouncement of such a gospel in the article that I quoted to you. It is rejected in terms of "the spirit of the age" and modern knowledge. "If you preach an authoritarian gospel," they say, "you will court disaster." What utter rubbish that is! What a complete failure to understand the very essence of the truth!

According to the modern idea, what we need is "the spirit of Jesus," and if you go to the Gospels for the ethical teaching of Jesus, you will catch His marvelous spirit. Then you denounce theology and do not like the apostle Paul because he was a theologian, a legalistic Jew, who foisted his legalisms on this simple gospel, the ethical and wonderful spirit of Jesus. But when you do that, all you are left with is a kind of mixture of socialism and pacifism. Yet that is regarded as the message of the Christian church, the only teaching the modern man is ready and prepared to believe.

But in actual fact, modern men and women are not ready and prepared to believe this modern gospel. Indeed, thank God, they do not seem to be as ready to believe that as to believe the authentic Gospel. They are wiser than some of the men who praise them seem to think. But I am here to say that it does not matter what people think. Our business is to preach "the word of God," and it is not a nebulous "spirit of Jesus" or some general disposition, but a message that can be defined, a message that is stated in propositions. This is of the very essence of the New Testament position.

Notice the terms that are used with respect to this word. It is called "the faith": "And the word of God increased; and the number of the disciples multiplied in Jerusalem greatly; and a great number of the priests were obedient to the faith." It is also called "the truth," as we see from endless examples. In his letter to Timothy, the apostle Paul puts it like this: "For this is good and acceptable in the sight of God our Saviour; who will have all men to be saved, and to come unto the knowledge of the truth" (1 Tim. 2:3-4). "The truth"—it is a particular and specific teaching.

Furthermore, what is the Christian church? Listen to Paul again: "But if I tarry long, that thou mayest know how thou oughtest to behave thyself in the house of God, which is the church of the living God, the pillar and ground of the truth" (1 Tim. 3:15). It is that great turret that has been erected where the truth is placarded and displayed; it is the pillar, the support, that which holds forth "the truth." This is something specific. Indeed, Paul goes on to define it. "Without controversy great is the mystery of godliness: God was manifest in the flesh [proposition], justified in the Spirit [proposition], seen of angels [proposition], preached unto the Gentiles [proposition], believed on in the world [proposition], received up into glory [proposition]" (v. 16). Fact! And that is the way in which you always find the Gospel presented in the whole of the New Testament. The faith! The truth!

Or, again, see how Paul puts it in his second letter to Timothy: "And the things that thou hast heard of me among many witnesses, the same"—these things, these particulars—"commit thou to faithful men, who shall be able to teach others also" (2 Tim. 2:2). But in the eighth verse there is something even more specific. "Remember"—remember, Timothy, whatever men may say, whatever these gainsayers Hymenaeus and Philetus and all the rest of them may say—"that Jesus Christ of the seed of David was raised from the dead according to my gospel." "My gospel"! This is something specific, is it not? This is not a vague feeling.

I remember once reading a sermon on the words, "my gospel," and this is how that preacher interpreted them. He said, "The great thing is, are you able to say 'my gospel'? Of course, it may not be somebody else's, but the question is: Is it yours?" And he meant: Have you had some sort of an experience? It does not matter whether it tallies with that of another person. It does not matter whether you stand for the same truth as the worshiper in the pew next to you. It does not matter if you attended last night's religious service along with Anglicans, Roman Catholics, members of the Orthodox Church, followers of Confucius, Buddha, or Mohammed.

God have mercy on us! No, no. The Gospel is "my gospel." It is particular, separate, and definite.

Paul constantly says this, and these truths mean the difference between eternal life and death everlasting. He writes to the Corinthians:

> *Moreover, brethren, I declare unto you the gospel which I preached unto you, which also ye have received, and wherein ye stand; by which also ye are saved, if ye keep in memory what I preached unto you, unless ye have believed in vain. For I delivered unto you first of all that which I also received, how that Christ died for our sins, according to the scriptures [proposition]; and that he was buried, and that he rose again the third day according to the scriptures [propositions]: and that he was seen of Cephas, then of the twelve.*
> —*1 Cor. 15:1-5*

Facts! What could be clearer than this? These are the positive statements of the Scriptures. But in a very interesting manner, the propositional character of the faith is implicit in the way in which the Scriptures deal with false teaching. There were false teachers at the beginning, as there are now; there is nothing new about today's heresies. Surely one of the most laughable of all ideas is the suggestion that it is the hallmark of modernity to deny the facts of the Gospel and to say, for example, that you do not believe in resurrection. It was not believed at the beginning either. Everything that is being denied today was denied in the first century.

In dealing with this false teaching, the apostle Paul wrote:

> *I marvel that ye are so soon removed from him that called you into the grace of Christ unto another gospel: which is not another; but there be some that trouble you, and would pervert the gospel of Christ. But though we, or an angel from heaven, preach any other gospel unto you than that which we have preached unto you, let him be accursed. As we said before, so say I now again, If any man preach any other gospel unto you than that ye have received let him be accursed. For do I now persuade men, or God? or do I seek to please men? for if I yet pleased men, I should not be the servant of Christ.*
> —*Gal. 1:6-10*

Paul goes on to say in effect, "If I were a man-pleaser, I would not preach the cross." And in chapter 5 he talks of the "offence" of the cross (v. 11). People don't like it—they hate it. But he says he is not there to please men; he is not there to pander to their taste. And no preacher of the Gospel should be. We have no right to trim the Word of God or change it in any way to make it suit the modern palate.

What about the antichrists? "Don't listen to them," says the apostle John. And he tells us how to test the difference between Christ and the antichrists, these false spirits that have gone abroad. Here is the way:

> *Beloved, believe not every spirit, but try the spirits whether they are*
> *of God: because many false prophets are gone out into the world.*
> *Hereby know ye the Spirit of God: Every spirit that confesseth that*
> *Jesus Christ is come in the flesh is of God: And every spirit that con-*
> *fesseth not that Jesus Christ is come in the flesh is not of God: and*
> *this is that spirit of antichrist, whereof ye have heard that it should*
> *come; and even now already is it in the world.*
>
> —*1 John 4:1-3*

Indeed, John goes further in his second epistle—evangelicals, listen to this, for you are beginning to forget it, I am afraid—"If there come any unto you, and bring not this doctrine, receive him not into your house, neither bid him God speed" (v. 10). He has no right on your platform. If he denies this doctrine, you must not receive him anywhere. You must have nothing to do with him; he belongs to antichrist, and we have no right to compromise the Word of God. This is how the early church began and flourished.

In the following centuries the early church, in her wisdom, was led by the Holy Spirit to draw up her three great creeds: the great Athanasian Creed, the Nicene Creed, and the Apostles' Creed. These creeds all give definitions of the truth. Because of false teaching creeping in, because of antichrists, the leaders of the church met together, and, under the influence of the Spirit and enlightened by the Word, they said, "The Christian faith is this; it is not that." They were clear and definite, whatever the cost. Athanasius stood alone against the whole world because he knew that he must not compromise the truth. He was not a man-pleaser; he was not interested in popularity or even in majorities; he stood on the Word because it was the Word of the living God.

And likewise, at the time of the Reformation, the Reformers drew up their great and mighty confessions of faith. Church leaders are changing those confessions today; they are shortening them, trying to manipulate them. And that is why the church is as she is; that is why the world is as it is. And there is no hope until we come back to this Word, which is definable in propositions. So we must know *what* we believe as well as *in whom* we have believed. These are the bare essentials, the skeleton of the whole position, without which the church is finished, whatever she may try to do. These are the absolutes.

What, then, is the truth? We must be clear about this. The apostle Paul was very glad that he could say to the elders of the church at Ephesus, "For I have not shunned to declare unto you all the counsel of God" (Acts 20:27). And the church must always be doing this. She did it at the beginning in spite of persecution and opposition: "all the counsel of God."

What is the message of the church? The first principle is that she must never add to the revelation given in the Scriptures. We are told that most solemnly at the very end of the book of Revelation. You cannot mix God's Word with your word. There is nothing known to modern man that in any way adds to this Gospel. You cannot amplify it. It is all here. It is complete, final, absolute. Be careful! Honest men, good men, have sometimes tended to add to it—that is the besetting sin of theologians. We press forward our logic, not stopping when the Scriptures stop, so that we sometimes add to the Scriptures. That is wrong; it is reprehensible. Some statements made by theologians can certainly not be substantiated from the Scriptures.

But, still more important, do not subtract from the Word of God. This is the particular danger at the present time. The man in the article I quoted from talks about what "the modern man" can and cannot take. The modern man, come of age, does not believe in the supernatural and cannot take the miraculous. Drop your miracles, therefore; demythologize your gospel. In the name of God, I say, be careful—do not reduce the Gospel. Hold to "the whole counsel of God"—everything that has been revealed.

The moment the preacher begins to look at his congregation and to think about what they will like and dislike and to ask himself, "What can I get them to believe and accept?" he has already betrayed the Gospel. "Do I seek to please men?" asks Paul, "for if I yet pleased men, I should not be the servant of Christ" (Gal. 1:10). Paul's refusal to water down the Gospel is seen in all his great testimonies. He preaches God, the God who has given him the message of the Gospel, the God to whom he is answerable. So the second principle is that whatever men may say, we must not subtract from the Gospel.

We are in danger of subtracting from the Gospel, the Word of God, in many ways and for many reasons. There is always the possibility of a truncated gospel. In order to please the intellectuals, some people take out the miraculous and the supernatural. "Out of a desire to please non-intellectuals," others say, "we must simplify the Gospel." It is as wrong and dangerous to subtract from the Scriptures to please the ignoramus as it is to please the intellectual.

"But," you say, "the ignorant man won't believe it."

Won't he? Where is the Holy Spirit? We are too clever; we seem to think that we are making people believe. But we are not. Look at these apostles. Look at the apostle Paul preaching to slaves, to soldiers, to servants, to people who knew nothing about these things. He gave them "all the counsel of God" (Acts 20:27), and they were able to take it in. Why? "God hath revealed them unto us by his Spirit" (1 Cor. 2:10).

To me, there is nothing more fascinating and romantic in the Christian ministry than seeing how men and women, who I would have thought, by my human judgment, incapable of following a sermon, being able to follow it, and follow it very much better than supposed intellectuals—as I have later found out when talking to them. There is a Holy Spirit, my dear friends! The Gospel is not dependent on the preacher but comes "in demonstration of the Spirit and of power" (1 Cor. 2:4). The whole Gospel—send it out. The Spirit will apply it; He will enable people to understand it.

The third principle is that the gospel message must not be distorted by human ideas. There are many warnings in the Scriptures not to make the Gospel "of none effect" through human philosophy. In 1 Corinthians 1:17, Paul says he was sent to preach the Gospel "not with wisdom of words, lest the cross of Christ should be made of none effect." He says the same thing in his letter to the Colossians: "Beware lest any man spoil you through philosophy and vain deceit" (2:8). Do not be deceived by human wisdom and understanding and knowledge. Do not let anyone pervert your Gospel; do not let anyone change it into something else. There are people who are preaching the cross of Christ as the most beautiful thing in the world: "A most marvelous thing—it will make people weep." But as we have seen, Paul talks about "the offence of the cross" (Gal. 5:11). It is ugly! If you make it beautiful, you have been indulging in philosophizing and have made it of none effect.

In the same way, we must not make the Gospel of none effect through our psychology. A great deal of Christianity is being taught in terms of psychology. "Are you having trouble with insomnia? Let me introduce you to Jesus—He will soon deal with your insomnia. As for your aches and pains, and this and that problem, come to Jesus. Meet Him and all will be well." That is not the preaching of the Gospel—it is psychology.

So much modern preaching does not start where the Gospel starts. There is nothing more important than the start, is there? It is the most important part of a journey. And it is the same with preaching. The Gospel starts with God. At the risk of being misunderstood, let me put it like this: The Gospel does not start with the Lord Jesus Christ, with Jesus. If you think it does, you do not know your Bible, you do not know your New Testament. Still less does it start and end with men and women and their needs and foibles, their aches and pains and their twentieth-century knowledge. No, no! The Gospel is a revelation of God. It is the Word of God, and it always starts with Him, the eternal Father, the everlasting God!

The Gospel starts with the Old Testament. If you read these chapters of Acts, you will see the truth of what I am saying. Apostolic preaching started with God, with the Old Testament background. Of course, the apostles were bound to start in that way because there is no meaning nor sense in the Gospel without this background. Likewise, the preaching of John the Baptist was repentance. And when our Lord first began preaching, He said, "The time is fulfilled, and the kingdom of God is at hand: repent ye, and believe the gospel" (Mark 1:15). Repent! To whom? What for? You do not understand repentance unless you start with God.

Then take Paul. As he said good-bye to the elders of the church at Ephesus, he said, "I kept back nothing that was profitable unto you, but have showed you, and have taught you publicly, and from house to house, testifying . . . repentance toward God, and faith toward our Lord Jesus Christ" (Acts 20:20-21). Notice what comes first: "Repentance toward God"! And if we do not start there, it is not the Word of God.

We must start with "the living and true God" (1 Thess. 1:9), the acting God, God the Creator, God the sustainer of the whole universe. We must know Him in His glorious character, everlasting and eternal. In John's Gospel we read, "No man hath seen God at any time; the only begotten Son, which is in the bosom of the Father, he hath declared him" (John 1:18). The Son has revealed God. The Son has taught us; He has come to tell us about Him. This is where you start: God's glorious character.

And then we see God as Judge—the Judge of every person who has ever been born into this life. That is what the apostles preached. Read how Paul preached it in Lystra to pagans, and how he preached it both in Athens and in Thessalonica to pagans. He told them to turn "from idols to serve the living and true God" (1 Thess. 1:9).

"But," you say, "they couldn't have understood this terminology."

I know. But the Spirit enabled them to believe it. The Spirit gives the understanding. Give them the knowledge of God, preach the whole counsel, and the Spirit will apply it. So let us be clear about the message that is given— it is about this eternal God who is our eternal Judge.

But, you continue, modern people don't believe in God. Can't you give some proof?

Well, we can and do present arguments for the existence of God. But ultimately only the Spirit can convict people of God's reality. If we could prove these truths beyond doubt, everybody would believe them. But the Bible tells us they cannot be proved in that way. Is there any kind of proof? Oh, yes, there is. But, remember, I cannot call upon my experience as proof. I have sometimes heard people saying, "Ah, you ask me how I can prove this. Well, my answer is that my experience tells me that I have met God—I know God." But that does not satisfy the psychologist. He can play with that very easily. He simply says, "Of course, deluded people are always very confident of these things," and he dismisses your experience as a mere psychological complex.

No, no; if you want proof, then it is to be had. Creation! Design! Order! Arrangement! I have often said from this pulpit that if I had no other proof, the human eye would be more than enough for me—its delicacy, its balance, its subtlety. It is sheer nonsense to suggest that this is an accident. It is inconceivable. Sir James Jeans was driven to belief in God by his scientific discoveries.

Of course, there are these great arguments, the so-called "proofs of God." But they are not the best proof. The Bible itself is a greater proof. Look at these books, all forming one Book, written by different men, with different temperaments, written in different circumstances, in different centuries—and all with the same essential message. The marvel, the miracle, of Scripture is a proof of God. Look at history. Look at the Jew—he is a proof of God and the truth of the Bible. You cannot explain the persistence of the Jew in any other way.

But if you want the biggest proof of all, it is the proof of prophecy, the proof that Peter employed in the first chapter of his second epistle. You cannot explain the prophecy found in the Scriptures in any other terms than that God revealed the facts to men and enabled them by His inspiration to record them in the accurate manner in which they did, down even to the small details.

So when you start preaching, you start with God. And then you go on to the doctrine of man. What is man? What is man's origin? What are men and women meant to be? How are they meant to live? What is the prospect for them? The Bible alone can answer these questions. No theory of evolution, no human theory, is at all satisfactory. These theories leave greater problems than the explanation given by the Scriptures.

Similarly, the doctrine of the Fall, as it is taught in the Word of God, is the only adequate explanation for the troubles of the world. Why, with all our cleverness and learning and advanced science, is the world as it is? Look at what is happening in Vietnam and in other parts of the world, including our own country. What is the explanation? There is only one. The devil, "the prince of the power of the air, the spirit that now worketh in the children of disobedience" (Eph. 2:2), came and tempted Adam and Eve, and they, listening in their folly, rebelled against God and fell into sin.

The Word of God tells of the judgment of God upon Adam and Eve and the consequences that have ensued to the race of Adam. What are they? Spiritual death and blindness; sin as slavery; sorrow and trouble; selfishness and immorality and vice; all the lusts of the flesh and of the mind; all that you see in the modern world. God's Word gives the only explanation of the universality of sin and of the state of the world. People laugh at this, I know. They have always done so. They laughed at Noah; they laughed at Lot; they laughed at the Son of God. But each time the judgment came! And it will come. The end of the world, the return of Christ, the final judgment, and the eternal punishment are all part of the message of the Gospel.

So that is where the gospel message starts—not with your particular problems and mine. What is important for you is not whether or not you can sleep, not whether or not you fall into some particular sin; what is important for you is your whole position and standing before God. That is what you need to think about. We all have our particular troubles and problems, but this is common to us all: "There is none righteous, no, not one" (Rom. 3:10). We are all under the wrath and the judgment of God.

Start with God. And the moment you do that, people are ready to listen to the gospel message. But until they have believed in God and in these other propositions of this truth, this faith, there is no sense or meaning in the death of Christ. You can say to people, "Come to Jesus," but they say, "I couldn't care less! I don't need Him. I'm having a very good time." But show them that when they die they will face God in the judgment and that they are faced with an eternity of misery and useless remorse and suffering, then they will be ready to listen; they will want to know about Him whom God raised up "to be a Prince and a Saviour, for to give repentance to Israel, and forgiveness of sins" (Acts 5:31).

If you have seen something of the glory of the everlasting and eternal God and your ignorance of Him and your self-centeredness, if you see yourself as a condemned sinner, listen to this message of the Word of God: "God was in Christ, reconciling the world unto himself" (2 Cor. 5:19).

Believe that God so loved you that He sent His only Son into this world for you, to bear your sins, to bear their punishment, to set you free, to give you forgiveness, to give you new life and a new start, to take you through the judgment, and eventually to receive you into the eternal glory. Just as you are, believe it, give obedience to it, and you will receive the knowledge that your sins are forgiven and that you are reconciled to God.

Thank God for the Word of God—the old, old story that is ever new and ever true, which is truth unchanged, unchanging, unchangeable, because it is the truth of God.

18

AN EXCLUSIVE MESSAGE

And in those days, when the number of the disciples was multiplied, there arose a murmuring of the Grecians against the Hebrews, because their widows were neglected in the daily ministration. Then the twelve called the multitude of the disciples unto them, and said, It is not reason that we should leave the word of God, and serve tables. Wherefore, brethren, look ye out among you seven men of honest report, full of the Holy Ghost and wisdom, whom we may appoint over this business. But we will give ourselves continually to prayer, and to the ministry of the word.

—Acts 6:1-4

We come back for the third time to a consideration of the opening verses of chapter 6 and their very important message. I ended our last study by saying something in general about the content of the great message of the Bible, and that is the point at which we resume. We saw that, in the first instance, the Gospel is always a message that starts with God.

As men and women, we differ in many respects; we differ in nationality, in appearance, in our backgrounds, in our ability or lack of it, in how much money we have. And we have many varying problems. We are all concerned about our own particular difficulties and differences. But this is where we are all making a mistake. What is important is what we all have in common, and that is our standing in the presence of God. The moment we realize that, we see that all these other matters are comparatively superficial, however big they may appear to be. All of us are in the same position; we are all face-to-face with God.

And it is just at this point that the Christian message comes in. This is what made these apostles feel that they must continue telling everybody about it. We have seen already that they were arrested, thrown into prison, and put on trial before the court. Furthermore, the great Sanhedrin repeatedly prohibited them from speaking or teaching any longer in the name of this Jesus. The Sanhedrin did everything it could to put an end to this preaching. And here now were these Grecians unconsciously becoming the tools of the devil and trying to say the same thing. They said, "Why don't you deal with this problem of our widows? Why don't you give the whole of your time to this?"

There is only one answer to the objections both of the Sanhedrin and of the Grecians: The preaching must come first. Why is this? It is because of the glory of the message, because of its uniqueness, and because humanity needs this message above and before every other message.

That is not to say that other things are not important. Of course they are. Health is important; having enough food is important; looking after widows is important. But remember this: "What shall it profit a man, if he shall gain the whole world, and lose his own soul?" (Mark 8:36). Even if you are rid of all your aches and pains and personal problems, you still cannot evade the coming day of judgment, as is stated so plainly by the writer of Hebrews: "It is appointed unto men once to die, but after this the judgment" (9:27). And when you are on your deathbed, it does not matter very much what put you there, whether a flaring pneumonia or a cancer eating your vitals away; your personal problems no longer matter. It is all irrelevant. The one question that matters is: "What shall it profit a man . . .?"

"No, no," said the apostles, "we cannot put the ministry of the Word of God to one side, even for the sake of doing that good work; we must and we will go on preaching." This alone can speak to a soul—a soul on its deathbed, a soul face-to-face with God.

Or to put it another way, the apostles had to continue preaching because they were declaring a gospel. Now the word *gospel* is just old English for "good news." "We cannot put this on one side," they said in effect, "because this is good news, the greatest, the best, the most glorious good news that has ever come into this world. People are dying," they said, "and they do not know about it. So we must give ourselves to this proclamation, the ministry of this Word. We must blazon it forth; we must shout it and herald it. We are the people called and sent out to preach by Christ, the living God, the Master." "Comfort ye, comfort ye my people, saith your God" (Isa. 40:1). Here it is. It is good news. And the good news is that there is a way of escape, a way of deliverance, and that is the most marvelous truth that the world can know.

The world is weary. Look at it! Look at what is happening in it! Is this a civilization to boast of? Is this some great achievement in which we can take pride? Look at the international situation; look at the problems within the nations. Look into your own heart. Civilization is a disastrous failure. Yes, go to the libraries, look at the works of the great philosophers, read the writings of the present philosophers, read the biographies of great statesmen, men who have grappled with the problems—they have all failed. The world is wretched; it is bankrupt; it does not know what to do. That is why it plunges into pleasure and turns to alcohol and drugs. It is all escapism.

And it is to a world like this that preachers say, "We must give ourselves to this ministry of the Word because we alone know there is a solution; there is a way of escape; there is a way of deliverance. We have been sent, we have been called, we have been commissioned, to proclaim glad tidings of salvation."

"How beautiful upon the mountains are the feet of him that bringeth good tidings" (Isa. 52:7). Preachers are messengers of peace. Now that is what the apostles saw so clearly, and they said, "Since we alone have the answer, we cannot put anything before this; we must give ourselves exclusively to the message of the Gospel."

So what is this way of deliverance? It is in the Lord Jesus Christ, and in Him alone. There is no other hope for the world apart from this blessed person, this one and only Savior. He alone can save. The apostles constantly repeated this message. We have seen it in every previous chapter of Acts, apart from the first, and even there it is implicit because our Lord sent them out to preach and promised the power to do so. And notice that the preaching was to be all about Him: "Ye shall be witnesses unto me" (Acts 1:8). Christ is the only, the exclusive, Savior.

But why must we say that our Lord is the exclusive Savior? Why were the apostles so sure of this? Why did they emphasize this exclusiveness? Remember, this was the great battle they had to fight against the Sanhedrin, which consisted of Pharisees, scribes, Sadducees, members of the Herodian party, and religious people of that kind. Those rulers wanted to hold on to their old religion. They wanted to hold on to the religion of the temple, a religion that had a magnificent building and many rituals—Hebrews 9 describes some of the ordinances.

Around the temple building there was a very large walled area, open to the sky, which was divided into various "courts." First, there was a large outer court, the Court of the Gentiles, where anybody could enter; then the Court of the Women, where all Jews could go. Further in was the Court of

Israel, open to Jewish laymen; then came the inner court, the Court of Priests, which was normally only for the priests. The temple building itself was divided into two by a veil, a curtain, that separated the inner room, called "the Holiest of All," from the outer room, "the Holy Place." Only one man could go into "the Holiest of All," and then only once a year, and that was the high priest.

The Jews also had their offerings and their sacrifices. Once a year, on the Day of Atonement, the high priest took a young bull, and also a goat, killed them, and sprinkled some of their blood on the cover of the mercy seat in the Holiest of All. This was to make atonement for his sins and the sins of all the people. All that is described in the ninth chapter of Hebrews.

Now the rulers of the Jews wanted the temple rituals to continue, but the apostles said they had to come to an end. That was their message. There was now only one way into the Holiest of All, and it was by this Jesus, by His blood. The apostles had to fight for this; they alone had seen it. It had been given to them to see it, and they preached it. They said, "This is the way of salvation. If you cling to that other way, you are clinging to something that will lead you to perdition. You must realize that He has put an end to the temple sacrifices. He is the way, and the only way."

So why did the apostles preach with such confidence and certainty, and why must we do the same? Why must we say that this is an exclusive message? Why have I the boldness to stand up in 1966 in this pulpit and say, "Do not turn to any other religion. Do not turn to Confucius; do not turn to Buddha; do not turn to Mohammed; do not turn to Hinduism and all its ramifications and subdivisions; do not turn to your philosophers; do not turn to anybody. Look only unto Jesus." On what grounds do I say that? Is it just arrogance?

Well, let me give you the answers that these men were always giving and that we must still give. The Gospel is an exclusive message because it is God's way. We have seen that the apostles constantly said this. When they were on trial, and their accusers said, "Did not we straitly command you that ye should not teach in this name? and, behold, ye have filled Jerusalem with your doctrine, and intend to bring this man's blood upon us," Peter and the other apostles replied, "We ought to obey God rather than men. The God of our fathers raised up Jesus, whom ye slew and hanged on a tree" (Acts 5:28-30). "The God of our fathers"! This is God's way of salvation.

We have come to the very essence of the Gospel. It is exclusive because it is what God has prepared. The apostle Paul, as is so often the case, puts this in a particularly clear way. In his second letter to the Corinthians he says:

And all things are of God, who hath reconciled us to himself by Jesus Christ, and hath given to us the ministry of reconciliation; to wit, that God was in [and through] Christ, reconciling the world unto himself, not imputing their trespasses unto them; and hath committed unto us the word of reconciliation. Now then we are ambassadors for Christ, as though God did beseech you by us: we pray you in Christ's stead, be ye reconciled to God.

—5:18-20

That is it! "God was in Christ, reconciling the world unto himself." And Paul constantly says this. "But we preach Christ crucified, unto the Jews a stumblingblock, and unto the Greeks foolishness; but unto them which are called, both Jews and Greeks, Christ, the power of God, and the wisdom of God" (1 Cor. 1:23-24).

Here is the answer, and it is a very serious matter. "The God of our fathers hath raised up his Son Jesus." All other teachings and all other proposals are only human ones. All other religions are man-made. So here is the first and the great answer for claiming an exclusiveness for the Christian message. Indeed, this is stated in the whole of the Bible, is it not? The Bible is not a record of man's search for God, but of God coming down to save man.

The Bible starts by giving an account of creation and of how God made everything perfect—paradise. He set Adam and Eve in the Garden of Eden, and all was well. And then came the Fall, and God came down to the garden. Oh, thank God that He did. If it had not been for this, we would have no message at all. Adam and Eve, in the chaos that they produced in the garden, did not know what to do or where to turn, and when they heard the voice of God they even ran to hide.

God came down! The whole biblical record is the record of God coming to save humanity, and it begins there, way back in the third chapter of Genesis—the promise concerning the seed of the woman that is finally going to bruise the serpent's head.

And God's first promise to Adam and Eve was followed by repeated promises that He would come. God had to make a nation in order that He might come. He had to take a man like Abraham and turn him into a nation and out of him produce a great progeny. God even made a nation in order to bear this message, and He gave parts and portions of this great promise to different people in different centuries and in different ways, but they were all saying the same thing. All God's messengers were telling of a world that had fallen away from God and brought chaos upon itself.

But God's messengers also announced that He would send a Redeemer, His Messiah. Some said this about Him, others that, but all were talking about Him and looking for Him. "Comfort ye, comfort ye my people, saith your God . . . make straight in the desert a highway for our God . . . and all flesh shall see it together" (Isa. 40:1-5). The whole of the Old Testament looks forward to the arrival of this mighty deliverer. It is all from God.

And then, as the apostle Paul writes, "When the fulness of the time was come, God sent forth his Son, made of a woman, made under the law, to redeem them that were under the law" (Gal. 4:4-5). That is it! From beginning to end salvation was the action of God. He announced the Son's coming, His birth, by sending an archangel. To think that the Christian message was man's teaching and ideas, that Jesus of Nazareth was but a religious genius, is to miss the point of the whole Bible. It is the supernatural action of God. Everything is miraculous, angelic, divine. All the power of the Godhead is involved in your salvation and mine. That is why the apostles felt they had to preach it. Nothing must come before this. No one can stop this. It is God's way of salvation.

And we must all the more realize the exclusiveness of the Christian message as we face the fact that everything else has failed. That is the importance of knowing your Old Testament. People still seem to have the idea that if they are only told what to do, then they can get up and do it; that if they are only told how to live, then they can use their willpower and they can live it.

But the only people who can believe in man's ability to save himself are those who have never read the Old Testament. In the pages of the Old Testament we read of some of the greatest and most wonderful people that the world has ever known, and yet we find that every one of them failed. They were defeated; they were sinners. God gave a law to the children of Israel, and when He gave them that law through Moses, He said, "If you can keep that law, it will save you."

The people had said, "Show us how to live," just as people say today. So God showed them how to live—He gave them the Ten Commandments. But no one could keep those laws. "By the law is the knowledge of sin," wrote Paul (Rom. 3:20). The law does not give you power and strength to keep it. The law will tell you what you ought to be, but that does not enable you to be it. It is one thing to know what is right; it is a very different thing to be able to do it. That was the whole experience of Paul: "For I delight in the law of God after the inward man: But I see another law in my members, warring against the law of my mind, and bringing me into captivity to the law of sin which is in my members" (Rom. 7:22-23). "For the good that I would I do not: but the evil which I would not, that I do" (v. 19). Here I am—a mass of contradictions. I cannot live as I should. I fail. "O wretched man that I am!" (v. 24).

But that failure not only applied to the children of Israel—it was equally true of the Greeks. There they were, the great thinkers who could delve into the mysteries of thought; but not one of them could find God. "The world by wisdom knew not God" (1 Cor. 1:21). One of the great problems in Greece at the time when our Lord came was the terrible problem of the modern world—the problem of suicide, and the suicide rate was highest among philosophers. Moreover, many of the greatest philosophers were leaders in the practice of sexual perversions.

Every philosophy and religion that human beings have ever thought of—Confucianism, Buddhism, Hinduism—are ultimately all religions of misery; they are all negative and depressing. They do not liberate people but keep them in bondage and slavery. There is no happiness; there is no joy there. They are man-made, and men and women cannot carry out their laws and precepts. They cannot save themselves; so how can they possibly save others?

And so I put it to you positively like this: The Gospel is an exclusive message because it alone tells us of the only way whereby we can receive salvation. What is the task and the problem? What is the need of humanity?

Again I must start with a negative: Our need is not simply to be cured of our sickness. Sin is sickness, but it is not only sickness. Sin does make us ill; it does make us weak and unhappy; it does produce failure. But the primary task of the Gospel is not to make us better. And that is what the world does not like. The world is interested in being better, in being made to feel happy. The world is ready to listen to the cults and their teaching, because the cults say, "Come to us, believe what we say, and then you will no longer be a worrier, you will no longer have insomnia, you will no longer feel out of your depth, and you will no longer be afraid of life. Come to us; we will put you right." The world never objects to that because it knows it is sick.

But thank God, the Gospel does not come in that way. The Gospel does deal with our sicknesses and diseases, but it does not start with them. The first great problem of all human beings is the problem of the guilt of sin, and their first need is to be delivered from this guilt. If we do not start there, then what we regard as the Gospel is nothing but some psychological technique that makes us feel a little bit better for the moment. The true Gospel starts with the basic problem—the honor of God, the glory of God, the justice and the righteousness of the everlasting and eternal God.

Sin is rebellion. Sin is transgression. Sin is an insult to the honor and the dignity and the glory of God. It is an insult to the majesty and the excellence of His holy law. Our first problem is that we have offended God. If you break the law of England, you are arrested and put on trial. And what will it avail you if you stand up in court and begin to talk about your illnesses and your diseases? No, no; you will be told, "The charge against you is that you have broken such and such a subsection of such and such a law. Here it is. This is the charge, and you must answer it."

And the charge that is brought against every one of us is that we have insulted God. His glory and honor are to come first. God in His infinite glory has made men and women for Himself. In the words of the Shorter Catechism, "Man's chief end is to glorify God, and to enjoy him for ever." That is the purpose for which we were made—and we have all failed. We are all guilty before God. "For all have sinned, and come short of the glory of God" (Rom. 3:23).

Now lest you may think I am simply voicing my own theological opinions on this matter, take the words of our Lord. When a man came to Him and asked how to inherit eternal life, and Jesus asked him what the law said, that man rightly replied, "Thou shalt love the Lord thy God with all thy heart, and with all thy soul, and with all thy strength, and with all thy mind" (Luke 10:27). That is the first commandment. Have you kept it? Have you loved God with the whole of your being, and then gone on to love your neighbor as yourself? That is what God demands of us; and the first problem is that we have all fallen short of it. So the whole world is guilty before God (see Rom. 3:19), and "The wages of sin is death" (Rom. 6:23).

"But," you say, "God is love, and He is ready to forgive me."

But it is not as simple as that. What about the justice of God? What about His righteousness and holiness? God is not only love, remember. "God is light, and in him is no darkness at all" (1 John 1:5). If you say, "The love of God will put things right for me," then there is no Gospel to preach, no Savior to proclaim. The Lord Jesus would not have come. Why did the Son of God ever leave the courts of heaven and be born as a babe in Bethlehem? Why was the Incarnation a necessity? Why did He have to die upon the cross? These are the questions that must be answered.

The Son of God had to come into the world and be born as a babe—"The Word was made flesh" (John 1:14)—because not one of us can ever save ourselves, let alone anybody else. The two perfect people in paradise sinned and went wrong. And if God had created two more perfect people, they would have done exactly the same thing. Perfect man has already had a chance, and he has failed. The devil is too strong; the power of evil is too great. There is only one way of salvation, and that is the way that was thought out by God in His eternal wisdom.

This is the great message of the Bible—God's way of salvation. The babe of Bethlehem is the eternal Son of God. He is God the Son, co-equal, co-eternal with His Father, of the same substance. God, everlasting and eternal! Mighty God! Everlasting Savior. Jesus is God *and* man. "The Word was made flesh, and dwelt among us" (John 1:14). Here is a new being; He is man, but He is more than man—He is God. He is pure, undefiled. He is "that holy thing" that was born of Mary (Luke 1:35). He is "the Lamb of God" (John 1:29).

Oh, follow that mighty argument of the Epistle to the Hebrews: "The blood of bulls and of goats, and the ashes of an heifer" (9:13) could not cleanse us from our sin. Even if you were to slay a human being, his blood would be inadequate. It is impure; it is polluted; it is vile. We need a new man! And God has made the new man, but He has combined Him with the Godhead. God had ordained the sacrifice of bulls and goats; lambs were slain morning and evening, and their blood was taken. Yes, but these sacrifices were all simply prophecies, adumbrations; they pointed forward to "the Lamb of God, which taketh away the sin of the world" (John 1:29)—and the Lamb of God is the Son of God!

But the Son had to be made man because we are human. He must be human in order to save us. God cannot save by appearing! He comes and is "made flesh." And so He stands as our representative.

And yet man is not enough. If any man could have saved us, the Incarnation would never have taken place. More is needed, and there is more—God and man. The Godhead guarantees the manhood and lifts it up in this indissoluble linking. The Lord Jesus Christ is enough to bear the punishment, to go through death and out the other side to save us, to redeem us, to represent us before God, and to present us at the end perfect in His holy presence. That is the message, and it is only true of Him; there is nobody else. I am not detracting from the greatness of other religious leaders. You may praise your religious exemplars—I do not quarrel with you. But all I say is this: Not one of them could save himself, still less save me.

So the message to the Sanhedrin was, "The God of our Fathers raised up Jesus, whom ye slew and hanged on a tree. Him hath God exalted with his right hand to be a Prince and a Saviour, for to give repentance to Israel, and forgiveness of sins." The apostles said, "We must go on preaching. We have the only message that can save any individual. God has made a way of escape, a way of salvation, a way of deliverance, a way of forgiveness, and He has done it by sending His only Son into the world in the likeness of sinful flesh."

This was the gospel message: The Son of God humbled Himself and became a man. He "made himself of no reputation" (Phil. 2:7). He was buffeted by the world, "in all points tempted like as we are" (Heb. 4:15). But He never sinned. He bore it all; He "endured such contradiction of sinners against himself" (Heb. 12:3). And He "steadfastly set his face to go to Jerusalem" (Luke 9:51). His followers warned Him that Herod was waiting for Him, that His enemies were plotting to catch Him. "Don't go," they said. "Stay away."

But our Lord knew that His death in Jerusalem was the only way whereby a single individual could ever be saved. Come with me for a moment to the Garden of Gethsemane, and there see Him alone, sweating drops of blood. Listen to what He is saying: "Father, if thou be willing, remove this cup from me: nevertheless not my will, but thine, be done" (Luke 22:42). He asks, "Is this the only way?"

And the answer comes back, "Yes, it is."

And our Lord says that He is willing, He is ready. He crosses the Kidron brook and goes on to Calvary, "as a lamb to the slaughter" (Isa. 53:7). He does not defend Himself. He goes in apparent weakness and helplessness. And they nail Him to the tree!

What is happening here? Is it just men misunderstanding, not recognizing a great leader and teacher? No, no! It is God who "hath made him to be sin for us, who knew no sin; that we might be made the righteousness of God in him" (2 Cor. 5:21). The prophet Isaiah wrote, "We did esteem him stricken, smitten of God" (Isa. 53:4). It is the Father who is striking Him! It is God who is pouring out upon Him His wrath. It is God punishing our sins in the person of His own Son! So Peter wrote, "Who his own self bare our sins in his own body on the tree, that we, being dead to sins, should live unto righteousness: by whose stripes ye were healed" (1 Pet. 2:24). That is the meaning of the death of the Son of God on Calvary's hill. That was the message preached by the early church, by the apostles—"Jesus Christ, and him crucified" (1 Cor. 2:2). "Christ the power of God, and the wisdom of God" (1 Cor. 1:24). The cross!

Our Lord's last words on the cross were these: "It is finished" (John 19:30). What was finished? He had finished bearing the punishment of your sins and mine. He had gone through with it all. He had drunk the cup to the very dregs, and there was nothing left to be done.

And the absolute proof is the resurrection. The resurrection of Jesus

Christ is proof positive that He has borne the complete punishment of our sins, that the law of God is satisfied and that God is satisfied. In the resurrection God declares that His Son has finished and completed the work: "who was delivered for our offences, and was raised again for our justification" (Rom. 4:25).

And our Lord did rise! He manifested Himself to the apostles and to other chosen witnesses. Then, after forty days, and in the very presence of the apostles, our Lord ascended from Mount Olivet up into heaven, and there He presented His own blood. Then He sat down at the right hand of the majesty of God in the glory everlasting. And there He now sits, and there He reigns, and there He waits until God finally sends Him back again to complete this grand redemption and to restore a renewed universe to God the Father.

So the message to the Sanhedrin was: Stop going to your temple; stop trusting in your priesthood; stop trusting in the killing of bulls and goats. Stop all your ceremonial, and turn to the Son of God, the Lord Jesus Christ, "the Lamb of God." And, most marvelous of all, believe that He is "the end of the law for righteousness to every one that believeth" (Rom. 10:4).

And the message for us is not, Decide to live a better life; join a church; try to please God. No, no! That is religion. The message is that all we have to do is realize that we have offended the majesty and the honor and the glory of God, and that we are hopeless, helpless, damned sinners, but that Christ, the Son of God, has died for us and borne our punishment, and that here and now, just as we are, without doing anything, we simply believe in Him and trust our eternal future to Him.

That is the word that must be preached at all costs. It is the only hope for every individual in the universe at this moment. Have you believed this word?

19

PRAYER

And in those days, when the number of the disciples was multiplied, there arose a murmuring of the Grecians against the Hebrews, because their widows were neglected in the daily ministration. Then the twelve called the multitude of the disciples unto them, and said, It is not reason that we should leave the word of God, and serve tables. Wherefore, brethren, look ye out among you seven men of honest report, full of the Holy Ghost and wisdom, whom we may appoint over this business. But we will give ourselves continually to prayer, and to the ministry of the word.

—Acts 6:1-4

Now I want again to deal particularly with that fourth verse: "But we will give ourselves continually to prayer, and to the ministry of the word." We have seen the importance of knowing exactly what that "word" is, and now I want to emphasize the first part of this verse: "We will give ourselves continually to prayer . . ." Why do the apostles include prayer, and why, indeed, do they put it before the ministry of the Word? I have deliberately reversed the order because I want to draw attention to this question: Why do the apostles give such prominence to prayer?

Here again we come across an aspect of the truth that is very important for us. As we look at it, we shall be further reminded of the character of the message of the Gospel itself, and at the same time we shall be reminded of something that is equally important—namely, how it is to be preached and how it is to be presented.

Now the message must always be right. If the message is not true, nothing else is of any value. We must be orthodox; we must know what the Gospel is. A church that does not know that is a travesty; she is not a church. But while orthodoxy is absolutely essential, orthodoxy alone is not sufficient. Even orthodoxy cannot do the work if it is left in isolation. "We will give ourselves continually to prayer, and to the ministry of the word." This Gospel cannot be preached properly and truly except it be in an atmosphere of prayer. And I repeat that it is of urgent importance that we understand this. At the present time it is misunderstood as much, probably, as any other aspect of the work of the church and the preaching of the Gospel.

For some time now we have been hearing a great deal about what is called "the problem of communication." People say, "This is the message that the world needs, but the problem is how to get it over. How can you get people to listen to it and accept it?" "The problem of communication"—a new title but an old problem, is it not? It has always been a problem throughout the whole history of the Christian church. But, we are told, today, because of the new conditions in which we find ourselves, it is the problem of problems.

We are told that we are confronted by a situation such as the church has never known. This is because we are living in an atomic, a scientific, age, an age that makes all previous ages look rather childish. In the past we were ignorant, but now we have conquered the force of gravity and split the atom, releasing tremendous powers. Because of scientific advances, humanity, we are told, has developed to the extent that men and women are no longer what they were, with the result that an entirely new situation confronts the church. In the past they believed in some sort of three-tier universe, but modern scientific people cannot possibly believe that, nor can they believe in the supernatural and the miraculous. They know that many things were once regarded as miraculous that can now be explained quite easily. So if you are to appeal to modern men and women, then you must just stop talking in those pre-scientific categories and find a new way of communicating.

We are also told that we are in a world in which the old religious language no longer counts. That is why many become so excited about new translations of the Bible. "At last," they say, "we have a Bible that the people can understand." Tom, Dick, and Harry, poor boys, do not understand about justification, sanctification, and glorification. But now they have the Word of God in their own language, and so they will now believe it. This is what is needed to solve the problem of communication; this is how to bring the truth to people who are ignorant of our very phraseology and terminology.

Now there are two main reactions to that kind of thinking. There are, of course, many views in between, but I shall put before you the two extremes, the two main teachings in the church today on how this new situation is to be dealt with. The first is well advertised in this country. Its proponents seem to be the people of whom the controllers of the various television channels are most enamored. They say that you must approach this situation in a more intelligent manner; you must approach it along the lines of the mind. Some notorious books have been published in the last few years in an attempt to do this—*Honest to God* and *Down to Earth*, among others. One such author—I quoted him earlier—says that modern men and women have certain built-in scientific convictions, and if you do not recognize that is where they are but just preach the Bible, you will make no contact with them, and your evangelism will be a complete failure.

This whole tendency in the church has been going on for over a century. A great change in the church herself took place about the middle of the nineteenth century. The church, which had felt the power and the fervor and the zeal of the Evangelical Awakening of the eighteenth century, began to say, "People are being educated now; so you must not preach to them in that old way; you must have men who are cultured who can present the Gospel in a scholarly way."

So more and more emphasis was placed upon—what? Well, not upon whether the preacher was filled with the Holy Spirit, but whether he was filled with a knowledge of philosophy and the sciences, so that he could speak to people on their own level and reason with them and argue with them in terms that were acceptable to them.

And the church has increasingly said that you need preachers who have been well trained in philosophy, psychology, and sociology. Psychology, an understanding of how the human mind works, is becoming increasingly important. Thus equipped, preachers will be able to speak to people in their own jargon. This is the way to evangelize. This is the way to get people to listen.

Some who hold this view go so far as to say that you need a new message, that obviously the Bible is dated, being written in the jargon and terminology of its own age, the pre-scientific era, and that therefore you must modify it if there is to be any hope for modern people to listen to it, let alone believe it.

That, then, is one reaction—cultivate the mind, approach people directly in terms of reason and logic and understanding. But side by side with this intellectual emphasis, there is the approach that says, "Don't be interested in the mind—that doesn't matter. It is the heart (or some say the will) that counts. So you put your emphasis upon the heart or the will, in that way meeting people as they are."

Let me give you a perfect example of this second approach. It may be extreme, but it covers everyone who thinks and argues in this way. This is a newspaper article about a television program that was shown for the first time last week. This is what I read:

> Identikit pictures of God and the devil are to be shown in a new type of religious programme, "Heavens Above," over the whole Independent Television Network on Sunday at 6.35 p.m. The pictures were drawn, with others of heaven and hell, by Peter Cocker, from descriptions from youths and girls of how, in childhood, they imagined God and the devil. One girl described God as, "Rather a cross between Father Christmas and my mother, a sort of friendly, jovial character with massive hands." The programme, produced by Southern Television and introduced by Kenneth Horne the comedian, is described as an almost revolutionary break-away approach to religious broadcasting. [This is religious broadcasting!] The director said yesterday, "We are really producing a twenty-five minute religious variety show, with comedy and musical novelty spots."

Now let us be fair—these people are perfectly sincere. They say that they are anxious to get the message over to men and women and children and that it is no use preaching in the old way out of the Bible and expounding doctrine because no one can understand it. You must come down to their level; you must give them something they know and understand and can appreciate; you must bring in the element of entertainment. The terms that are used are very interesting: "We are really producing a twenty-five minute *religious variety show*, with comedy and musical novelty spots." One turn comes on, followed by another and another—religious entertainment. That is the second approach.

I am anxious to deal with the underlying principle. This second approach may not always be expressed in such a blatant form, but it always uses the same reasoning, the same argument—that you must deal with people as they are; you must come down to their level in order to interest them, to attract them, even to entice them. Let me repeat, I am not concerned about the honesty of people who use this approach. I will grant them full honesty and sincerity. But what I want to do is to show you that this is a complete departure from the method of the apostles. And until we come back to the apostolic method and pattern, there is literally no hope.

Of course, you can achieve results with such methods, but the question is, Are they the work of the Spirit of God? Look at the apostles. How did they deal with the problem of communication? This was their answer: "We will give ourselves continually to prayer"—prayer!—"and to the ministry of the word." Not a variety show, not entertainment, not wheedling the people, not pandering, not reducing the message, but prayer.

So the question is, Why did the apostles emphasize the all-importance of prayer? Why did they pray continuously? Well, the answers are here before us, and we have already come across them in the earlier chapters. Let us look at these great principles again. Every time there has been a revival of religion, men have returned to this apostolic method and pattern. Is there anything that is more urgently needed today? This is God's own way, and there is no other.

The apostles emphasized prayer, first, because of their realization of their own impotence and their absolute need of the power of God. The Sanhedrin, you remember, described these men accurately as "unlearned and ignorant men." And they were. They had no knowledge, they had no understanding, they had no innate power; and even if they had, and had used their power to the maximum, they would have been quite useless. And they knew that. They knew there was only one hope, and that was that they should be filled with the power of God. So they gave themselves continually to prayer.

These were the men, remember, who on the Day of Pentecost had been baptized by the Holy Spirit; they had been filled with the Spirit until they were overflowing. Then they had a similar filling when they were praying together in that upper room and the very building was shaken (Acts 4:31). It is interesting that these men, who had been so filled with the Spirit, nevertheless found prayer an absolute imperative, an utter necessity.

We have already seen that at every crisis the apostles turned to prayer. You remember that after their first arrest, Peter and John had been set at liberty but were warned very plainly and clearly not to continue preaching and teaching in the name of Jesus. The apostles knew their lives would be in danger if they continued. So what did they do? We are told, "Being let go, they went to their own company, and reported all that the chief priests and elders had said unto them" (Acts 4:23).

And when the others heard the apostles' report, what did they do? Did they have a conference? Did they say, "We seem to be failing; we're not so successful. We've been too blunt and too direct. Let's start again, and mod-

ify our methods; let's go more slowly and try a little diplomacy"? Nonsense!
"When they heard that, they lifted up their voice to God with one accord,
and said . . ." (v. 24). They prayed! The first thing they did, always, was to
pray. Indeed, we have already been told in the second chapter that "they continued steadfastly in the apostles' doctrine"—teaching—"and fellowship, and
in breaking of bread, and in prayers" (Acts 2:42).

People filled with the Spirit find that prayer is absolutely essential. But
why is this? It is because you are not given the power of the Spirit all in one
go and never any more. No, no. You constantly need to keep in touch; you
constantly need to be in an attitude and condition of prayer; you constantly
need to be receiving fresh supplies. And these men knew that. They saw the
problem confronting them and knew they were inadequate. They realized
they needed more knowledge and understanding of the Gospel, the truth that
had been committed to them. So they said, "O God, teach us and give us
understanding. Enlighten the eyes of our understanding; open them. Give us
the Spirit. Give us the unction, this blessed anointing that will make the Word
plain and clear to us. Lord, give it to us!"

So the apostles prayed. They needed understanding; so they asked for it.
And they needed power to preach. They were not trained orators, they were
not rhetoricians like the Greek philosophers, but were simple men—fishermen, artisans, and others. Do not misunderstand me. I am not condemning
teaching or knowledge or culture. What I am condemning is reliance upon it,
putting your faith in it or in any other human expedient. The apostles did not
do that. Their faith was in the living God, and that is why they prayed. They
needed power to preach, and they needed authority.

Let me take you to the great example of dependence on God alone. Look
at that mighty man, the apostle Paul. Here was a man of ability, a man of
knowledge and of culture, one of the great geniuses of all the centuries. But
notice what he said about himself when he went to preach in Corinth: "I was
with you in weakness, and in fear, and in much trembling" (1 Cor. 2:3). What?
The apostle Paul? Yes. He did not bounce into the pulpit or onto a platform
in supreme self-confidence. "Weakness"! "Fear"! "Much trembling"!

How do you explain Paul's sense of weakness? Oh, there is no difficulty
about the explanation. This colossus, this mighty genius, was aware of the
terrible responsibility that rested upon him. That is why he was fearful; that
is why he was trembling. It was the responsibility of realizing that he was
preaching to dying souls who may be going to an eternity of misery. A man
who realizes that cannot be light and trivial and jocular; he is filled with a
sense of inadequacy. What a desperately serious thing it is!

What would you think of a surgeon who came to you when you were very ill to advise you of your need for a serious operation and who cracked jokes about it? It is unthinkable. No surgeon would dream of doing such a thing. But a preacher is a man dealing with the souls of men and women. It is not a question of a temporary improvement or of life for just another few years but of an everlasting destiny. The preacher is in the middle position between this judgment and the people. And he is overwhelmed by the thought of it.

Paul was afraid of misrepresenting the message, afraid of standing between people and the truth, afraid of being a hindrance to these souls. He constantly says this, but he expresses his sense of weakness and responsibility perhaps most plainly in his second letter to the Corinthians. Here is a description of the preacher:

> *Now thanks be unto God, which always causeth us to triumph in Christ, and maketh manifest the savour of his knowledge by us in every place.*

Then notice this:

> *For we are unto God a sweet savour of Christ, in them that are saved, and in them that perish: To the one we are the savour of death unto death; and to the other the savour of life unto life.*

Then Paul asks this question:

> *And who is sufficient for these things?*
>
> —2 Cor. 2:14-16

My dear friends, have you ever known what it is to be conscious that you are in the presence of the living God? And we are in his presence this evening [in Westminster Chapel, London]; this is a religious service. It is not made sacred by the building; it would be the same if we were in the open air or anywhere else. It is not buildings that determine your form of worship. There are people who, in certain places and with stained-glass windows, insist upon a certain type of service. Put the same people in another kind of building, and they behave entirely differently. They are not governed by the presence of God but by buildings. We are in the presence of the everlasting and eternal God. He is looking down upon us, and our whole eternal future is here; it is being decided by our reaction to this Gospel.

That was what made the apostle Paul feel such "weakness, and . . . fear, and . . . trembling." He was literally trembling! He was terrified, he tells us, that the people might believe in him and not in his Gospel. He says, "that your faith should not stand in the wisdom of men, but in the power of God" (1 Cor. 2:5). He deliberately eschewed human wisdom. He says in the next chapter of 1 Corinthians, "If any man among you seemeth to be wise in this world, let him become a fool, that he may be wise" (3:18). Paul did not care what they thought about him but wrote to the Corinthians, "I determined not to know any thing among you, save Jesus Christ, and him crucified" (1 Cor. 2:2). He relied upon the Spirit of the living God, so that the glory might be God's and God's alone.

These apostles gave themselves continually to prayer because they needed God's power, God's authority, God's unction. They needed that which alone could demonstrate to men and women the realization of God's glory and His authority and His eternity and His mighty power unto salvation. And so they gave themselves continually to waiting upon God, and this has been the characteristic of all men whom God has used signally and mightily throughout the running ages.

We are told of Robert Murray McCheyne, that saintly Scottish preacher of the 1840s, that very often, the moment he entered his pulpit on Sunday mornings, people began to weep. Why? Because he had come from the presence of God, and there was something of the radiance of God on his very face, in his whole deportment, in everything about him. Oh, the seriousness, the solemnity, the majesty of it all! An emissary from God, an ambassador of Christ! ". . . in demonstration of the Spirit and of power" (1 Cor. 2:4). That is only obtained in prayer—continual prayer.

Second, the apostles gave themselves to prayer because they realized the state of all humanity by nature. In other words, they had a true understanding of the task of evangelism, or, if you like modern jargon, the problem of communication. Here is the Gospel—there is humanity. What is the problem? Is it the twentieth century? No, no! Is it the problem of new knowledge, science, learning, philosophy? No; the problem does not change, and it is not new. It was as difficult to preach the Gospel in the first century as it is in the twentieth. It has never been easy to preach this Gospel. All the modern-day modifications of the message, all the new methods—including the pathetic "religious variety show" on television—are all nonsense and are, ultimately, a denial of the nature of the Gospel. These men gave themselves continually to prayer because they knew the problem of evangelism and of communication.

There are many ways in which the problem can be stated. First, the apostles realized, as the apostle Paul has again expressed it authoritatively once and for all, that "We wrestle not against flesh and blood"—our problem is not human nature—"but against principalities, against powers, against the rulers of the darkness of this world, against spiritual wickedness in high"—heavenly—"places" (Eph. 6:12). That is the problem.

We are fighting not man but the devil. We are fighting hell; we are fighting spiritual forces second only in power to God Himself. We are fighting a power that has defeated every man, even Adam in a state of perfection, that has defeated all the patriarchs and all the prophets and the psalmists, that has defeated them all. Though the apostles had a new message, as it were, who were they to deal with such powers? It could not be done. They needed divine power to meet a devilish power. All human cleverness, whether it be manifested in the realm of the mind or the heart or the will, is of no value.

But the apostles also knew that not only were they fighting the terrible powers that were at the back of the problem, they were dealing with humanity under the nefarious influences of these evil forces. Let me give you a description of what humanity is like as the result of the Fall, as the result of sin.

> *This I say therefore, and testify in the Lord, that ye henceforth walk not as other Gentiles walk, in the vanity of their mind, having the understanding darkened, being alienated from the life of God through the ignorance that is in them, because of the blindness of their heart: who being past feeling have given themselves over unto lasciviousness, to work all uncleanness with greediness.*
>
> *—Eph. 4:17-19*

That was Paul's description of the Gentile world in the first century, and it is a perfect description of London this night [June 26, 1966]. There is no difference whatsoever. Do not talk to me about splitting the atom and all these other marvelous advances that I am as aware of as you are. Here is humanity, this is the problem—their minds are darkened.

If you read the second half of the first chapter of Paul's letter to the Romans, you will find an account of life as it is being lived in London today, and in New York, and in Washington. Men and women, the slaves of the devil and of hell, of sin and lasciviousness, sexual immorality, sexual perversion—the whole gamut is all described there perfectly.

The world today is exactly what it has always been. That is the problem of evangelism. Man is "dead in trespasses and sins" (Eph. 2:1). "The carnal [natural] mind is enmity against God: for it is not subject to the law of God, neither indeed can be" (Rom. 8:7). "The fool hath said in his heart, There is no God" (Pa. 14:1). They were denying God a thousand years before Christ was born, and modern men and women think they are clever when they reject God today! Hallmark of modernity? How old-fashioned unbelief is! How blind, ignorant, and spiritually dead!

Paul tells us, "The natural man receiveth not the things of the Spirit of God: for they are foolishness unto him" (1 Cor. 2:14). That was said in the first century. People did not believe in God then. They did not believe in Christ as the Son of God; they did not believe in two natures in one person—it seemed utterly unreasonable. Men and women have always rejected the miraculous and the supernatural.

The apostles, here in Acts 6, realized that no argument or demonstration could persuade people. If a man or woman could be reasoned into belief, then why is it that all reasonable and learned people are not Christians? But it cannot be done. What is the value of reasoning in these matters? This is a great question. I suppose, in many ways, the most acute problem of all at the present time is the problem of deciding the place and value of reason when proclaiming the Gospel. And there is no difficulty about discovering the answer given by the Bible. It is this: At its best, the value of reason is only general. It has its value, but it is mainly negative and condemnatory.

Again Paul has put this perfectly in Romans 1:

> *Because that which may be known of God is manifest in them; for God hath showed it unto them. For the invisible things of him from the creation of the world are clearly seen, being understood by the things that are made, even his eternal power and Godhead; so that they are without excuse: Because that, when they knew God, they glorified him not as God, neither were thankful; but became vain in their imaginations, and their foolish heart was darkened. Professing themselves to be wise, they became fools, and changed the glory of the uncorruptible God into an image made like to corruptible man, and to birds, and four-footed beasts, and creeping things.*
>
> —vv. 19-23

Paul is saying there that because the evidence of God is all around us in creation, we are without an excuse if we do not believe. Reason can bring us to that position. Reason is of value as far as it goes, but it can never go far enough. It can show us how wrong it is not to believe in God; it can show us the futility of trusting in human wisdom and understanding. The modern world is showing us all this. Reason can demonstrate the reasonableness of believing the Gospel, but it cannot persuade us. It does not touch people; it leaves them exactly where they were.

Why does reason have no effect? Our Lord has given the answer: "And this is the condemnation, that light has come into the world, and men loved darkness rather than light, because their deeds were evil" (John 3:19). The light has come—it is more than sufficient to enable people to believe. But they will not have it; they reject it. Why? Because their natures are rotten; they are perverted, blinded by sin.

So you can modify your message, and you can put it in terms of philosophy, but you will not save a single soul. You can go to the other extreme and bring in your jazz bands and all the tomfoolery of the new television program, and again you will not save a single soul. Nothing that you can do will ever save a soul. The Spirit alone can do this work. It is His. There is nothing and no one that can convict a person of sin except the Holy Spirit. I can prove that you are wrong in many respects, but I cannot convict you of sin. I can make you miserable perhaps or make you happy, but I cannot convict you of sin. Every man or woman born of Adam needs to be broken down, to be convicted of sin. People everywhere need to realize the state of their hearts, to realize they are at enmity against God, to realize they are hateful and that there is no good in them. They need to say with the apostle Paul, "In me (that is, in my flesh,) dwelleth no good thing" (Rom. 7:18).

Nothing but the Spirit of God can enlighten your mind with regard to God. So why give your time and attention to these other things? Why bother with your modern methods and intellectual arguments? Nothing can avail. Knowledge of God is totally beyond the reach of human ingenuity. I repeat, only the Spirit of God reveals God and our need of God. "God hath revealed them [the things of God] unto us by his Spirit: for the Spirit searcheth all things, yea, the deep things of God. . . . Now we have received, not the spirit of the world"—the hallmark of the things of God is that they are totally unlike the world—"but the spirit which is of God; that we might know the things that are freely given to us of God" (1 Cor. 2:10, 12). And God alone can give faith. Therefore we must pray to Him, and like the apostles, we must give ourselves continually to prayer, as well as to "the ministry of the word."

That brings me to the third reason why the apostles prayed. They not only realized their own weakness and impotence, they not only had a realization of the state of men and women by nature, but they also understood the nature of this great salvation that we are given by the Lord Jesus Christ. Now here is the very heart and center of this matter. Salvation is not merely help; it is not merely assistance; it is not merely comfort; it is not merely happiness and joy. What is it then? What has our Lord given us? What do we really need? And there is only one answer—regeneration. Nothing less.

Regeneration—here is the very truth that is stated by our blessed Lord Himself in his famous interview with Nicodemus: "Verily, verily, I say unto thee, Except a man be born again, he cannot see the kingdom of God. . . . Verily, verily, I say unto thee, Except a man be born of water and of the Spirit, he cannot enter into the kingdom of God" (John 3:3, 5). He can have nothing to do with the kingdom unless he is "born again." That is the very essence of the Christian message, and that is what differentiates it from all cults and religions. It is not help, it is not aid that we need—it is to be "born again," to be "born of the Spirit," to be born from above.

The necessity of being born again is repeated constantly in the New Testament. The apostle Paul says to the Ephesians:

> *And you hath he quickened, who were dead in trespasses and sins. . . . But God, who is rich in mercy, for his great love wherewith he loved us, even when we were dead in sins, hath quickened us together with Christ, (by grace are ye saved;) and hath raised us up together. . . .*
> *—Eph. 2:1, 4-6*

Or come back to our Lord's words to Nicodemus:

> *That which is born of the flesh is flesh: and that which is born of the Spirit is spirit. Marvel not that I said unto thee, Ye must be born again. The wind bloweth where it listeth, and thou hearest the sound thereof, but canst not tell whence it cometh, and whither it goeth: so is every one that is born of the Spirit.*
> *—John 3:6-8*

It is a miracle, a mystery. Human beings cannot give new life; it comes from the Spirit of God. "If any man be in Christ," says Paul, "he is a new creature"—a new creation (2 Cor. 5:17). A Christian is not merely someone who has made a decision. No, no; God has acted. "For God, who commanded the light to shine out of darkness"—that is creation at the beginning—"hath shined in our hearts, to give the light of the knowledge of the glory of God in the face of Jesus Christ" (2 Cor. 4:6). In regeneration, the God who made us is making us anew, re-creating us, remaking us from the very depths, giving us a new life, a new nature, a new disposition; not improving us, not doing this or that, but doing what God alone can do—planting in us a seed of the divine nature, putting a principle and a disposition of the life of God into our very beings. And that is the need of humanity.

And if that is the need—and it has been the need ever since the Fall—it does not change because we are now in the twentieth century. That is why modern methods and new gospels are valueless. So these apostles, realizing these things, said, "We will give ourselves continually to prayer, and to the ministry of the word."

The supreme need of the preacher is to be filled with the Spirit of God, and he obtains that by waiting upon God, by spending time in prayer, by opening his mind and his heart and the whole of his being and pleading with God to fill him, to energize him, to put into him the dynamic energy that alone can save souls, that alone can bring men and women to a new birth.

Then, indeed, the gospel message comes back to this: "Our gospel came not unto you in word only, but also in power, and in the Holy Ghost, and in much assurance" (1 Thess. 1:5). Here it is again: "My speech and my preaching was not with enticing words of man's wisdom, but in demonstration of the Spirit and of power" (1 Cor. 2:4).

I am told that teenage hoodlums and rock and rollers do not understand Christian terminology. I know; it does not matter. The Holy Spirit can make them understand. The Holy Spirit of God can enlighten blind eyes; He can give understanding to the ignorant; He can give insight to those who are utterly bereft. It is His power, and in Him nothing is impossible.

The Spirit of God is in every believer, so that all those who listen see not man but the power of God—"that your faith should not stand in the wisdom of men, but in the power of God" (1 Cor. 2:5).

20

CALLED TO OBEDIENCE

And the word of God increased; and the number of the disciples multiplied in Jerusalem greatly; and a great company of the priests were obedient to the faith.

—Acts 6:7

We have been considering together the crucial decision taken by the apostles at this early juncture of the life of the church to make it their primary task to give themselves to preaching the Word, and also to give themselves to prayer because they knew that it was through prayer that they would be given the power of God. Clever speakers can persuade people to do many things, but no human being can change a soul or change human nature, and that is what is needed. Humanity is dead in trespasses and sins. And this Gospel offers regeneration.

That is the point at which we have arrived, but Acts 6 also shows us how to become a Christian and what that means. Now this follows directly from our last study, and therefore the first proposition that I wish to lay down is that Christians are people who have undergone a very profound change. This one statement, here in the seventh verse, is sufficient to demonstrate that, and that is why I chose it. Notice particularly the words, "and a great company of the priests were obedient to the faith." That is a staggering statement.

We read a lot about priests in the Bible, in the Old Testament and in the Gospels also. They were the men whose function it was to maintain the services in the temple, to receive offerings from the people, and to conduct sacrifices. That system of worship had been ordained by God Himself. He had taught Moses, the great leader of the children of Israel. It had not been Moses' idea, and he never claimed that it had been. God had revealed it to him and had sent him down from the mountain, telling him, "See . . . that thou make all things according to the pattern showed to thee in the mount" (Heb. 8:5). And Moses had done that. The Israelites had built a tabernacle first, and later a great temple.

But by the time of our Lord, the priests had departed very far indeed from the original pattern. You can read in the Old Testament how they had always had a wayward tendency. Humanity has always had this tendency—we even see it in the Christian church, which is always trying to turn herself into something essentially different from the church as she was at the beginning. It is almost impossible to reconcile certain aspects of what is today called the Christian church with the accounts of the church in the early chapters of Acts. I am not here to defend any institution, and I say that organized Christianity is often a denial of the New Testament church.

Now in New Testament times the Jewish priests were often very worldly, mercenary men, and they were a disgrace to the original priesthood. They were some of our Lord's bitterest and sharpest opponents. They objected to this man who had suddenly come from nowhere. They were startled at this fellow. He had not had any training; yet He taught with authority. They hated Him and conspired with the other religious leaders, including the Pharisees, to bring about His death. But here we are told this astonishing fact: "A great company of the priests were obedient to the faith." Now you cannot imagine a greater change than that. That was a revolution.

In other words, I am presenting the principle that to become a Christian is not something superficial; it is the most profound and most radical change that can ever take place in the universe. Let me remind you again of the terminology that is used in the New Testament. Becoming a Christian is called being "born again," "born from above," "born of the Spirit." "Therefore," says Paul, "if any man be in Christ"—what is the truth about him?—"he is a new creature"—a new creation—"old things are passed away; behold, all things are become new" (2 Cor. 5:17). I want to emphasize this, and I could illustrate it endlessly by making comparisons.

You can change your opinion about many things in this world. Having been brought up in a family that was liberal, you may become a conservative; or you may have started as a socialist and became a liberal. It is a change of political party, a change of opinion. In the same way, you can change from one social class to another, and you can change your work or your home. These changes all have their significance and importance; yet when you compare them with becoming a Christian, they are nothing. They are just like changing your clothes.

Becoming a Christian affects the whole being; it affects one's mind and thinking. Consider what it meant to these priests. Because they had come to see that "Christ is the end of the law for righteousness to every one that believeth" (Rom. 10:4), they had to give up all the ceremonies and rituals of the temple. That was finished. It was fulfilled. The Lamb of God had come; so the representations were not needed. What a revolution in thought! And it was exactly the same in worship, in conduct, and in every other respect. Becoming a Christian is not an easy or superficial change because it is, as we saw, the result of the operation of the Spirit of God.

The apostle Paul expresses the change that takes place in what is, perhaps, the most glorious statement that he ever made: "For God, who commanded the light to shine out of darkness"—that is a reference to the original creation when the Spirit brooded over the chaos, the abyss, and God the Creator said, "Let there be light"—"hath shined in our hearts, to give the light of the knowledge of the glory of God in the face of Jesus Christ" (2 Cor. 4:6). There is nothing bigger or deeper than that. Something has come into being that was not there before.

You see illustrations of the new creation in many places in the New Testament. Look at Saul of Tarsus. What a change! An about-face—a new direction, new thinking, new teaching, new service. It is not surprising that Paul says that when a man is in Christ, he is indeed a new being, a new creation. It is as different as that.

But, second, how does this newness of being manifest itself? That is the important point for us to grasp and to understand. The answer is given in this verse: "a great company of the priests were obedient to the faith," and the operative word is "obedient." This is important because were we to leave it at what I have just said, there might be considerable confusion. We know there are many agencies and teachings in this world that can have an effect upon people, that can give them experiences and change them. The cults would never be successful were it not that they can do something.

Numbers of people testify that Christian Science has made all the difference in the world to them. Whereas they used to be miserable and worried, always defeated and suffering from insomnia, now, as the result of this teaching, all that has gone. They say that even their physical illnesses have gone, and now they are well and healthy. And various other cults and teachings are able to achieve the same results. Furthermore, psychotherapists are doing quite good business and, especially in a century of wars like this one, can help people with their teaching, their listening, and their drugs. People say, "Well,

I'm absolutely different since I had that treatment. I'm well again, and my whole outlook has changed."

So if I had merely preached to you about a great change, a great experience, I would not be giving an accurate definition of what it means to be a Christian. I remember years ago reading a book, a symposium, written by a number of people who all gave accounts of a turning-point in their lives. It was most illuminating. I think that only one of the contributors claimed to be a Christian. The others were all able to give a most amazing story of a dramatic change they had experienced. One man described how he was walking down Villiers Street off the Strand when suddenly something flashed into his mind, and he was never the same again.

I myself remember meeting a man who had been a hopeless drunkard, and he told me in the most dramatic manner how one morning, having been drunk the night before, he got up, had a wash, and was trying to brush his hair when he suddenly saw his own face in the mirror, and it so shocked him that he never drank again. He had not become a Christian; in fact, he was an opponent of Christianity and was arguing with me against regeneration and the rebirth. The basis of his argument was that he had undergone a profound change similar to the one I was talking about, but without believing my message.

So it is important to understand that the mere fact that our lives have changed does not prove that we are Christians. What, then, is the proof? It is that our experience is the result of and leads to obedience to the faith. This is the acid test. The Scripture is careful to say that the priests were "obedient to the faith," to the message that was preached. There must be no confusion about this. The devil, according to the apostle Paul, can turn himself into an angel of light. He can quote Scripture. He can delude us. The devil will do anything he can to give us a false peace and a false comfort. He will do anything to make us think that all is well with us and that we need not worry anymore; that is what he does as an angel of light. He has often done it, and he is still doing it. We must be clear about these things. The thing that marks out the Christian from all others is that he has rendered obedience to the faith.

What, then, does "obedient to the faith" mean? First, let me take for a moment the word *obedience*. This word is used throughout the Scriptures. The Bible is not content, as I shall show, merely with using the word *believe* but also uses the word *obey*. The apostle Paul, writing to the Romans, says, "By whom we have received grace and apostleship, for obedience to the faith among all nations, for his name" (1:5). In the same epistle he says, "But God be thanked, that ye were the servants of sin, but ye have obeyed from the heart that form of doctrine which was delivered you" (6:17). That is what makes men and women Christians.

Take Paul's words at the beginning of the tenth chapter of Romans: "For Christ is the end of the law for righteousness to every one that believeth" (v. 4). Later on in that same chapter, in describing preachers of the Gospel, Paul says, "But they have not all obeyed the gospel" (v. 16). You find the same emphasis in the last chapter of Romans: ". . . but now is made manifest, and by the scriptures of the prophets, according to the commandment of the everlasting God, made known to all nations for the obedience of faith" (16:26). That is why it has been made known—in order that we might be called to obedience.

Now in case somebody might think this is just a special emphasis in the preaching of the apostle Paul, listen to Peter. Writing to Christians, he says, "elect according to the foreknowledge of God the Father, through sanctification of the Spirit, unto obedience and sprinkling of the blood of Jesus Christ" (1 Pet. 1:2). This tells us that it is not good enough just to listen to the Gospel. There are people who have spent a lifetime listening to the Gospel Sunday by Sunday, out of tradition, habit, and custom; but that does not make them Christians, it does not put them right, it does not save them.

You say, "Oh, but I like to listen to the Gospel!" I know you do, but what has it done to you? What has it led to? The Gospel is not only to be listened to. Nor is the Gospel merely a question of opinion. It is not just something to be discussed and argued about and written about and thought about. There are a number of people doing that at the present time, and I agree it is very interesting to listen to their ideas. Some will tell us quite frankly that they are not Christians. They nevertheless express their opinions on modern Christianity and the modern church, and sometimes they are very illuminating and well worth reading. Sometimes one almost thinks that these people have a clearer insight than many who are inside the church. But their trouble is that they tend to stop at giving their opinions. They have their discussions; they write their articles and give their interviews. But what does it do to them? Later on you see them in an entirely different type of television program, and you hear them using language that is not always right and showing a similar interest in problems to do with sex and other issues. So the Gospel is not merely a subject for discussion.

Nor is the Gospel merely to be accepted in an intellectual sense. Let me be clear about this. It must be accepted by the mind. Indeed, the intellect comes first. The first thing that happens to people, as I shall show you, is that their minds are illuminated. People who do not know what they believe are surely not Christians. But many people have fallen into the error of thinking that the Gospel is only a matter of intellectual assent. God knows, I myself was once in that position. I was interested in theology, in religious arguments and disputations; but these discussions had no influence at all upon my life. That is why the word *obedience* is important.

Let me quote Romans 6:17 again: "But God be thanked, that ye were the servants of sin, but ye have obeyed"—there is the will—"from the heart"—what have you obeyed?—"that form of doctrine"—teaching—"which was delivered you." That is how it works. You start with the mind, and the mind influences the heart, and the heart moves the will. So Christians are men and women who have made a total response to the message.

Christians do not only respond with the heart. There are many whose hearts have been moved. As a result, they think they are Christians, but they are not. They are just sentimentalists. Perhaps a direct appeal has been made to their feelings. They have been affected by some hymn or chorus or by a moving story that an evangelist has told. And because they weep, they think they have undergone a profound change. But they cannot give a reason for this change. It is only in the heart.

And in the same way there are some who are only moved in the will. They were ready to do something, and they have done it, but they do not know why they acted as they did, and there was no emotional response. The Christian faith always produces emotion. It is the Word of God; it is the truth of God; it is the action of God re-creating us. It involves the whole person. The mind is engaged, the heart is engaged, and the will is engaged. Unless your entire personality has been captured and involved, then you are not a Christian. You must obey "from the heart that form of sound doctrine which was delivered you," and anything short of this is not consistent with the New Testament teaching concerning the essence of the Christian faith.

Now why is this question of obedience so important? Why does the Scripture so constantly use this term? And why is it all-inclusive, as I have just been showing you? Here again is something that it is vitally important for us to understand. We must be quite clear here; otherwise we will never see why the word *obedience* is used. The essence of sin is disobedience to God. Many people seem to think that sin is that which makes me miserable, that which gets me down, that which gives me the feeling of the morning after the night before, that which makes me kick myself for being such a fool. They think sin is a habit, something that makes me ill at ease. Now I grant you that sin has all those consequences, but that is not the essence of sin.

The essence of sin, I repeat, is rebellion against God. It is transgression of the law of God. That is what makes sin sin. And this is vital, for this reason: The Pharisees and the scribes and priests resented our Lord's teaching and finally brought about His death upon the cross because His preaching made them realize that they were sinners—and they did not like it. The Pharisee was a very self-righteous person. He felt he was all right. There was nothing wrong with him. Why? Because he had never gotten drunk. He had never committed adultery. He had never committed murder. He did not break the law; therefore he was not a sinner. It was intolerable that he should be regarded as a sinner like the tax-collectors and "sinners" so-called. He felt it was insulting; he could not stand it. So the Pharisees conspired to crucify our Lord.

But sin is not merely a sickness or a failure; it is not a mere blemish or a defect. It is an attitude of heart toward God. And that is why obedience is emphasized. "The carnal mind"—the natural mind—"is enmity against God: for it is not subject to the law of God, neither indeed can be" (Rom. 8:7). "The natural man" (1 Cor. 2:14) hates God and will do anything he can to try to drag God down. And, therefore, the very essence of becoming a Christian is the rendering of obedience.

God is our Maker. He is our Lawgiver and eternal Judge. He has a right over us. This is not some arbitrary action on the part of God. He is just and right and holy, and His purpose for men and women is that they too should be holy. He gave them the great dignity of having something of His own image within them. God, as it were, was trying to hold up the dignity of human beings. They were meant for communion with Him. So men and women, in rebelling against God, not only disobeyed Him but dragged themselves down. But God's purpose for them has not changed, and He demands obedience from them in order that they may live and function as human beings created in the image of God and worthy of Him.

So the essence of becoming a Christian is to obey God, and that includes believing the Gospel. Our Lord Himself put it like this to the people following Him:

Labour not for the meat which perisheth, but for that meat which endureth unto everlasting life, which the Son of man shall give unto you: for him hath God the Father sealed. Then said they unto him, What shall we do, that we might work the works of God? Jesus answered and said unto them, This is the work of God, that ye believe on him whom he hath sent.

—John 6:27-29

That is God's command. The work God wants us to do is to believe in His Son.

Then there is another statement at the end of the third chapter of John's Gospel:

> *He that hath received his testimony [the testimony of Jesus Christ]*
> *hath set to his seal that God is true. . . . The Father loveth the Son,*
> *and hath given all things into his hand. He that believeth on the Son*
> *hath everlasting life: and he that believeth not the Son shall not see*
> *life; but the wrath of God abideth on him.*
>
> —*John 3:33, 35-36*

God has sent His only Son into the world, and He has said of Him, "This is my beloved Son: hear him" (Mark 9:7). "Listen to Him. Obey Him. Here He is, My representative."

God commands us to believe the Gospel, and He commands us all to repent. Paul told the Athenians, "[God] now commandeth all men every where to repent" (Acts 17:30). As He is the eternal Lawgiver, so we are called to this obedience. That is why we must put emphasis upon the necessity for obedience. "A great company of the priests were obedient to the faith"—to the teaching, to the Word.

Now I am trying to be practical. I want you to know of a surety that you are a true Christian. Do not rest upon an experience you have had. Do not rest upon your good works. Do not rest upon your upbringing. Do not rest upon your church membership. This is the test: obedience.

But what is this obedience? The first step in obedience is to stop resisting the message. In the next chapter of Acts, we have a great sermon preached to the Sanhedrin by Stephen, one of the seven men chosen to "serve tables." As Stephen was preaching, he said, "Ye stiff-necked and uncircumcised in heart and ears, ye do always resist the Holy Ghost: as your fathers did, so do ye" (7:51). Now there is no difficulty about this. As we have seen, the Bible tells us that every one of us, by nature, resists this message. As Paul writes, "But the natural man receiveth not the things of the Spirit of God: for they are fool-ishness unto him: neither can he know them, because they are spiritually dis-cerned" (1 Cor. 2:14).

Men and women as they are by nature do not like this teaching about God and His holiness and about their need for righteousness. No, no! They love sin, and that is why they commit it. People do what they like. They are guided by their desires, their instincts, and their impulses. That is why, in the midst of this twentieth century, with all our education, able men and women, learned and good men and women, from a human standpoint, are still drinking themselves to death. Look at the way people live. Is this intelligent? Why do they do it? Well, it is what they like.

Further, every one of us, by nature, hates the thought of God. God is a sort of enemy. God is someone who stands between us and what we really want to do. God is against us. He is cramping us, holding us down. He is a tyrant. That is how people think, and so they are always resisting Him. Then something happens, and they are shaken. Perhaps they are taken very ill, and their conscience begins to trouble them. So for a while they say, "All right, if I get well, I'm going to live a better life." But they get better, and they forget all about their resolve.

Or it may be that someone who is very dear has been taken away by death, and again people are pulled up short. The Word of God speaks to them; their consciences speak; everything that is good and decent in them speaks. But they do not like what this will involve; so they resist the Spirit who has spoken through their consciences.

It may be that something disturbs people and appeals to them in a church service. They get a glimmer of a life lived better and higher, and they know within themselves that they ought to be like that; but then they resist this impulse. They say, "Oh, it was just something passing, something that was getting at me in the wrong way." So again they resist the Holy Spirit. People come under the power of the Gospel in a service, and, seeing something of the immediate consequences, they deliberately pick up a hymn-book and start turning the pages, or they look at somebody and wink and smile and laugh. They shake themselves and will do anything at all to stop this movement of the Spirit. You know about that, do you not? So the first step in obedience is to stop resisting God.

But that is not enough. That is negative. The next step is repentance. The Latin word from which our word *repentance* has come means "think again"—and this is a very simple but profound step to take. You have your scheme of things, you have your philosophy of life, and you say you have worked it out. You are an intelligent person, up-to-date in your reading and well aware of modern theories. You know all about Hinduism, Confucianism, and other religions, and you know all the arguments that can be brought against Christianity. You have decided there is no God, there is no salvation. And there it is.

And the first positive step in obedience is to be prepared to think again. Do you still have an open mind? It is commonly said that people who are

Christians have closed minds, whereas those who are not Christians are open-minded. Open-minded? Come, just be honest. Are you open-minded, or have your closed your mind against God, against the whole notion of the soul, and against the glorious doctrine of salvation through the death of the Son of God? That is nothing but prejudice. It is not ability, it is not understanding, it is not knowledge, for there are men of ability and knowledge and under-standing who believe the Gospel. No; it is a prejudice that blinds the eyes and shuts the mind.

Repentance begins when you say to yourself, *I must be honest. I really must listen to this message and examine it.* So many people dismiss the whole of the Bible who have never even read it. They do not even know the New Testament. They have dismissed it in general, on principle, out of prejudice. And so the first step is the readiness to think again.

The second step is allowing the Spirit, this Spirit that brings conviction and enlightenment, to persuade you to change your mind—that is the mean-ing of the Greek word *metanoia*, which is translated by our word *repentance.* You must not only think again, but having done that, you must be ready to change your opinion. This means being ready to confess that you are wrong. It is the most difficult thing in life to say that, is it not? No one, by nature, likes to admit that he or she is wrong. But it is essential. You cannot give obe-dience to this faith, to this Word of God, unless you are big enough and hon-est enough to confess to having been wrong.

> *Our little systems have their day;*
> *They have their day and cease to be:*
> *They are but broken lights of thee,*
> *And thou, O Lord, art more than they.*
>   Alfred Lord Tennyson

Read again "Bishop Blougram's Apology":

> *Just when we are safest, there's a sunset-touch,*
> *A fancy from a flowerbell, some one's death,*
> *A chorus-ending from Euripides,*
> *And that's enough for fifty hopes and fears*
> *As old and new at once as nature's self*
> *To rap and knock and enter in our soul. . . .*
> *The grand Perhaps!*
>   Robert Browning

All I am asking you is this: Are you prepared to admit this "Perhaps"? Are you prepared to break through your rigid little system and admit its possible failure and incompleteness?? Are you prepared to listen to those deeper intimations and feelings, those aspirations and longings after "an ampler ether, a diviner air" (Wordsworth)?

Well, there it is. Thinking again, changing your mind, acknowledging and confessing that you have been wrong. But still that does not make you a Christian. No; what makes you a Christian is this: "For whosoever shall call upon the name of the Lord shall be saved"—calling upon the name of the Lord!—"How then shall they call on him in whom they have not believed?" (Rom. 10:13-14).

Having considered your life and your experience, you see yourself becoming old and decrepit and dying, your body buried in a grave, and your soul going on—where? Well, you do not know. You cannot be very proud of your past. You know in your heart of hearts that you are not what you were meant to be, that you are a failure, that you fall into sins. You can do nothing about your past, and you know that making resolutions is of no value. You have often made them, but you have never kept them, and you know it will be the same in the future because as you get older, it is more and more difficult to break ingrained habits, and life becomes increasingly complex. Having considered all this, you know there is only one thing for you to do, and that is to "call upon the name of the Lord," to cry out to Him.

You have heard about the Lord Jesus Christ. The preachers have been sent by God to tell you that "God so loved the world, that he gave his only begotten Son, that whosoever believeth in him should not perish, but have everlasting life" (John 3:16). In our Lord's famous parable of the Pharisee and the tax-collector, who both went up into the temple to pray, the Pharisee stood up and said, "God, I thank thee, that I am not as other men are, extortioners, unjust, adulterers, or even as this publican. I fast twice in the week, I give tithes of all that I possess." As for the other poor fellow, the tax-collector, there he is at the back by the door. He cannot even so much as lift up his head because he is so ashamed of his sin, his unworthiness, his failure. And this is what he says: "God be merciful to me a sinner" (Luke 18:11-13). That is what it means to call on the name of the Lord. That man says, "I am undone if You do not have mercy on me."

Have you ever been there? That is what makes you a Christian. You are convinced of your sin, your helplessness, your failure, of the fact that you deserve hell and damnation. You admit it all. You cry out to God for mercy. That is repentance. And obedience to the Gospel demands this repentance.

But repentance does not stop at crying out to God. The next step is to believe what God says to you when you cry out to Him. For if you do cry out, He will hear you—it is my privilege to give you an assurance of that. Our Lord Himself said, "Him that cometh to me I will in no wise cast out" (John 6:37). So you come to Him. You call on the name of the Lord, knowing that He will answer you. He will answer you with the word of this Gospel, this message, that these priests in Acts obeyed. What is this message? Oh, it is that although we have all sinned and come short of the glory of God, and though we all deserve the punishment of hell, God has so loved us that He sent His only Son into this world and laid on Him the iniquity of us all. That is the message you are to believe.

You believe that when you cry unto the Lord for mercy and compassion, He will say, "I have given it to you. I have already done it. I have laid your sins on Him. He has taken your punishment. You are free. You are pardoned. I put upon you the righteousness of My only begotten Son." To believe this is a part of repentance. We come to Him knowing we are nothing. We have no plea except that Christ died for us and bids us come.

But even to come to Christ in faith is only a part of repentance. You then give absolute proof of the genuineness of this repentance. You give proof that it comes from your heart and not merely from your head, not merely as a mechanical action of your will. And you give proof of it in this way—you leave the world. You leave the idols of the world, the false religions and the cults. You leave your sin, turn around, and turn to Him who is alone the living and true God. This is the essence of repentance and obedience.

There is one further step, and it is given to us in that tenth chapter of Romans where Paul says:

> *But what saith it [this message]? The word is nigh thee, even in thy mouth, and in thy heart: that is, the word of faith, which we preach; that if thou shalt confess with thy mouth the Lord Jesus, and shalt believe in thine heart that God hath raised him from the dead, thou shalt be saved. For with the heart man believeth unto righteousness; and with the mouth confession is made unto salvation.*
>
> —*vv. 8-10*

This means that you cannot confess the Lord Jesus with your mouth unless you understand something of the doctrine and the truth concerning Him. You have not made merely a decision from the will, nor only responded with the heart. You do not merely say that Christianity is wonderful, and you want to show that. No; you must have understanding and confess "with the mouth." But neither does this mean that you get up and say like a parrot, "I believe that Jesus is the Son of God." No, no; confessing Him with the mouth means that you are able to give a reason for the hope that is in you, that you are able to give other people an account of why you are a Christian. As we have seen, the mind, the heart, and the will are all involved. You are a new being, and your whole personality is manifesting the change.

And, finally, you give obedience by aligning yourself with all others who are in exactly the same position. In that lyrical account of the early Christians at the end of the second chapter of Acts, we are told, "They, continuing daily with one accord in the temple, and breaking bread from house to house, did eat their meat with gladness and singleness of heart, praising God, and having favour with all the people. And the Lord added to the church daily such as should be [were being] saved" (2:46-47).

It was the characteristic of these people at the beginning, as it has continued to be of Christians ever since, that once they had obeyed the faith, they knew that they no longer belonged to the world but to the church. They became part and parcel of all who had given the same obedience, who believed in the same Lord, who gloried in Him and wanted to live for His praise. They were "added to the church," and if you do not desire to belong to the church, if you do not desire to be taught and trained by the church, to imbibe her teaching and to be built up and rooted, grounded, and established in this faith, then you had better examine everything all over again. This coming together is instinctive in all who are born again. With all the saints everywhere, they want to learn of Him that they may magnify His grace and live to His praise for the remainder of their lives.

So there it is. Great numbers, "a great company of the priests," were "obedient to the faith." Are you ready to give obedience to it? Have you repented? Have you humbled yourself? Have you admitted and confessed your sin? Have you exercised faith in the Lord Jesus Christ? Are you as a total personality captivated by this message, this faith, this Gospel? Does this dominate your life? There is no value in anything less than that. To be a Christian is to know whom you have believed, and to know what you have believed, and with all your might, by the aid of God's blessed Holy Spirit, to live unto righteousness. By His stripes we have been healed in order that we might live unto righteousness, to the obedience and the glory of God.

21

THE GLORY OF THE GOSPEL

*And in those days, when the number of the disciples was
multiplied, there arose a murmuring of the Grecians against the
Hebrews, because their widows were neglected in the daily
ministration. . . . And the word of God increased; and the number
of the disciples multiplied in Jerusalem greatly; and a great
company of the priests were obedient to the faith. . . . Then there
arose certain of the synagogue, which is called the synagogue of
the Libertines, and Cyrenians, and Alexandrians, and of them of
Cilicia and of Asia, disputing with Stephen.*

—Acts 6:1, 7, 9

We are now examining chapter 6 for the sixth time, and I have constantly
been at pains to point out its importance. It is interesting from the mere standpoint of church government and church order. Here you see the beginning of
the diaconate, of deacons in the life and organization of the church. But it is
much more important for another reason, and that is the one on which we
have been concentrating. The events outlined in verses 1-6 really did consti-
tute a turning-point in the whole history of the church. The church here met
a temptation connected with the question of looking after the widows, and
if she had succumbed, the whole story of Christianity would have been very
different; indeed, it is doubtful whether there would have been a story at all.

In resisting the temptation, the apostles established once and forever the
fact that the primary task of the church is not to change social conditions,
not to do acts of kindness and mercy, but to preach the Gospel. Yes, charitable work has to be done, and the church has always done it, but it is not the

primary task. "It is not reason that we should leave the word of God, and serve tables," said the apostles. That establishes the great principle.

So we have considered what the message is, and then we have seen why these men felt that they must give themselves continually to prayer, as well as to the ministry of the Word. Nothing can be done apart from the power of God. And then, finally, we have considered how one becomes a Christian and have seen that it is through giving obedience to the faith.

All these are fundamental doctrines. Let me remind you again that we are studying these early chapters of Acts for the one reason that we are anxious to know what Christianity really is. There is considerable confusion in the world today as to what the church is and what her message is, and here is the only authentic, and therefore the only authoritative, answer. This message calls upon us not merely to give it a passing glance, not merely to give some emotional response that we forget the next day, but to obey it. It demands obedience with the mind, the heart, the will, the whole self.

That is the point at which we have arrived, and I want now to look at the church and her message as a whole, and to do so in particular in the light of the opposition that arose against the Gospel. This opposition is described in the second half of chapter 6, from verse 9 to the end. In verse 9 we are told, "Then there arose certain of the synagogue, which is called the synagogue of the Libertines, and Cyrenians, and Alexandrians, and of them of Cilicia and of Asia, disputing with Stephen," who was one of the men chosen to do the work of a deacon.

I am focusing on the church's message in this way because I want to try to show you the essential, the true character of the Gospel. I have a feeling that our main trouble today is that we forget that it is "the power of God unto salvation to every one that believeth" (Rom. 1:16). I think the main charge that will be brought against this generation—not only against those who are outside the church, but against many of us on the inside—will be that we have reduced the Gospel to something human, and sometimes even a very poor version at that, and have missed the glory and the greatness and the grandeur of it all.

It is because we have missed the essential nature of the Gospel that we tend to put such emphasis upon "the modern man." That is all you hear today, is it not? Some emphasize modern man's knowledge. They say, "It's no use preaching as you used to preach, no use preaching from the Bible, no use preaching the old message, because modern man has grown out of it." You are familiar with this argument. Many start there, and that is what controls their thinking.

Then others at the opposite extreme tell us that we must take into account modern man's ignorance. They say, "Of course there are some people who fall into your first category—scientists, philosophers, and so on; but the masses of the people are not like that at all. They are completely ignorant. They don't know what all these learned terms mean. The church is failing today because she doesn't understand the situation of the average person." That is the second emphasis.

Then there are others who tell us that we must pay attention to what people like. They say, "People no longer want to listen to preaching. They like pictures, singing, entertainment, and drama. You must take people as they are, with these likes and dislikes."

Now as a result, the whole emphasis in this century has been on what is called "the need for a new message." This is the great message among the intellectuals. You are intelligent people, and I know you watch television—I am not saying you are intelligent because you do that!—but if you do, you may have heard someone talking about "secular Christianity," a Christianity that gets rid of the supernatural. I think it is very good for us to hear the alternatives that are being put forward to the Gospel. How pathetic they are! The people who propound these ideas want a new message; so they are trying to work out a new gospel that they think will appeal to the "modern scientific man" who does not believe in the supernatural and the miraculous.

At the opposite extreme are the people who advocate new translations of the Bible, and new translations are appearing one after another. "This is all you need," they say. "Tom, Dick, and Harry do not understand the Authorized Version, and that is why they do not believe the message. So give them new translations—the New English Bible or so-and-so's translation of the New Testament. Once they get the Bible in a language that they commonly use, the language of the kitchen, if you like, or even the kitchen sink, then people will believe this message."

Then others say, "No, what we need is more entertainment. People like that, so let them have it. Once you come down to their level and do things that they normally do, you can slip in your gospel, as it were, and succeed in that way."

I do not want to weary you with all this. All I am trying to show you is that these advocates of change all have one thing in common: They have never seen the greatness of the Gospel. My objection to them all is that they are turning the Gospel into something small, something ordinary, something cheap and easy. This one chapter alone, chapter 6 of Acts, is enough to give the lie to all this modern thinking, for it holds before us the glory of the Christian message.

This Gospel is "the power of God unto salvation" (Rom. 1:16). You must not start with humanity, but with God. If you start with men and women, then of course you will do what I have been describing. You will be interested in new messages or in new methods or in psychological approaches. But all that is a travesty of the Gospel; indeed, I feel it is an insult to the Gospel. This is the charge, I fear, that modern Christians will probably have to face at the bar of eternal judgment—that by reducing this glorious Gospel to the level of modern men and women, they have cheapened it.

Here in Acts 6, especially in the second half of the chapter, where we see the Gospel in conflict with opposition, we are shown the essential nature of the Gospel, which is its grandeur and glory. How do these verses reveal that? I want to show you that something of the glory of the Gospel is seen even in the method used to spread the message. Now there is much talk and interest today in method, in new methods. People say, "How can we get the Gospel over?" The so-called "problem of communication" is the big thing. So much expenditure of energy on methods! Oh, let us go back to the New Testament, let us go back to this book of Acts, and here we will see the method.

In this chapter we are told two main things about the method used by the apostles. The first is that it was the proclamation of a word, and it was the proclamation of a word that is truth. "It is not reason that we should leave the word of God, and serve tables . . . we will give ourselves continually to prayer, and to the ministry of the word." And in the dispute that took place between Stephen and the members of the synagogue and others, we are told, "They were not able to resist the wisdom and the spirit by which he spake." He was speaking to them; he was teaching and expounding.

These first Christians were not interested in gadgets or in entertainment; their whole emphasis was upon the message. And this is the claim of the whole of the New Testament. On one famous occasion our Lord in His preaching had been drawing back the veil a little to give a glimpse of the relationship between the Father and Himself, and we are told, "As he spake these words, many believed on him" (John 8:30). And then we go on to read, "Then said Jesus to those Jews which believed on him, If ye continue in my word, then are ye my disciples indeed; and ye shall know the truth, and the truth shall make you free" (vv. 31-32).

What makes anyone free? Psychological experiences? Certainly not. It is this truth, this word. "The truth shall make you free." And there is nothing under the sun that can make men and women truly free except this word, the word of the apostles, the word of the Gospel. We know that men and women are in slavery. You do not start with them, we know that; but we do need to consider what we have to give to them, and it is this truth. Or again, take our Lord in His high-priestly prayer. He says, "Sanctify them through thy truth: thy word is truth" (John 17:17). What is it that sanctifies us and delivers us from sin and its thralldom? What is it that makes us more and more like the Lord Jesus Christ? It is the truth; it is this message.

The apostles put their faith in the very character of the message. That was the method they used. In other words, their method was to give teaching, to give instruction, to impart knowledge. Now we are told that modern men and women prefer entertainment to preaching. But I do not care what they like. I am saying that it is not what they like or want that is important, but what they need—and that is knowledge and enlightenment. Men and women by nature are ignorant and in sin. They say there is no God. "The fool hath said in his heart, There is no God" (Ps. 14:1). So they need instruction.

It is no use starting with what "modern man" wants and then trying to conform to that. That is an insult to the truth of God. We are called to proclaim the truth, to be heralds of the Gospel. "Whether they will hear, or whether they will forbear" (Ezek. 2:5), says God as He gave His commission to Ezekiel, and I believe that the same commission is given to every true preacher of the Gospel today. Men and women are not the judges of what they need because they do not know. Look at their world! They must be taught the truth, the Word of God. Here is the first thing that Acts 6 reveals about the method used by the apostles.

The second factor is that the apostles preached with power. This is most important. Power! "Stephen, full of faith and power, did great wonders and miracles among the people" (Acts 6:8). And we are told that those who opposed him "were not able to resist the wisdom and the spirit by which he spake." This is something that we need to grasp all over again.

The Gospel, of course, is a teaching; it is, as I said, the impartation of knowledge. But there is an essential difference about the Gospel, and this sets it apart from everything else that is being offered to the world today. Because of this difference, the method of the preacher should be unlike that of the politician or the salesman. Politicians and salesmen are anxious to please people. If you are trying to sell a commodity or get votes, it is the essence of wisdom to come to people's level and give them what they want. That is the whole art of selling.

But the gospel method has nothing to do with the approach used by the salesman or politician. Why not? Because in the realm of politics or salesmanship, success depends upon human ability and human persuasion. But that is not so with the Gospel. Human persuasion can do nothing here, nothing at all. A man may be a born salesman, he may be an orator, skilled almost to perfection in the art of reasoned debate; but he will never save a soul. It is impossible. In the preaching of the Gospel there is a need for something greater, something more profound, and, thank God, we have it. That is why we need not borrow the methods of big business or anything else. "Stephen, full of faith and power, did great wonders and miracles among the people."

Power! What power was this? Well, we are told something about Stephen earlier on. Confronted by the problem of the widows, the apostles said to the church, "Wherefore, brethren, look ye out among you seven men of honest report, full of the Holy Ghost and wisdom." Then we read, "And they chose Stephen, a man full of faith and of the Holy Ghost." And it was because he was filled with the Holy Spirit that Stephen was filled with power, power not only to work "wonders and miracles," but power in his speech. Here were these clever people, and here was one man standing against them all. "And they were not able to resist"—what? Well, the power! ". . . the spirit by which he spake."

Let me put this in another way, because this is where we must start. The method of the Gospel is the method of the supernatural power of the Spirit of God. It is nothing less, because nothing less would be of the slightest value. Years later Peter put it like this: "Unto whom it was revealed, that not unto themselves, but unto us they did minister the things, which are now reported unto you by them that have preached the gospel unto you with the Holy Ghost sent down from heaven" (1 Pet. 1:12). That is it—"the Holy Ghost sent down from heaven."

The letter to the Hebrews puts exactly the same message in these words:

> How shall we escape, if we neglect so great salvation; which at the first began to be spoken by the Lord, and was confirmed unto us by them that heard him; God also bearing them witness, both with signs and wonders, and with divers miracles, and gifts of the Holy Ghost, according to his own will?
>
> —2:3-4

That is the method of the Gospel. It does not ask, "What will men like? What do men want?" and then say, "Let's give them that, thus reducing the glory." No, no! The truth! The Spirit! This is, let me repeat quite clearly, a supernatural Gospel, a supernatural message. It is miraculous. That is the whole point about it. That is why it is what it is. That is why it has done what it has done. That is why it will do what it will do, as I shall show you. We are dealing here with what Paul describes as "the power of God." He was writing to Rome, the seat of government of the whole Roman Empire. But Paul says, "I am not ashamed of the gospel of Christ"—why not?—"for it is the power of God unto salvation to every one that believeth; to the Jew first, and also to the Greek" (Rom. 1:16).

This is no human teaching, no mere philosophy. This is God's truth, and He sends His Spirit upon it, and the Spirit does the work. It is the Spirit alone who can enlighten a man or woman; it is the Spirit alone who can change people. This is a miraculous, supernatural Gospel, and if the modern man tells me that he does not believe in the supernatural, so much for the modern man! That is why he and his world are as they are. There is no hope for people until they realize their perilous condition and in utter helplessness cry out unto the Lord and begin to experience the power of this blessed Spirit of whom we read in this chapter.

So that was the apostolic method, and you see how different it is from so much that is popular today. Oh, the cheapening of the Gospel! Oh, the reduction of the message and the reliance upon human methods and expedients instead of upon the power of the Spirit of the living God!

But let me show you also the greatness and the glory of this Gospel in the work that it does in the believer. This is amazing. We have much too cheap an idea of who a Christian is. If you would only look at this chapter, you would see who a Christian really is. We see here that Christians are men and women who have been dealt with by this supernatural and miraculous power; it has filled them and changed them completely. We are not talking about a superficial decision, a little improvement here or there, stopping doing one thing and taking up another. No, no! That is true, of course, but that is merely the surface.

So what is Christianity? As our Lord taught Nicodemus, it is being born again; it is being made anew; it is being created afresh. It is something that God does again as He did in the original creation, bringing something new into being out of nothing—that is Christianity, and nothing less. There is no other definition. We must not reduce the Christian faith. You do not decide to be a Christian; you are *made* a Christian, and you are made a Christian by nothing less than the Spirit of God Himself.

Now then let me show you this simply by calling your attention to different terms that are used in this one chapter. Take, first of all, the term *brethren* in the third verse. The apostles say, "Wherefore, brethren, look ye out among you seven men of honest report, full of the Holy Ghost." They were addressing these people as "brethren," and it is a most wonderful word.

Who were these "brethren"? Well, they actually came from different nations. In Jerusalem at this time there were people from different parts of the world. We are given an account of them in chapter 2, verses 9 and 10: different nations; Greek-speaking, Hebrew-speaking; some Jews, others Romans.

The marvelous thing about the early church is that it broke down all the barriers that nations erect between one another. The Gospel brings down "the middle wall of partition" (Eph. 2:14) and makes "brethren" of Jew and Gentile, Greek and barbarian, Roman and Scythian. What an astounding thing! That is the major problem in the modern world, is it not? We talk about our great advances, but the nations are still quarreling today as they quarreled two thousand years ago. What have we achieved? What have we learned? We do not seem to have learned how to live together, have we, nor how to respect one another. But here is something that can bring people of different nationalities together—"brethren"! Members of the same family.

But not only were there different nationalities in the early church, there were also people of different callings. Many among the priests became believers, but also there were fishermen; men from many backgrounds were "brethren," believers together, sharing all things in common. Not only that, it is wonderful to notice, in the New Testament alone, the differing abilities of these early believers. We see a towering genius like the apostle Paul, and then we see Peter. Now Peter was a strong character and a leader, but I do not think you would give him very high marks in the matter of sheer intellect. He was a fisherman, an ordinary man—and yet Peter and Paul were "brethren." Peter talks about "our beloved brother Paul" (2 Pet. 3:15), and Paul would doubtless have referred to Peter in the same way.

So this term "brethren" is the answer to most of the modern misunderstandings about how to communicate the Gospel. The Gospel of Jesus Christ does not care at all about your ancestors or your nationality, your color, your culture, or your intellect. The Gospel of Jesus Christ does not say, "What exams have you passed? What were your grades? Do you have a good degree?" That does not matter. It makes no difference. The Gospel does not say, "Have you read the latest textbook on astronomy or on some abstruse branch of mathematics?" It does not say, "What is your political allegiance?" None of these things matter at all because we are dealing with the power of God.

Now the attack upon the Gospel in this century has come very powerfully from psychology. It is said, "Oh, yes, certain people are religious. They cannot help themselves; they were born like that. Religion is all right for them. We don't want to quarrel with them. But they mustn't say that everyone should be religious." Religion is dismissed in terms of temperament, natural makeup, and emotional needs. But here is the answer: "brethren."

I do not care whether you are a paragon of all the virtues or whether you have come out of one of the gutters of London. I am proud to be able to say to you that this Gospel makes you one with all other Christians. You are one in your failure; you are one in your ignorance of God; you are one in your helplessness. This Gospel makes "brethren" of all types and conditions of men and women. The Holy Spirit makes all people one. "Brethren"! What a Gospel!

And then notice the second term. I find it in several places in chapter 6, including the first verse: "And in those days, when the number of the disciples was multiplied . . ."; and in the second verse: "Then the twelve called the multitude of the disciples unto them. . . ." *Disciples!* This word means "learners," scholars, if you like, or pupils. This, too, is a wonderful concept, and it gives the lie to the modern approach; indeed, it makes it quite laughable.

The modern approach says, "There are those people—Tom, Dick, and Harry—who know nothing about the Gospel and do not understand the Authorized Version and its language. You must come down to their level. You must speak their language; otherwise it will be impossible for them to follow you." But if you are going to reduce your message or even vary your methods because of that argument, you are denying this essential teaching. "Disciples"!

Many of these people in the early church had only had a very basic education. But they were learners, and this was because of the miracle of redemption, because of the power of the Holy Spirit. The Holy Spirit can make anyone into a new person. He can regenerate an ignoramus quite as easily as a great philosopher, perhaps even more so. It is the Holy Spirit who creates a desire and an appetite to know more about the truth. The moment men and women become Christians, the moment they are regenerate, they desire to be learners.

Peter, writing his epistle much later, puts it like this: "As newborn babes, desire the sincere milk of the word, that ye may grow thereby" (1 Pet. 2:2). And in writing that, he remembered what had happened at the beginning. At the end of the second chapter of Acts, we read of those people who had believed his preaching on the Day of Pentecost, "Then they that gladly received his word were baptized: and the same day there were added unto them about three thousand souls." Then notice: "And they"—these three thousand souls—"continued steadfastly"—in what?—"in the apostles' doctrine"—teaching—"and fellowship, and in breaking of bread, and in prayers" (Acts 2:41-42). And the teaching, the doctrine, is put first. These people who had suddenly turned from ignorance and darkness, from the vileness of their lives, what did they want? They had an appetite and a desire for more teaching.

Have you ever heard of such a thing? People who had never read, who had never thought, people who had lived for gambling and for sex and for drunkenness, suddenly wanted teaching. They said, "Let's have more of this." And we are told that they "continued steadfastly," meeting "daily with one accord in the temple" (vv. 42, 46).

The desire to learn more about the faith is one of the miracles of redemption and is proof of the fact that a man or woman has become a Christian. Many people have professed decisions, but they do not want to be taught. They do not like teaching; they grumble at it. They say sermons are too long, and they want something nice and simple, something bright and breezy and short. Ah, but when men and women are Christians, when they are born again, they are disciples. They want to know; they want to grow; they want to learn. It is inevitable. The new principle is put into them, whatever they were by nature.

But the new birth not only puts within people the desire for teaching—it gives them a faculty that enables them to receive it. This is a wonderful fact, and I glory in it. If you followed the modern ideas, you would think that people could not possibly understand the great teaching of the Gospel unless they were expert philosophers or scientists or academics. It is very difficult to understand the books of some theologians; it is very difficult to follow their statements on television and in other places. But that is just a proof that they are not teaching the Gospel. "And the common people heard him gladly" (Mark 12:37). They listened to the Son of God, and they could follow Him.

So it does not matter what you are by nature. It does not matter whether you are poor in brainpower or have little learning; once you get this new life, you not only want the teaching, you will be able to receive it. I am sometimes told that a particular person will not be able to take in my sermons, and yet I think—let me say this to the glory of God—that this one place of worship alone proves that view to be wrong.

There have been people who have come here knowing nothing, and yet they have listened to me preaching for an hour and have got something out of it. "At first," someone has told me afterward, "I didn't get much, but I felt something. I knew I was getting something, and I wanted more. I knew it was reality, and I had a hunger for it within me." And gradually understanding has come. Why is this? The apostle John gives us the answer. Speaking of false teachers, he says:

> *Little children, it is the last time: and as ye have heard that antichrist shall come, even now are there many antichrists; whereby we know that it is the last time. They went out from us, but they were not of us; for if they had been of us, they would no doubt have continued with us: but they went out, that they might be made manifest that they were not all of us. But ye have an unction from the Holy One, and ye know all things. I have not written unto you because ye know not the truth, but because ye know it, and that no lie is of the truth.*
>
> —1 John 2:18-21

Further on, John says again:

> *But the anointing which ye have received of him abideth in you, and ye need not that any man teach you: but as the same anointing teacheth you of all things, and is truth, and is no lie, and even as it hath taught you, ye shall abide in him.*
>
> —v. 27

"Disciples"! They are not only given a hunger for the word—they are given the power to receive it. And more, they are given the power of discrimination, so that when clever men are misunderstanding the Gospel, some poor ignoramus who has been born again can tell them they are wrong. On countless numbers of occasions throughout the centuries simple Christian people, enlightened by the Spirit, have proved wiser than their teachers.

Then the next fact that I read about these people in Acts 6 is that they became people of character. "Wherefore, brethren, look ye out among you seven men *of honest report*" (Acts 6:3). Oh, what a Gospel this is! Here is a Gospel that can change people, do away with prejudice, make "brethren" of enemies. It can give them a desire for the truth and make them disciples. And it also reforms them; it makes them "men of honest report." When you consider what some of these had been, you see exactly what that represents.

Let me put this to you in just one great statement made by the apostle Paul to the church at Corinth:

> *Know ye not that the unrighteous shall not inherit the kingdom of God? Be not deceived: neither fornicators, nor idolaters, nor adul-*

*terers, nor effeminate, nor abusers of themselves with mankind, nor
thieves, nor covetous, nor drunkards, nor revilers, nor extortioners,
shall inherit the kingdom of God. And such were some of you: but
ye are washed, but ye are sanctified, but ye are justified in the name
of the Lord Jesus, and by the Spirit of our God.*

—1 Cor. 6:9-11

Here is a power that can take a moral weakling and make him strong
and mighty. It washes him, it cleanses him, it renews him, it gives him moral
vigor and a moral fiber—it makes him a man of character.

Then, further, we read that it is possible for a man or woman to be filled
with the Spirit and to receive the gifts of the Spirit. I read here that the
Christians were to choose "seven men of honest report, *full of the Holy Ghost
and wisdom*"—and wisdom is one of the gifts of the Holy Spirit. Here is a
baptism of power that can give men and women abilities that they have never
had. Stephen was "full of faith," trusting God, able to rely upon God's Word,
venturing out on God. Faith, wisdom, understanding, knowledge, miracles,
healings, tongues—all these are gifts of the Spirit.

Notice the wonderful statement at the end of the chapter: "All that sat
in the council, looking steadfastly on him [Stephen], saw his face as it had
been the face of an angel." Stephen was on trial before the Sanhedrin, and as
his enemies looked at him, they saw a radiance, a shining. There was a glory.
Was it Stephen? No, no; it was God shining through the face of Stephen. He
was a man who was filled with the Holy Spirit of God. That is what this
Gospel does. We need not worry about modern method; we need not reduce
the Gospel to the level of human understanding. The Gospel is the truth of
God, and it has the power of the Spirit.

So I come to my last point, which I am anxious to emphasize. It is that
in this chapter we see the glory of the Gospel in its invincibility. What a
Gospel! And how pathetic are those little modern men who are nervously trying to reduce it to suit the palate of modern pseudo-intellectuals or are searching for ways to make it cheap and acceptable and easy for the man in the
street. Oh, shame on them! Shame on them! How have they missed the glory?
Have they never seen it? This wonderful Gospel—the Word and the Spirit—
is invincible.

So look at chapter 6 of Acts. The Gospel has had to face opposition
and difficulties from the very beginning. It is all here. Let us be honest; let
us face the facts. It is marvelous that there is still a church at all because at
the very beginning trouble and opposition arose even in the bosom of the

church herself. "In those days, when the number of the disciples was multiplied, there arose a murmuring of the Grecians against the Hebrews." If the church were a human institution, she would have gone out of existence centuries ago. If men could have destroyed the church, they would most certainly have succeeded.

Do not misunderstand me. When I say that the Gospel creates a person anew, I am not saying that it immediately makes him perfect. Not at all! Here were very imperfect Christians, as so many of us are today. That is why Paul wrote, "We preach not ourselves, but Christ Jesus the Lord" (2 Cor. 4:5) and why he relied on the power of the Spirit. Difficulties within!

And then there were difficulties without: "Then there arose certain of the synagogue, which is called the synagogue of the Libertines, and Cyrenians, and Alexandrians, and of them of Cilicia and of Asia, disputing with Stephen"—trying to bring an end to the faith. The church has had to fight for her life from the very beginning. We have seen how the apostles were arrested and thrown into prison, how they were threatened, how they were commanded to stop preaching. From the moment it was born, the church has faced a world that has done everything it could to exterminate Christianity.

And what has been the story? It has been this: There were eras and epochs when the church seemed to be defeated. There were times when it looked as if the world and the flesh and the devil were triumphant and the church was just a little, weak, and feeble remnant. Many and many a time the world thought that it had conquered Christianity. But despite all appearances, the end never came. It never has, and it never will. Here in Acts 6 the situation was desperate—Stephen was put to death. But that was not the end. The church went on, and it will continue until God's plan is brought to an ultimate triumph and to a final completion.

Why must this Gospel continue and triumph? At the present time it does not look as though it will succeed, does it? In this country [England] only 10 percent of us claim to be Christians. Success seems to be all on the other side. People are laughing at the church. They say it is monstrous to expect anyone to believe the gospel message in the twentieth century. And yet I say that this is a passing phase, that the Gospel will go on and on and will triumph, bringing God's great program to a perfect conclusion.

On what grounds do I base my optimism? The answers are here in this chapter. Let me just note them for you as I finish. The church will prevail because of the Word and the truth of God. Truth must triumph. If evil were to triumph, it would mean the defeat of God, and that is impossible. God must prevail. God is truth, light, righteousness. God is holy and eternal. In His inscrutable will He permits evil to triumph for a while, but only for a while. Final success is guaranteed because of who God is, because of the character of the message.

The Gospel states that this is God's world and not man's. Human inventions should not turn our heads—we are only discovering what God has already put in the world. As more discoveries are made, more is revealed of God's glory. God made the world, and God's character is therefore involved in it. And God has given us the message of the Gospel. What is the message? It tells us that though man has fallen and brought chaos down upon himself and this world, God will redeem it. He gave the promise way back in Eden. In Acts we see it being worked out, and it is still being worked out.

The Gospel tells us that God is so involved in this world that He sent His only Son—"The Word was made flesh, and dwelt among us" (John 1:14). God's Son died to redeem us, the world, and the universe. And God has pledged Himself to this redemption. The Gospel announces that God not only forgives us but re-creates us; He gives us new life, new natures, new understanding. It is the truth of God, and it must triumph. God must triumph because He is God.

But let me show you God's ultimate triumph in another way. Look at the feebleness of the opposition—I commend this to you for your consideration. I do not know what would happen to me if I were not a Christian because I could not believe what is being offered as an alternative. Look at the opposition as it is depicted here in Acts 6. The members of the synagogue started disputing with Stephen, but we are told:

> *And they were not able to resist the wisdom and the spirit by which he spake. Then they suborned men, which said, We have heard him speak blasphemous words against Moses, and against God [an absolute lie]. And they stirred up the people, and the elders, and the scribes, and came upon him, and caught him, and brought him to the council, and set up false witnesses, which said, This man ceaseth not to speak blasphemous words against this holy place, and the law: for we have heard him say, that this Jesus of Nazareth shall destroy this place, and shall change the customs which Moses delivered us.*
>
> —*vv. 10-14*

That was the opposition. Do you see its character? Opponents of the Gospel are not quite so blatant at the present time, but they come very near it. They do everything they can to make the Gospel seem ridiculous—lying, twisting the facts, using dishonest reasoning. They play to the gallery, getting popular applause; they would stoop to any deceit.

But here we are told, "They were not able to resist the wisdom and the spirit by which he [Stephen] spake," and they really could not. Nobody can overcome the Gospel. What is your complaint against it? What is wrong with a Gospel that offers us free pardon and forgiveness? What is wrong with a Gospel that offers to make us anew? What is wrong with a Gospel that calls upon us to keep the Ten Commandments and to live the Sermon on the Mount? What is wrong with it? I say again that if only the whole world were living according to this teaching, there would be no problems in the international realm; the world would be paradise again. What can you say against the Gospel? And there is no answer, none at all.

A book has been published quite recently, a symposium with the imposing title *What I Believe*. To start with, in many of the cases you will find it very difficult to understand what the writers are saying. But when you do understand, you will find that they are actually writing about what they do *not* believe! There is nothing there; it is all negation. They do not know what they believe. They say they see no meaning, no purpose, in the universe. It is all accident and chance; there is nothing in life at all for any of us. "What do I believe? I believe nothing! I don't know!" That is virtually what they are saying.

Oh, the feebleness of the opposition! "They were not able to resist the wisdom and the spirit by which he spake." There is no answer to the wisdom of God that is in the message of this Gospel. That is my second reason for my optimism.

But, finally, my confidence is in this: The Gospel is the power of God Himself. And that is more than sufficient. It is not only the truth of God—it is "the power of God unto salvation to every one that believeth" (Rom. 1:16). The power that created the universe out of nothing; the power that brought the Lord Jesus Christ up from among the dead. What a power! It is a resurrecting power, an invincible power. It is indeed the power of God.

Not only could Stephen's enemies not resist the wisdom of his words—they could not resist "the spirit by which he spake." And anyone who is trying to reject the Gospel is doing nothing but resisting Almighty God. Those who object to the Gospel are hurling themselves against the everlasting God, and they will only dash themselves to pieces. They will end in ultimate and everlasting destruction.

His kingdom cannot fail;
He rules o'er earth and heaven;
The keys of death and hell
Are to our Jesus given:
Lift up your heart, lift up your voice,
Rejoice, again I say, rejoice.

Charles Wesley

Let God's enemies rise up against Him. They defied Him at the beginning and have continued to defy Him. The Jews were opposed to the Gospel; the Romans rose up afterward; the Goths and the Vandals came. All the hordes of evil and of hell have been let loose against this Gospel, this message; they have all done their utmost to destroy it. But the gates of hell shall not prevail against this proclamation that Jesus Christ, and Him crucified, is "the power of God, and the wisdom of God" (1 Cor. 1:24).

Cannot you see it? Have you ever felt it? I want to put some personal questions to you. Have you ever felt the power of this Spirit dealing with you? There was the Spirit in Stephen dealing with these people, and they could not resist. In spite of all their efforts, they had no reply. And yet they would not believe it.

Have you been doing that? Have you felt the power of this Word? Have you seen the wisdom? Have you seen the glory, the perfection, of it all? Have you seen God in it? Have you felt the Spirit, the power, dealing with you, pleading with you, showing you your emptiness and woe, showing you your need of salvation, displaying to you the glory of the Son of God dying on a cross that you might be forgiven, offering to make you a child of God? Have you felt it?

You know you are a failure. You put up your intellectual camouflage, but you know it is only a pretense. You know the running sore of your soul. Are you still resisting—still resisting the Holy Spirit of God? I warn you that you are pitting yourself against the All-mighty and you and the clever people of the modern era will go down to destruction. You are hurling yourself against the Rock of Ages, against the immovable God.

My friend, have you given obedience to this Gospel? Have you yielded yourself to it? Have you become a disciple? Do you want to keep learning more and more about this message? Have you become one of the brethren? Do you feel that you are made anew in such a sense that you belong to the family of God and that you look forward with them to the glory everlasting?

Shall I ask you a final question? Do people sometimes express amazement as they look at you? Do they say that at times they see your face as if it had been the face of an angel? Do people come to you and say, "What is the secret of your life? What is the peace and the quiet and the equanimity that I see in you? How can I get that?"

The twentieth century and all the glory of its civilization will pass away, as the glory of every other civilization has already passed away. "But the word of the Lord endureth for ever" (1 Pet. 1:25). It has been preached to you. My dear friends, recognize the wisdom; yield to the Spirit, the Spirit of God. And then you will know for yourself the glory of the power of the Lord as He was preached by the early church.

NOTES

1. *Courageous Christianity*, published in the UK by The Banner of Truth Trust and in the USA by Crossway Books.
2. Jodrell Bank, south of Manchester, is the site of the world's first giant radio telescope.
3. The high court and governing authority of the Jews.
4. Michael Ramsey.
5. There was a general election in Britain at the time.
6. There was a general election in Britain in March 1966.
7. The Second World War.
8. This sermon was preached on the Sunday before the British general election on March 31, 1966.
9. This sermon was preached on Easter Sunday evening, 1966.
10. "Conversions—Psychological and Spiritual," in *Knowing the Times*, Banner of Truth Trust, 1989.
11. This book was written by Rosalind Murray about her father, Gilbert Murray.
12. "Conversions—Psychological and Spiritual."
13. On June 3, 1966, Eugene Cernan and Thomas Stafford were launched into space in Gemini 9. The purpose was to develop techniques for functioning in space.